The working-man's way in the world; being the autobiography of a journeyman printer

Charles Manby Smith

BIBLIOLIFE

Copyright © BiblioLife, LLC

This book represents a historical reproduction of a work originally published before 1923 that is part of a unique project which provides opportunities for readers, educators and researchers by bringing hard-to-find original publications back into print at reasonable prices. Because this and other works are culturally important, we have made them available as part of our commitment to protecting, preserving and promoting the world's literature. These books are in the "public domain" and were digitized and made available in cooperation with libraries, archives, and open source initiatives around the world dedicated to this important mission.

We believe that when we undertake the difficult task of re-creating these works as attractive, readable and affordable books, we further the goal of sharing these works with a global audience, and preserving a vanishing wealth of human knowledge.

Many historical books were originally published in small fonts, which can make them very difficult to read. Accordingly, in order to improve the reading experience of these books, we have created "enlarged print" versions of our books. Because of font size variation in the original books, some of these may not technically qualify as "large print" books, as that term is generally defined; however, we believe these versions provide an overall improved reading experience for many.

THE WORKING-MAN'S WAY IN THE WORLD

BEING THE

AUTOBIOGRAPHY

OF A

JOURNEYMAN PRINTER

REDFIELD
110 & 112 NASSAU-STREET, NEW-YORK
1854.

PREFACE.

THE time has been when an apology would have been thought necessary for obtruding on the notice of the public these passages in the life of a Working Man: that time is, however, past, and there are now an abundance of precedents to keep any man in countenance who, for reasons good, bad, or indifferent, may choose to draw aside the veil from his personal history, and publish it to the world. My own reasons for so doing the reader will find out in the course of the following pages, if he think it worth his while to peruse them; and therefore I need not state them here. Neither shall I endeavor to secure his favorable opinion by palliating my own blunders. Like poor Goldsmith, I know "there are a hundred faults in this thing"—but, unlike him, I do not know that anything could be said to prove them beauties. One thing

I know; and that is, that if what is here written and printed be not worth reading, nothing that can be said in apology will make it so. I might say, truly enough, that what I have written I have seen; but the question is, whether what I have seen and been in the course of my life is worth writing about? Of that the reader is perhaps the best judge. I ask but his candid consideration, and shall submit to his verdict, whatever it be, with the best grace I may.

I did not intend to preface these desultory sketches with a single introductory remark; having a conviction that all such premonitions to works of this kind are needless. But the printer warns me that there are two blank pages which must be filled, as, being a printer myself, I know perfectly well—and therefore I fill them up with a Preface, which, if it have no other merit, has at least that of stopping a gap, and therein resembles ten thousand other Prefaces; or else I know nothing of my trade.

CONTENTS.

CHAPTER I.

I am born, and brought up to rely on self-exertion—I go to school, through wet and dry, and learn a little cheap Latin and gratuitous Greek—My first sorrow and separation—My father's misfortunes—His household homily, which affords a glimpse of his character—I set out in search of a trade—Destiny makes me a Printer—I begin life as a Devil, and win favor—My master's religion and business—The Fish—I am apprenticed, and begin to know the world—Dangerous companions—The tramping system—I find out my ignorance, and commence study—A club of seven—End of my apprenticeship—I start for the metropolis 13

CHAPTER II.

I arrive in London and commence the search for employment—No Printers wanted—A remnant of a Compositor—His history and prospects—Despair in a business way—The use of a flat iron—His good advice to me—He pays himself for it—Farewell for seven years—My first Sunday in town—A charity sermon—I carry my pigs to a fine market—Renewed search for work—I am picked up in the park—Solve a riddle, (not the Sphinx's,) and dine and drink like a lord—Effects of champagne—No work for me in London—I resolve to start for Paris—Journey to Dover—No lodging, how to manage without a bed—Bob Jones, a benefactor—Smuggling manœuvres—Living bonnet-boxes and a Petticoat Captain—Custom-house nuisances—Gallic Tritons—I embark for France... 28

CHAPTER III.

The Straits of Dover, and of Nottingham weavers—The virtues of bread and butter—Unanimity among the passengers—A cheap voyage—Calais touters—I mount a knapsack, and start for Paris on foot—Last view of Old England—How the gens-d'armes turn a penny—I make an acquaintance—A French country wagon and team—My first lesson in the language—French farming—Triumphant and distressing entry into Abbeville—Road-side inn and its inmates—Supper and song—Singular sleeping quarters—Primitive price of accommodation—We proceed on our way—I find myself in possession of a wagon and five horses—Grandvilliers—Beauvais—I lose my only friend—I arrive in the Palais Royal—An English home in Paris—I commence the study of the language—How I managed it—A scoundrelly Parisian shark feeds me with false hopes, with the view of plundering me—Odd sort of dramatico-gastronomical entertainment—I scent the designs of the shark, and escape his fangs—One of his victims—Am introduced by M Galignani to Count D——, who gives me employment. 45

CHAPTER IV.

Paris on a summer's morning—A gratuitous bath, for which I am very near paying too dear—An innocent pickpocket—The Breakfast of the operative Masons—The custom of *faire greve*—A French Printing office in 1826—Pirated editions of Scott's novels—I pay my footing, and am hoaxed according to rule—My English acquaintance in Paris—Gentlemen R————Franks the old Peninsular campaigner—A Duel of a French and English trooper—The man of many tongues—N——, the infidel philosopher and republican—A tippling Cockney and his notions of prudence—A French workman of the old school, and his reminiscences of the Revolution of '89—Olfactory misdemeanors—M——, the type-farmer—I apply for work at press—Vanity of the overseer—Unexpected encounter with the Fish—His past history and present confidences—The Fish in love—I am introduced to his Inamorata—A trip to Versailles—Extraordinary experience in returning to Paris 68

CHAPTER V.

The Loves of the Fish—A musical acquaintance—Extraordinary Musical Performance—A trap for the widow—I urge my companion's suit—The friend of the family—The widow not to be caught—The Fish disappears in dudgeon—I grow fond of billiards—The Pool and the Pole—A Duel by moonlight—New resolutions—A new study—Pursuit of knowledge under a blanket—A literary auction—My friend N—— and his extempore Homilies on Politics and Religion—Their effect upon me—N—— turns author, and I commence as Professor of English—My first pupil—Difficulties of teaching; the Future tense and the Subjunctive mood—Account of my Patrons............ 93

CHAPTER VI.

Thoughts of home—Reminiscences of Parson C——, the gambling Divine—Death of a Country Squire—Weak resolutions—The Sampford Ghost—An apology for Gaming—Interior of a Gaming-house—Interview with C——His suicide—Charles X. and his advisers—The Ordonnances—N—— joins the Republicans and I take care of myself—Barricades, Bullets, and Dragoon-pepper—First and second days of the Revolution—Cockney mettle—Night of the 28th—Victory of the Republicans on the 29th—Lafayette and the Duke of Orleans—The Chances of War—A sudden stop to my professorship—I start for home with half a passport—A fond Irish husband—A capsized Diligence—An affectionate re-union—I arrive at home........118

CHAPTER VII.

The Pleasures of Home—Prospect of employment—A new Patron and a new engagement—The Doctor, his house, and his hobbies—A finny Compact—A trip to London and back—A private Printing Office—I find myself in clover—And in love—The Doctor and the Methodists—A Primitive Preacher—A Fire in the Village; the Doctor's humanity, and the gratitude of his pensioners—A visit to Bristol—Feeling on the subject of Reform—Arrival of Sir Charles Wetherell—Reading the Riot Act—The Bristol Riots—Plunder of the Mansion House—Burning of the Gaols—Burning of the Mansion House—Conduct of Colonel Brereton—Burning of the Bishop's Palace—Sacking of Queen's Square—Destruction of the Custom House—Conduct of the Mob—Cunning and Cowardice of Mob-leaders

CHAPTER VIII.

French and English Mobs—I resume work at F———Second Journey to London to seek my Fortune—Make my *debut* in a London office—Parson Smart—The art of extempore preaching—How to "dish" the Cash—Admirable management of an Overseer—a Greek compositor—

1*

"Writing horse"—I am out-generalled by the Grecian—The Sheep's head Delinquent turned Gentleman—He gives me employment—His clever Tactics—I am out of work and miserable—the Cutler Editor and amateur Printer—How to get up a Country Newspaper—The late County Advertiser—Sketch of a Country Market-town—I am cut by the Cutler—Return to Town—Clever and profitable Dodge of colluding Printers—The Latin language not worth sixpence to a Journeyman Printer—I am enlightened on the subject of the Compositors' System of Protection—Which defrauds me of my labor—An offensive Cockney—I 'lick" him, and am chapelled and fined—Resolve to give up my berth—Apply for a situation in a School 175

CHAPTER IX.

I am engaged at the Grammar School—Farewell for a time to the Printing Office—Enter upon my new duties—My Companions and Coadjutors—Up in the morning early—The Mortal Body—"Plugger"—The life of an Usher in a School—Value of Time—Arrival of "Tater," and establishment of the drill—A mutinous Militia—The Whisker Synod—A domestic Revolution and a Barring out—Precautions against Starvation—Physical force triumphant—The Christmas Holidays—Parson Smart and my Sheep's-head Patron again—I go to work temporarily on a Weekly Paper—A Popular Author and Burglary Historian—The Mysteries of Romance Writing—The Mushroom Literature which springs up in a night—Desperate resources of Genius—I surrender my post. 202

CHAPTER X.

I return to the Grammar-School—New Regulations—I resolve to leave—Am paid off and return to London—Search for Employment—A model Master Printer, not for imitation—I find work on the Surrey side—Enormous gains of workmen—Cold Comfort—Pleasant Anticipations—A sudden check to them—Poor Parson Smart—"Wanted a Schoolmaster"—A Crowd of Competitors—A confident Character—A Parish Beadle—A Midnight Examination—Claims of Candidates—The Schoolmaster elect—Decree of Mr Bundle—Dissatisfaction and Tumult—Farce of advertising in some cases—A Roadside Professor—Geography made easy—"Strike flat the thick rotundity o' the Globe"—First Literary Attempts—A dishonest Patron—I am employed in a Government House—Economy of a "fast" Printing Office—A permanent Post—A home visit and dispositions for matrimony—I am married 229

CHAPTER XI.

Marriage and Manhood—I keep my own counsel—Memoir of Charley Crawfish, a "woman's husband" and a compositor of the old school—Doings of the "Cock Sparrow"—Charley's Portrait—Sixteen shillings' worth of Love—A Printer's Wedding—Grand musical procession—The Bride in hysterics—A 'Jerry"—Congratulatory address—Spiritual union—Pleasures of Housekeeping—Home Joys—Paternal Counsels—A public Execution—The Rush to the Gibbet—Conduct of the mob—The victim of the Law—Death in the air—The Gallows good for Trade—Reflections on British killing by Law—Executions in France—The Influence of the Hangman upon the crime committing class—Effects of "Gallows Literature" 258

CHAPTER XII

The Printing Season—A "regular Fly"—Blue-book Labors—Half a pint of Beer—Office suppers and night work—A Sleepy House—Birth of a Blue-book—Destiny of the majority of them—I am promoted and enter the closet—The Printer's Reader—His peculiar position, and the reputation he bears—A model Reader—Candidates for the Closet—His real Character—Slanders concerning him—His habits of neatness and punctuality—His amusements—His "den"—The Reader at work—The Reading-boy, and his predilections—His duties and habits—The reader his oracle—Specimen of the tribe—A stipendiary Billow—Virtues of the Wave—His one failing—I am called up to be reprimanded—Marvellous erudition of my Employer 283

CHAPTER XIII.

Overseers, their Duties, Temptations, Virtues, and Failings—Playfair—Screw-Screwdriver—The Printer's Weigh-goose—Who pays the piper—Non Nobis Domine—Silence for the Cha-a-ar'—The Governor's Speech—Incomprehensible Moonshine—The Overseer's Speech—Moonshine accompanied with muttered Thunder—Social Harmony—The Tables turned—Strange Gospellers—Laborious Fanaticism—Three in one pulpit—Oh for a dose of Physic'—Dearth of Religious Knowledge 310

CHAPTER XIV.

I cut off my own tale, and wind up that of others—My last visit to the paternal roof—A Domestic Scene—A Sabbath Evening Walk—

CONTENTS.

Worship *al Fresco*—Wagon-loads of Eloquence—a travelling Prophetess—a startling Surprise—My old Friend of the Revolution—An Infidel turned Evangelist—Death a stern Teacher—N——'s History—Consummation of Dick D——, the tippling Cockney—Profitable Policy of the "own Correspondent," and his mysterious disappearance—Last news of my Sheep's-head Friend—The Fish once more, his successful courtship and prosperous marriage—Parents and Friends in the Silent Land——Conclusion 332

APPENDIX.

A Workingman's Notions on Socialism 349

THE WORKING-MAN'S WAY IN THE WORLD.

BY A WORKING-MAN

CHAPTER I.

I am born, and brought up to rely on self-exertion—I go to school, through wet and dry, and learn a little cheap Latin and gratuitous Greek—My first sorrow and separation—My father's misfortunes—His household homily, which affords a glimpse of his character—I set out in search of a trade—Destiny makes me a Printer—I begin life as a Devil, and win favor—My master's religion and business—The Fish—I am apprenticed, and begin to know the world—Dangerous companions—The tramping system—I find out my ignorance, and commence study—A club of seven—End of my apprenticeship—I start for the metropolis

The condition of the laboring classes, their claims to the assistance and sympathy of the ranks above them, their political grievances, their social and moral degradation, their right to a voice in the election of representatives in Parliament, their demand of " a fair day's wages for a fair day's work," their moral and religious sentiments, their supposed revolutionary tendencies, and a host of similar or analogous subjects, all bearing a close reference to the question of industry and its rights, have now for some years been agitated in every possible form, and kept continually before the public view. Papers, sketches, and articles of every size and weight—disquisitions, philosophical or fanciful, and novels and romances not a few, have borne the same burden, and blown the same querulous blast; yet is the subject as unexhausted and unsettled as ever. I make no pretensions to settle it myself; I leave that to wiser heads and stronger hands, content if the record of such facts as have come under my own notice may contribute in any degree, however small, to shed a gleam of truth upon the popular question of the day.

I make no claims to literary talent, and must crave the reader's indulgence for my want of literary tact. I can forge no fiction upon which to hang any peculiar doctrines or dogmas of my own. Doctrines or dogmas, indeed, I have none to inculcate or announce, and no romantic story to tell. I am a working-man, in the plainest acceptation of the term, and one whose companionship, for more than thirty years, has been with working-men. My knowledge of the world is of the working-man's world, and my knowledge of books (the world of mind and of the past) has been derived from such books as a working-man could afford to buy or avail to borrow. So pardon, gentles all, and a plenary indulgence (if such a word may be mentioned in these papaphobic times), for all the sins I may fall into, and all the *lapsus pennæ* which must occur now and then to one but little accustomed to trail the quill

I was born on the banks of the Exe, in a pleasant town not a score of miles from the capital of Devon—a town in which a clear little brook, not a yard wide, ran babbling and sparkling through the streets, where it was not unusual to see a chase after a trout, of a summer's morning, among the lads and shopkeepers of the place. My parents were honest, industrious, and God-fearing, and brought up a large family (' we were seven,") though with but limited means, in comfort and respectability. We were taught to fear God and honor the King—which latter injunction we obeyed by making a holiday of the fourth of June—and were early imbued with the necessity of self-reliance, and thoroughly impregnated with the truth of what was a part of our family creed, that " Heaven helps those who help themselves."

In a meadow upon the skirts of the town, adjoining the road leading to Exeter, stood the grammar-school, from which the famous Bampfield Moore Carew, king of the gypsy tribe, eloped, when a school-boy, to join his gang of vagabonds. Here, in the good old days "when George the Third was King," my father being a freeman of the town, I enjoyed the advantage of hic-hæc-hoc-ing it for a couple of years. Messrs. Richards and Matthews were the classical masters at that time, and well deserved the good-will of the honest burgesses for the praiseworthy pains they took in the discharge of their functions. Though both were severe disciplinarians, and one, though I forget which, made a rather freer use of the cane than was agreeable to juvenile shoulders, they yet managed to make the boys rather fond of the school than otherwise. As a proof of this I may mention that upon one occasion, when the school was inaccessible, the meadow that divided it from the road being flooded by the heavy rains, many of the boys got across the water in tubs or on stilts, and I myself (which fixes the fact in my memory) got a ducking, through an abortive attempt to do the same.

Here, in the course of my two years, I picked up "small Latin and less Greek," together with as much mathematics and algebra as might have served to start me in those studies, had my after career allowed me leisure to pursue them. As it was, my Greek, small, indeed, at the best, soon came to the vanishing-point. My Latin, however, through all my after struggles for subsistence, I was unwilling to part with; and as I would not let it go, it grew by slow degrees into an accomplishment not common to my class, but a source of interest, perhaps too, of vanity, to myself, though I am not aware—and I make the avowal for the benefit of all those to whom the *cui-bono* is a rule of action—that it ever put a pound into my pocket.

When I had completed my second year at the grammar-school, having just turned thirteen, my parents, and of course, with them the whole family, none of whom were grown up, removed from Devonshire, and settled in Bristol. My father had suffered a loss which, though he had philosophy enough to bear with tolerable composure, it being only a loss of this world's goods, he did not yet choose to bear in the company of those who might seek to add the burden of their compassion and condolence to the weight of his own difficulties. He would have been grateful for the assistance of a friend, and had generosity enough to avail himself of it, but he loathed the lavish pity which costs nothing and is worth less; and so he flew from the face of it to try his fortune elsewhere. It was sad to part from the home of my boyhood, the green lanes through which I had wandered, the clear streams in which I had fished and swum, and the dear companions of childhood with whom I had tasted the first and purest pleasures of friendship unfeigned and unfaltering; but the contrast that awaited me at Bristol was sadder still. I had not been made aware of the real circumstances of our lot before leaving our old home, and it was not until we were settled in our new residence, a small cottage on the Gloucester road, within a mile of the city of dirt and smoke, that the whole truth was made known to us all. On the second day after our arrival, when we had by our common efforts succeeded in unpacking our goods, and putting our new dwelling into something like a condition of comfort, my father summoned us all to a family conference in the little parlor. I had recovered the spirits lost at parting with my old companions, and amused with the excitement of new scenery, and the bustle of moving and arranging the goods, broke in upon the group with a jovial laugh. My merriment was checked in an instant by the grave face of my father, as he pointed to a chair, and by the sight of my mother, who sat sobbing and shedding bitter tears over my youngest sister, who lay on her knees, while the two oldest, one on each side, strove in vain to comfort her.

My father began. "My children," said he, "I have sent for you all this evening, to tell you what it is but right that you should know. What I have to announce to you is, that a great change is come upon us as a family: most people in my case would say that a great misfortune has happened to us. Perhaps it is so; but that is more than I can undertake to say. It will be a misfortune to us, and perhaps something worse, if we persist in regarding it as such; but, as I have told you before to-day, it is in the power of each of us, while health and strength are spared to us, to get the better of circumstances, and to be happy, if we will, in spite of any calamity which we do not bring upon ourselves. We have left behind us in Devonshire the station which we once held, but we have also left behind us an unspotted character; and if we have lost all, we have at least the consolation remaining that nobody has lost anything by us. If we had stayed much longer where we were, you would have heard, in a much less pleasant manner than I now tell it you, that your father is a 'ruined man.' Such is the phrase the world uses in reference to cases like mine; but remember it is only a phrase, a piece of cant—the cant of the prosperous: a man is no more ruined because he is stripped of his means of spending than a tree is ruined because it is stripped of its foliage. The simple fact is just this, that we must work harder and live plainer than we have done; and we must *all* work, every one of us that can, to procure food and shelter for ourselves and for those that cannot."

Here my elder sisters broke in with a hearty declaration that they were willing to work at anything, and to begin at once; my brother and I were not slow in responding to the same purpose, and little Ned, who was hardly six, vowed that he could and would work as much as anybody.

My father continued: "I expected nothing less from you all, and that is the reason why I am not cast down in this strait, as some men might be. I have always laid good store by my girls and boys, and all I ask of them now is to stand by one another. Come, you see mother begins to put a smiling face upon the business at last. We will have no more of this talk to-day. To-morrow I go to the town to look out for employment—you, Tom and Charley, go with me; and who knows but we may drop upon a berth for each of us?"

The next day, in company with my father and elder brother, I perambulated the streets of Bristol, calling upon different persons to whom we carried letters of recommendation; and my father was fortunate enough to obtain an engagement for himself and my brother, who already possessed some skill as a cabinet-maker, the business which we had carried on in Devonshire. As neither of them could be employed before the commencement of the ensuing week, there was still time to look out for something for me. I knew well enough that the choice of a trade was out of the question, and that it was my duty to accept anything that offered; and I considered myself fortunate indeed when a printer, whom I shall call Cousins, offered to take me upon trial, and to bind me apprentice to himself in case of my giving satisfaction. Into a printing-office, then, at the age of thirteen years and three months, I entered, in the character of a *devil*, a term which, though now it is going out of use, and indeed among printers is gone out of use, was not at that time an unapt designation. The indescribably filthy processes which later improvements in the mode of doing business have altogether done away, were for the most part consigned to the luckless imp who enjoyed that infernal cognomen; and it is no slander to say that, when engaged in his daily occupation, he at least looked the character to perfection. Few boys, however, have any constitutional horror of dirt, and I did not allow its perpetual companionship to prejudice me against the duties of my function. I strove to give satisfaction, and did not strive in vain.

My master had the character of a religious man, and very possibly deserved it to a certain extent; but there were certain anomalies in his daily conduct which were unceremoniously discussed in the office among the journeymen and apprentices. He was a stationer and bookseller, as well as a printer, was a staunch churchman and regular communicant. He had family-prayer every evening after supper, and on Sundays after breakfast as well. But he supplied his customers with newspapers, and many of these were called for on Sunday morning; and it was no uncommon thing for the good man to rise from his knees in the middle of his prayer to go and serve a customer with a weekly paper. This I learnt from the conversation of the lads and the jeers of the men soon after I got there, and subsequently witnessed myself upon several occasions.

There were two journeymen and two apprentices besides myself, and there was a third hand who wrought occasionally both at press and case, as his services were required, and who had generally to be sought out at some one or other of his haunts in the town when anything was to be done in a hurry. It was my job, of course, to hunt him up when he was wanted. His real name was Cotton, but he was called by us and by all in the town who spoke of him, "The Fish," and an odd fish he certainly was. He was never drunk, from the simple fact that he had got over that weakness, and it was no longer in the power of any fluid to intoxicate him. Still he found a pleasure in the attempt, vain though it was, and drank everything he earned, and what else he could get besides. He plied for passengers occasionally on the river, and feathered his oars with the best. He piloted vessels down to the Channel, and drank his way home again in a period proportioned to their freight. He handled the hose at a fire, and enjoyed a pension from a gentleman whom he had rescued from a burning house some years before. One day, during the fair at St. James's, I found him in the garb of a beef-eater, blowing the trombone in front of a wild-beast show; on another, strapped to the back of a mad steed in a riding-school—the Fish being the only person who could be found daring enough to mount the savage brute. He had been a sailor; and, according to his own account, there was no country he had not seen, and no lingo he could not talk. At the time I first saw him he must have been about five-and-thirty; he was a strong, rather meagre but well-proportioned man, something taller than the average height, with a face of prepossessing mould, and brown as a berry His advent at the office was always hailed with a shout of welcome, and the time never seemed to pass so quickly or so merrily as when he was with us. He was an admirable pressman, but a poor hand at arranging the types (or what is technically termed composition), a process, indeed, for which he was not constituted either by education or habit. He had been under some obligation, we knew not what, to our employer, and would never allow a word to be uttered in his dispraise. The Fish was an embodied mystery to me during my boyhood, but, as he was invariably kind and generous, he grew into my good opinion, in spite of his incomprehensibility.

I passed nine months with Mr. Cousins before I was apprenticed, as it was not thought advisable to make out my indentures until I had reached fourteen, that I might be of age at the expiration of my term of seven years. Before the nine months had elapsed, my father's prospects had somewhat improved; and my master having expressed an inclination to take me as an in-door apprentice, an arrangement was made to that effect, and on my fourteenth birth-day I was regularly bound to learn the art and mystery of a printer. For three years I wrought daily in the office, and learned more of the world and the way of it than perhaps it was profitable to know. At that period the principles of infidelity were beginning their wide-spread diffusion among the working ranks. The works of Tom Paine—whose "Rights of Man" was regarded by a very large class, who considered themselves as foully wronged, in the light of a new-found charter, containing their natural privileges—were read with an avidity of which we can now scarcely form an idea. The "Age of Reason" was but a popular version of doctrines that had for ages before, arrayed in philosophical garb, been working their demoralizing effects in a different circle of society The advocates of disbelief now sought success, and found it to a desolating extent, among the humbler orders.

When I had just completed my sixteenth year, one of our apprentices, having finished his term, left us, and his place was filled by a London hand, who was a confirmed and hackneyed freethinker and leveller, and who labored hard to indoctrinate us with the then new notions. He was thoroughly master of all the deistical dogmas of the day, and would talk eloquently and well by the hour together upon the monstrous juggles of priestcraft, and the inconceivable folly of those who afforded them credence. He made selections from the Old and New Testament history, which he read aloud, and upon which he dilated with a force and eloquence that would have done honor to a barrister. With the most plausible reasoning he united the most cutting sarcasm, and with a show of the most generous candor he would invite our replies to his propositions, or challenge us to produce the arguments for our faith: woe to the unfortunate who had the temerity to accept his challenge! He was still better versed in disputation than in reasoning, and overthrew every objector by the force of metaphysical argument, and the power of his lungs. Though I had been too early and painstakingly instructed in the doctrines of the Christian faith not to be able to render a reason for adhering to it, I was yet too young to pretend to be its champion, especially against such an antagonist. I therefore held my peace, but unhappily did not continue to hold my faith in the same reverence as I had hitherto done. It would have been better for me if I had. I was not aware at the time that the tirades of Martin (such was the name of our deistical declaimer) were producing any effect upon my own mind. There were many points in his character which I could but admire. He was by far the best workman we ever had; he was open and generous, and ever ready to assist his fellows in any possible way. He possessed a fund of information upon all popular topics, and knew much of the personal history of the public characters of the day. He had travelled all over England, and wrought in most of the principal towns, and had received a substantial testimonial, at a period when testimonials were not hourly occurrences, for his successful advocacy of the rights of the working-man upon the occasion of a strike in the North. Upon every topic, moreover, except Christianity, he reasoned gently and modestly, and was the means and medium of much pleasant and useful information to his companions. He was a great admirer of Franklin, whom he was continually quoting, and whom he confessedly made his model.

When Martin had been with us about a year, and after I had passed full three years in the office, the work fell rather short; and my master, unwilling to part with Martin, whose services had stood him in good stead, proposed that I should take a turn for a few months in the shop, in the place of a shopman who was under notice to quit, in consequence of some unaccountable defalcations in the till. As I had not the slightest objection to a temporary change, I agreed to the proposition, stipulating only that I would not be absent from the office more than a year in the whole seven, lest, by want of practice, I might fail in my skill as a compositor. Accordingly, on the departure of the shopman, I installed myself in his place behind the counter. As the trade we did, though not contemptible in amount, was not sufficient to require my continual attention, I found time to read a good many of the books with which the shelves were stored. The "Age of Reason" was among the first, and, in order that both sides of the question might be fairly presented to my mind, was immediately followed by Bishop Watson's "Apology for the Bible." I should have read neither. What mischief the infidel writer effected, the bishop failed to repair. The iron blows of the former remained indented upon the tablet of my memory, while the godly rejoinder of the latter soon vanished like a summer cloud. Happily, the poisonous seed took no immediate root; my spirits were light and gay, and the thoughtless vivacity of youth, so often the source of evil, was, for a time at least, my protection from it. What sufficed, however, to give more force to the objector against Christianity than even his own matchless effrontery, was the insight which my new position gave me into the habits and practices of my employer, who himself enjoyed a high reputation as a religious and conscientious man. By his singular management, the same article was constantly sold to different parties for different prices. Like Robin Hood, he gave the poor, in some degree, the benefit of the contributions he levied upon the rich. Paper from the same ream was sold in quires at a price twenty per cent. less to the tradesman than to his more wealthy customers. He piously carried his gallantry to the ladies to a still greater extent, condescending to accept at their hands nearly double the value of their purchases. I confess that, on the first discovery of these peccadilloes, to which I was expected, and indeed compelled, to afford my complicity, I could not think of kneeling at his family-altar without a feeling of disgust and contempt. But, so true is it that habit reconciles the mind to everything, this feeling soon wore off. I began to consider such things allowable in business, and to look upon the inexperience and want of judgment of the buyer as the lawful prey of the shopkeeper.

At the end of a year I returned to my frame in the office, according to my stipulation. Martin was ill, often absent from weakness, and not able to do much work when present. He had caught a chill through incautiously bathing while hot, and the doctor had warned him that the consequences might be serious, if not fatal, unless he used great caution. As he used none, the admonition became a veracious prophecy; the cold settled upon his lungs, and he soon fell into a rapid decline. He would walk into the office in the fine summer days, and, seating himself among his old companions, would discourse, as he had been used to do, upon the folly of fanaticism—his term for religion—and the monstrousness of priestcraft. It is usual to describe the latter days and death of men of his character as scenes of horror, dismay, and despair. I know that in the case of Martin, there was nothing of the sort. The reason may have been, that he had no doubts. It was not in his nature long to doubt upon any question; if it was one in which he was concerned, he would have settled it speedily one way or another; and if not, he would have dismissed it from his mind altogether. He suffered but little violent pain until the day before he died. Up to that period he had sought amusement in cheerful and entertaining books. A child of his landlady read to him as he lay upon a sofa, while he endeavoured to fancy himself, as he said, a gentleman of fashion paying the penalty of a debauch. He sent for my master when his last hour was at hand, who hurried off to see him, in company with the parish parson; but Martin would hear no prayers. "I have no time to spare," said he, "for frivolities." Then, after a pause, "I have served you faithfully, Mr. Cousins. You will attend to my last request—will you not?" The old man gave his promise. "Post that letter after I am gone, and bury me at S——. It is a pretty place; and if my ghost walks, there will be pleasant places to walk in." The letter was addressed to a poor girl to whom he was betrothed, and reached her the next day. She came down to his funeral, and saw that his last desire was gratified.

The Fish was immensely moved at the sad fate of Martin, whom, though he had been long eclipsed by the other's superior talents, he admired exceedingly. He would have it that it was all owing to water-drinking (Martin took neither beer nor spirits), and warned each of us earnestly to beware of such a dangerous habit. We greatly felt the loss of our best hand, and, as work poured in upon us, we engaged a couple of tramps to recruit our working power. Both of them drew a few shillings in advance, "to procure a lodging," and neither of them appeared again to work it out. We succeeded, at length, in securing the assistance of one, through the precaution of not trusting him with anything till he had earned it. He managed, however, to obtain more money than he had earned on the first Saturday night, and of course failed to make his appearance on the Monday following.

Owing to the want of any efficient system of union among the members of the trade, the practice of tramping had, at the time I speak of, risen to a most disgraceful climax. A regular tide of lazy and filthy vagabonds, professedly of various trades, but virtually living without work, or the intention of working, flowed lazily through the kingdom from one end of it to the other. These were a continual and heavy tax upon the industrious members of the several trades upon whom they levied contributions for their support. Their laziness was comparable only to their impudence; it was impossible to get rid of them without a contribution, and if this fell short of their expectations it was not unfrequently received with contemptuous upbraidings. The greatest misfortune that could befall a regular tramp was the finding of employment; and it was rare, indeed, that any effectual assistance could be obtained from one of the tribe. It was necessary, too, to keep a sharp look-out upon their motions, as one and all seemed to possess an uniform habit of converting into cash, at the pawn-shop, anything and everything furtively portable. Like every other trade, that of the tramp has undergone the pressure of competition; they are as numerous as they ever were, perhaps more so; but necessity has taught them civility, and, finding the mere plea of want of work in most cases ineffectual to raise supplies, they invent wives and children starving, sick families or domestic calamities, and find it still difficult, at least according to the confessions of some of them, to escape the occasional pressure of hunger during their wanderings. There wants but the exercise of a little firmness and common sense on the part of the inmates of our workshops to put an end, at once and for ever, to this wretched trade—a trade by which thousands of indolent scamps contrive to get through life without discharging its duties, submitting to the vilest degradation, and enduring every species of discomfort—for all which they yet find compensation in the darling pleasures of a nomadic wayside existence. A point-blank refusal of money, in every case, would be an act of humanity to the tramps themselves, by putting an end to their miserable wanderings, and would relieve the working-classes from a burdensome tax, which it is injustice, not charity, to submit to.

During the first four years of my apprenticeship I received no wages, and as my parents could afford me but little out of their small store, it was not much that I was perplexed with expending. But at the end of my fourth year I drew a small weekly salary, one half of which my father allowed me for my own use. In addition to this, when we were busy, I earned a good deal in over-hours, and accordingly soon began to feel on a more independent footing. I bought books, and read as much as possible, and reflected upon what I read while engaged in my daily avocations. I found out what Martin had before caused me to suspect, namely, that I knew nothing, and had everything to learn. One holiday afternoon, while strolling among Clifton's rocky scenery, I met with a young man of about my own age, to whom I had occasionally spoken before. We fell into conversation, and I soon began to feel ashamed of my own inferiority in point of knowledge. He proposed to me to join a club of seven, which he was then endeavoring to organize with a view to mutual improvement. The plan was, to hire a room for three-and-sixpence a week, and to stock it with books, papers, and drawing-materials, each one contributing what he could. Subjects were to be discussed, essays written and criticised, the best authors read aloud, and their sentiments subjected to our common remark. I joined at once without hesitation, and have congratulated myself that I did so to this day. We got a room, with such attendance as we required at the sum above-named, and thus, for sixpence a week each, with an additional three-halfpence in winter time for firing, we had an imperfect, it is true, but still an efficient means of improvement at our command. Here we met nearly three hundred nights in the year, and talked, read, disputed, and wrote *de omnibus rebus et quibusdam aliis*, until the clock struck eleven. We had fines for non-attendance, and prizes, paid out of the fines, for the best-written productions. My father and Mr. Cousins approved of our club, and sometimes, together with a few friends of the other members, paid us a visit upon the occasion of a lecture or discussion upon any question upon which we considered ourselves up to the mark.

But it is time that this account of my apprenticeship should come to an end. I attended the club's sittings regularly during the remainder of my term, made as much acquaintance with the literature of the day as my means and leisure allowed, and took especial pains to qualify myself for any department of the business of a printer that it might be found advisable to engage in when I became my own master. The variety of my occupations, and the new interests which they created in my mind, seemed to add fresh wings to time. The last years of my term seemed not half the duration of the first. The second week in April, 1826, saw me free from all bonds and indentures, and ready to begin the world on my own account I would willingly have remained with Mr. Cousins for a season longer, but, unfortunately for me, the business had greatly declined a few months previous to my release, and there was now hardly sufficient employment to be found for the apprentices alone. The journeymen had been discharged for some time. The Fish had disappeared as well, after several vain applications for employment. This almost complete stoppage of business was one of the results of the dreadful money-panic of the day, which was the cause of severe deprivations to the working-classes throughout the whole kingdom. As I could obtain no employment in Bristol, and could not bear the thought of settling my feet under the frugal table of my parents, I resolved to seek an engagement in London; and for London I accordingly set out by the night-coach, within ten days of the expiration of my apprenticeship.

CHAPTER II.

I arrive in London and commence the search for employment—No Printers wanted—A remnant of a Compositor—His history and prospects—Despair in a business way—The use of a flat iron—His good advice to me—He pays himself for it—Farewell for seven years—My first Sunday in town—A charity sermon—I carry my pigs to a fine market—Renewed search for work—I am picked up in the park—Solve a riddle, (not the Sphinx's,) and dine and drink like a lord—Effects of champagne—No work for me in London—I resolve to start for Paris—Journey to Dover—No lodging, how to manage without a bed—Bob Jones, a benefactor—Smuggling manœuvres—Living bonnet-boxes and a Petticoat Captain—Custom-house nuisances—Gallic Tritons—I embark for France.

AFTER paying twelve shillings for an outside place by the Old Company's coach, which flew from Bristol to London nightly in sixteen or eighteen hours, as it might happen, I found myself in possession of nearly six pounds in cash. This, together with a dozen shirts, and two suits of clothes, about a score of well-thumbed volumes, among which my mother had packed a new pocket Bible, a set of drawing-instruments, and an old fiddle, constituted the whole amount of property which could be called my own. But, as the French novelists are fond of saying, I had my twenty-one years, and youth is a fortune in itself. I had no idea of poverty as attachable to my own case, and should have spurned the commiseration of any one who had presumed to offer it in reference to my prospects. I enjoyed my journey to town, in spite of the darkness and three or four sharp showers which wetted me to the skin; but must confess to losing heart a little when, after riding for more than a full hour through the interminable streets of London's western suburbs, the coach stopped at its destination, and I found myself alone in the populous desert of the capital.

After a hearty breakfast, not feeling in need of rest or sleep, I set out in search of a lodging; and having found the accommodations I required in a small street running out of the Blackfriar's road, transferred my luggage to a hackney-coach, and removed thither at once. I devoted my first day in town to holiday purposes, and walked along the leading streets to see what was to be seen. I bought a map of the city, and endeavored to imprint its leading features upon my memory by tracking my own route upon the paper. I further studied the map carefully in the evening, and addressed myself on the following day to the task of seeking employment. I had but one letter of introduction, and that was to my master's wholesale stationer, who resided in one of the old-fashioned narrow streets on the river side of St. Paul's, and who, Mr Cousins assured me, would forward my views as much as lay in his power. I called upon him accordingly, presented my credentials, and found him amazingly civil, and bland; but as his power happened to be *nil*, my views were none the better for his furtherance. He advised me to apply to the *Times* office. "You know," said he, "they are printing there every day, and all day long." To the *Times* office I went, and was, of course, summarily dismissed before I had half expressed my demand. As I had never worked on a newspaper, this did not much daunt me, and I proceeded to make application elsewhere. With some trouble I procured a list of London printers from my friend the wholesale stationer, who, having supplied me with that, and taken my address, informed me that I need not call again, as he would let me know so soon as he heard of any thing likely to suit me.

Armed with my list, I began my peregrinations, and in the course of the day called at above a dozen of the largest houses, without hardly obtaining a hearing. I returned rather out of spirits to my lodgings in the evening, and while taking tea with my landlord, who kept a sort of scrambling shop, filled with second-hand hardware and old furniture made him acquainted with my profession and wants. From him I learned that the printing business was just then in a state of the greatest depression, and that many hundreds of hands were out of employ, and thrown either upon the trade fund or their own wretched resources. I found his description but too true. My second day's inquiries were as fruitless as the first. Upon the doors of many of the offices notices were posted intimating that "Compositors and pressmen need not appply." This example, begun by some one weary of the incessant application of men seeking work, was soon followed by the whole trade, until at length the words "Printing-office" were nowhere to be seen without this awful appendage. In vain I walked from one end of London to the other, and trod the "stony-hearted streets" from morning to night, day after day. "We are doing nothing, and have not work for our old hands," was the stereotyped form of the reply I received at almost every house. Sometimes of an evening, after my miserable journeyings through the day, I would stand for hours in the Strand, leaning against the shutters of a closed shop, and watching the compositors at work by gas-light, on the opposite side of the way, upon a morning paper. How I envied them, and longed again to feel the familiar touch of type at my fingers' ends!

One night, while thus wishfully gazing at the active motions of my more fortunate compeers, I was accosted by a man in a sort of confidential whisper, who asked me, civilly and quietly enough, if I "would not stand a pint to a comp hard up and out of luck." The speaker was about thirty-five years of age, buttoned close to the chin in an old brown surtout, patched and greasy, his nether garments hung in shreds about his ankles, and his bare toes were visible by lamp-light through the rents in a pair of palpable charity boots. I took him at first for a beggar, not distinctly hearing his demand, and told him I had nothing for him. An involuntary gesture on his part made me aware of my mistake ere he replied, "I'm not used to beg, my friend. If I'm not mistaken, you are, like myself, out of employ; and I thought you might perhaps be willing to spare the price of a pint to a fellow-workman." "Is it possible," said I, "that you are a compositor, and reduced to such a condition?" "I leave other people to call me a compositor if they choose," said he, "I profess only to be a hand at case; but it's long enough since I had my fist in the space-box, and it's short sorts with me in the money-market for many a day, worse luck!" I told him to lead the way to some place where we could procure refreshment; that I was in need of supper, and would be glad if he would join me. Following him as he dived rapidly through a wilderness of narrow courts, I found myself in less than ten minutes in a little room, or rather closet, lighted by the smallest spur of gas, and seated in front of a hot baked sheep's head, a pot of foaming beer, and a small loaf. My new friend was not slow in appropriating the viands, which he despatched with a marvellous celerity, and with a knowledge of cerebral anatomy that was edifying to witness. I did my part with equal appetite, though with less dexterity, the want of which he gratefully supplied both by instruction and example. Our hunger appeased, I began to question him as to the state of the business we both pursued, and the cause of his dilapidated fortunes. "Oh," said he, "I'm not worse off than many others. If you'll order a pipe of tobacco I'll tell you how it goes with too many of us." I rang the bell; he called for a "screw," which the waiter having delivered, the poor fellow produced a short pipe from his pocket, filled it carefully, stowed away the remainder of the weed upon being informed that I did not smoke, and, between occasional puffs and sips at the can, delivered himself as follows.

"You see, my friend, that fathers and mothers, all of 'em, think that printing is a light and genteel business; and the consequence is, they are for everlastin' a-bringing their sons to be bound apprentice. There's three times the number of boys brought up to this trade that there's any occasion for; and that's the reason there are so many scamps and tramps to be found among them. In the busiest times, so far as I can recollect, and I'm getting on to forty, there are plenty of hands to be met with out of work—at least, I never heard tell of a dearth of compositors or pressmen either, and if the trade suffers a general depression, as is the case just now, full half, or even two-thirds, of the workmen are turned adrift. Being so often out of work makes a man apt to get fond of lounging about in tap-rooms, and tramping it, so that when he gets a job he don't care how soon he touches the tin for it, and gets off on the mop again. I like a drop of beer myself, (here's your health!) but I like work too—at the scale figure—and never shirked it yet to go on the swig. I'm a typo, I may say, bred and born. My father was a glass-cutter for twenty years on the *Morning* ———, he died before I was out of my time, or perhaps I might have taken his place. I was at S—'s then, comfortable enough; earned money, bought sticks, and, like a fool, took a wife. I don't say that out of any reflection upon the old 'oman, she's as good as me any day, and a better mother to the kids there never was."

"What do you mean?' I asked, "Have you any children?"

"Only four," said he, "now, we planted one last Sunday was a week."

"What do you mean by planted?"

"Lord! how green you are! (excuse me)—I mean buried, to be sure, and a good job too, hoping it's no harm to say so. Children are all very well where there's plenty for 'em, and a good trade to look to; but 'tis the devil and all to have half a dozen hungry mouths to feed, and never a mag in your pocket or even a shirt left to spout." Here the poor fellow unbuttoned his coat, and exhibited a patched flannel jacket next his skin. "I haven't earned a sixpence," he continued, "since November last, and we've been obliged to pop everything, all but the mattresses we lie on, and when they are gone, as go they will, I feel pretty sure of that, I don't know what's to follow. I suppose they won't take our carcases in pledge; it's a pity in this free country that the only thing that won't fetch a penny in the market is a fellow's own blood and bones. Here is a pretty portable catalogue of my property! Upon my life, I never knew, when I was well off, how rich I was. Look here!" So saying, he produced a bundle of duplicates thick as a pack of cards, and began reading them over. "This first one," said he, "is a four-post bedstead and hangings, bought for a ten pun' note in my courtin' days, and in for forty bob. That's the old 'oman's dress and shawl, in for nine and six. That's my best suit, in for a pound. All these is everything we had, in for next to nothing; down to this last one, a couple of flat-irons that little Jemmy spouted last night for fourpence a-piece. Mother would have been savage enough if he'd done that on a washing day; but when there's nothing left to wash, it's one consolation that a flat-iron is good for fourpence."

I asked him if he thought it would be of any use for me to continue my applications for employment.

"You have done the neighborly thing by me," he replied, "and I'll give you the best advice I can in return. You are a decent-looking cove, with a lot of tidy-looking togs, and might get taken on when a seedy hunks like me wouldn't stand a chance; but there's a hundred chances to one against you; and while you are waiting for the one, you may eat your pockets empty, and your back bare. Try it again for a day or two, if you like; and if that don't answer, and you don't want to go back to your friends, take yourself over to Paris while you have got the mopuses to get there. I know, for a certainty, that plenty of work is to be had there. I saw a letter from a chap yesterday, who is doing well, and says there's room for more hands. The work is English—mainly pirated editions of Scott, Byron, and others; and as English hands can get them out faster than the Frenchmen, of course they have the preference. That's my advice. I must be after wishing you a good night now, for the old 'oman will be coming home. She goes out a charing in the day, (God help me! I never thought to have let her)—and I mind the children at home. When it's dark, I get 'em to bed, and starts out for a chance. That's how I met with you. I've seen you two nights before, and knew you were a comp. out of work well enough."

I demanded what was to pay, and produced my purse, in which were a few sovereigns and one shilling. Handing him a sovereign, I requested him to pay the reckoning.

"You have a shilling there," said he, "that will more than pay it."

"No," said I, "I want change," (intending to help him with a few shillings, which I thought might be due from me to the necessities of his family.)

He took the sovereign and went out, *and I saw him no more till the year 1833, seven and a half years after our sheep's-head supper.*

I sat musing in my chair for some minutes, revolving in my mind the misfortunes of this poor fellow, whom every moment I expected to re-appear. I had resolved to spare him a crown from my stock in hand, and to make an appointment with him for another meeting. The waiter coming in, I asked what had become of my friend, and was informed that he had paid the reckoning and taken his departure. I was rather astounded on hearing this, but took care to betray no surprise. I waited a full half hour at the door of the house, which was in a court near Clare market, with some sort of expectation that he would return. At length I turned my steps homewards more in sorrow than in anger, regretting chiefly that I had not got more information out of him, since it had cost me so dear. That the man was not habitually dishonest I felt assured; and when I considered the temptations that four hungry children must have presented to his mind, I felt more inclined to blame my own want of caution than his weakness of principle.

The next day being Saturday, I knew it was of little use to apply for work; and being weary with a week's walking, I stayed at home and wrote to my father, describing the state of the business, and bidding him not to be surprised if I should see fit to go abroad for employment. I went out for an hour in the evening, in search of my delinquent companion of the night before, but, of course, without meeting with him.

I rose with a heavy heart on the Sunday morning, and read mechanically a chapter or two in the little Bible in which my mother had blotted my name upon the title-page; but my thoughts were far away, and I knew not what I read. It was on that morning that I really missed my home, for the first time; and some tears, not the first but the bitterest since I had left our snug cottage, started from my eyes. But the thought of home led me to do as I knew they were doing at home. So having breakfasted with my landlord, I dressed in my best, and set off to church, resolved if possible to banish all thoughts of business for that day at least. It was not to be so, however. Crossing the river, I walked into the first church I came to, and being well-dressed, was shown into a pew by the verger. The parson preached a charity-sermon in aid of certain poor Welch curates, who, he said, were doing duty in the Lord's vineyard for the wretched pittance of twelve pounds a year; and he urged with such length and strength the obligation we were all under to administer to their necessities, that I felt it would be difficult to pass the plate without giving. I felt offended, however, with his pertinacity, and more so with the ostentation of a huge diamond ring which he wore on his finger, and flashed in our faces twenty times a minute in the vehemence of his gesticulation—and secretly resolved that, as charity begins at home, and as his big diamond would be of more use to the poor Welshman than anything I could spare, pass the plate I would, cost what blushes it might. As fate would have it, the opportunity was not afforded me. No sooner was the sermon ended, than round came half-a-dozen ecclesiastical mendicants, each armed with a kind of pocket-pistol shaped like the bowl of a huge spoon. These were presented point-blank with a sort of stand-

and-deliver gesture to each inmate of every pew. At sight of these formidable weapons my uncharitable resolution took flight, and I began fumbling in my pocket for the identical shilling which the sheep's head delinquent had recognized on the Friday night. Just as I imagined it secure between my finger and thumb the pocket-pistol was at my breast, and I dropped in the coin, which, as it glided through a slit in the green baize lining of the begging-box, I had the mortification of perceiving was one of my few remaining sovereigns. I remember thinking I would have given the others for the pleasure of kicking the diamond-ringed parson round the aisles of his own church to the tune of Handel's Occasional Overture with which the organ was pealing us out. I walked back to my lodgings in a semi-savage mood, and began to think, to use a Devonshire phrase, that I had " brought my pigs to a fine market." Here had I been scarcely a week in London, without having earned a sixpence or finding the chance of earning one, and a good half of my funds had already disappeared. I told my landlord of both my losses; he derided my folly in trusting a fellow with a sovereign who had not a shirt to his back, and my want of spirit in not applying at the vestry and recovering the other from the collectors, who, he said, would willingly have returned it. I told him I could not have done it for ten times the sum, even though I had not another farthing in the world. ' Then,' said he, ' you won't be fool enough to fret about it."

I passed the rest of the day in revolving what would be the most prudent course to adopt, and came at last to the resolution not to remain longer in London than the end of the following week, unless I obtained or saw a pretty certain prospect of obtaining employment. I put myself also upon short allowance, setting a shilling a day at the most for my expenses so long as I earned nothing. I rose the next morning in better spirits, the result, no doubt, of having a decided plan to act upon. I made the best appearance I could, and repeated my applications at every office with as much earnestness as though it were my first time of calling. In two days I had canvassed the city district for the second time in vain, and on the Wednesday pushed my route further west, with the intention of calling at some small job-houses whose addresses my landlord had given me.

Finding myself about one o'clock in the neighborhood of St. James's Park, and not feeling so hungry as usual at that universal dinner-hour of the artisan, I persuaded myself that I could do without a dinner for once, and resolved to rest on one of the benches in the Park, and dine with Duke Humphrey. Accordingly, finding a seat to my liking, and stretching my limbs upon it at my ease, I pulled a small duodecimo Sallust from my pocket, and began to read. I had got through some ten pages, and was admiring the impudence of that redoubtable scoundrel Cataline, when I felt a gentle tap on the shoulder. Looking up, my eyes met those of a tall commanding personage, whose grizzled hair and profuse white whiskers gave token of a foreigner and a sexagenarian. He did not apologize for disturbing my studies; but smiling blandly, said, in a foreign accent—

"And so you read Latin?"

"Yes," said I, "for want of something better to do."

"You might be worse employed, young man. What are you reading?"

"The 'Conspiracy of Cataline,'" (handing him the book.)

"Ha! Sallust, a practical scoundrel, but not a bad historian. Can you understand him well?"

"I ought to—I've read him through half-a-dozen times."

"Come, then, my friend, I will give you a riddle. Can you resolve me this: *Sum principium mundi; sum finis omnium rerum; sum tria juncta in uno; attamen non sum Deus?*"

"When the ancients propounded a riddle," said I, "they always named a reward for the solution. What am I to get if I answer it?" This I said not with any idea of getting a reward, but merely to gain a moment for consideration.

'Ha! I like that well! Come, I shall give you a glass of wine."

"Well, then," said I, "*Impransus sum*. The answer to your riddle is the last letter of that declaration, which I dare swear you cannot and never could pronounce with the same truth as I do."

He laughed, told me I had earned a bumper, and invited me to follow him. I hesitated for a moment or two, as my pride revolted against being beholden to a stranger for a meal; but curiosity prevailed, and I followed him, wondering at my adventure, as he led the way out of the park-inclosure. Crossing the Mall, he stopped at one of the doors of Carlton Gardens, and, producing a key, opened it, and pushed me in before him. We were met in the gardens by a powdered gentleman's gentleman, from whose polite obsequiousness to my guide, I began to form a grand idea of the latter. The two spoke for a few moments in a language I did not understand, and the old gentleman then led the way up one flight of stairs to a large room, where was a fire, before which stood a table covered with books and papers, both English and German, as I supposed from the character. He pointed to a seat, and took one himself by the fireside. In a moment a servant in rich livery appeared bearing a tray well supplied with cold meats and a pasty; he was followed closely by another who brought wine and glasses.

"Now, my young friend," said my hospitable Amphitryon, "let me see that your appetite is equal to your scholarship; help yourself, and take your leisure."

I did as he commanded me, and began disembowelling a mysterious-looking pasty, in which, so exquisite was the flavor to my untaught palate, I soon made a most savage inroad. I thought I had made a meal which would have done honor to Dalgetty himself, when my host, pouring a bubbling colorless liquid into a glass full four inches deep, filling at the same time another for himself, bade me taste that, and try again. I obeyed, and enjoyed the luxury of champagne for the first time, and then renewed my assault upon the viands. When I had done my worst upon these, I rose to go, and tendered my thanks for his hospitality. But he insisted upon my fulfilling the conditions of the treaty, which he averred were that I should finish the bottle; and, upon his assurance that it would not hurt me, I consented to do so. We sat together for nearly an hour, during which he managed to get out of me my whole history and prospects. The treaty being fulfilled, he rang the bell, and, assuring me he was happy to have made my acquaintance, shook hands, and consigned me to the care of his waiting-gentleman, who very politely escorted me to the same door by which I entered.

I felt in a very merry mood as I walked the rest of my round, and no doubt presented a rather flushed and impudent appearance at the several places where I called to demand employment in the course of the afternoon. But no sooner were the fumes of the wine vanished from my brain than I began to feel discontented and half-ashamed of myself, as well as somewhat angry with the old gentleman, whoever he might be, for putting me in what my pride suggested was no very commendable a position. My feeling of independence revolted at the idea of having supplied my wants at the cost of another, and I was actually silly enough to feel mortified at the thought of having received a meal at the hands of a stranger. So strong was this feeling within me, that I took care not to go near that quarter again during the remainder of my short stay in town.

Notwithstanding the uniform ill success that attended all my inquiries, I persisted in my applications for work up to sunset on the Friday night Finding all my efforts useless, I formed the sudden resolution of starting for Paris on the following morning. With this view, I hastened to my lodgings, tied up my books, with the exception of my Bible and a Printer's Grammar, and lugging them off to a dealer, sold them for a fourth of their value. Half-a-dozen of my new shirts were made over to my landlord at a moderate price; and having thus lightened my luggage, and reinstated my funds, I wrote a few lines to my father, informing him of my destination, and went early to bed, to recruit for the morrow's journey.

I was the first passenger that stepped on board the Margate steamer on the Saturday morning. I sat watching my two boxes for a full hour before the company for the day had arrived, and the paddles were in motion. We had an agreeable and rapid voyage, and arrived at Margate between four and five in the afternoon. While looking about for a conveyance to Dover, I was accosted by a post-boy, who said he was going back with a return chaise, and would take me and my boxes for eighteen-pence, provided that I would close the window-blinds as we passed the pikes. I made no objection, and thus, simulating nobody, had a pleasant and cheap ride, with my reflections on the probable future for my sole company. I put up at a small inn in Snargate-street, and bespeaking supper, but omitting to mention a bed, took a walk through the town and on the pebbly beach, amid the roar of the dashing surges, under the light of a waning moon. I returned about ten o'clock to my supper; having leisurely discussed that, I took up a newspaper, to wile away the time until retiring. When at length, it being near midnight, I called for a candle, and requested to be shown to my chamber, the landlord informed me that he had no bed to spare, and that I had not bespoke one. I immediately set off in search of other accommodation, and had the agreeable fortune of finding that none was to be had at that late hour. So putting the best face I could upon my mischance, I resolved to outface the night for once, and, as to-morrow would be a day of rest, to retire early and make up for it. It grew, however, dismally cold, and walking rapidly along the beach, I was challenged by one of the Preventive men, to whom I told my misfortune. He recommended me to go up to the Castle, where I should find some of the soldiers in the canteen, and where I could sleep comfortably enough by the fire. Following his advice I ascended the hill, and accosting the first sentinel I saw, acquainted him with my wishes. This civil fellow told me to go straight on, and if any one spoke to me, to ask for Bob Jones, who would be sure to be there, and would give me a shake-down. I found Bob Jones a decided member of the civil brigade—told him what his friend had said, and offered to wet his whistle if he would make it good, as I felt very weary—adding that I had come from London that morning. Bob declined to wet his whistle just then, but heaping half-a-dozen watch-coats upon a broad bench near a large blazing fire, advised me to go to sleep while I was in the mood; he would see that no one should disturb me. In five minutes I was fast asleep, and did not wake until the sun was high in the sky, and the band was playing in the parade-ground. Bob Jones had vanished ere I awoke, and I have had no opportunity of returning thanks for his courtesy from that time to this. I returned to my inn; the landlord was full of apologies, and showed me to a room whither he had carried my boxes, and where I could sleep so long as I stayed in Dover. I asked what time the packet sailed for Calais next morning, and understanding it would sail at ten, made arrangements for departing with it.

After church in the afternoon, I encountered the Preventive-man of the night before, and thanked him for his good counsel. We walked together on the beach; and wishing to get at the feeling of his profession, I asked him how he liked his occupation, and said that I supposed it must be a mere ceremony in such a place, close to a town where there were so many soldiers and a custom-house.

"You don't know much about it," said he. "What do you think that is?" pointing to the half of a boat sticking up among the pebbles.

" Why, a piece of an old boat."

" No, it aint; try again."

" No?—if that's not a part of an old boat, I can't believe my own eyes."

"Believe what you like, that there's no part of an old boat, for a very good reason ; 'tis part of a new un, unless you call six weeks or two months, mayhap, very old."

I was still incredulous.

" Look here," said he. " These planks is about the thickness of shoe-leather. This boat was built (and there's lots more like her) for one voyage and no more. She would carry three or four hundred tubs, besides her hands. Well, she starts from the opposite coast just before dark; she gets within signal distance, and there she lies till her friends ashore give the signal, when in she pulls, and mayhap lands her cargo under our very noses, in a dark night, before we get sight of her. I've known a boat shoot the harbor while there were Preventives on each pier, and they neither see nor hear her. In the morning we find the boat, and that's all. The boat suffers the sentence of the law, at which the free-traders laugh as long as they win; but they mostly come to our net sooner or later."

We passed the severed carcases of several of these executed small craft, by which I judged that a brisk smuggling trade was there carried on in small bottoms. Turning my eyes seaward, I fancied I saw a dim line of smoke upon the horizon. "Is not that a steamer, yonder?" said I to my companion.

"Yes," said he, "it is the French steamer, and if you wait till she comes in you'll see another system of smuggling that the Government is obliged to wink at in spite of their teeth."

We walked on, and my companion being off duty, ascended the high grounds leading to the Castle, where, seated upon a rusty gun, we began spying alternately at the approaching vessel, through my companion's glass.

"Ha! There they are, sure enough!" he exclaimed; "the whole regiment of drabs. Don't you see," he continued, handing me the glass, " a waving straw-colored line just under the smoke? You can see that, though you can hardly see the deck as yet."

I fancied I saw what he described, and asked what it meant.

"It means bonnets," said he.

"Bonnets!" said I, "and petticoats to match, of course."

"No 'of course' about it," he replied. "Petticoats *not* to match, if you like."

"Don't bother me with riddles; let me know all about it."

"That's soon told," said he. "'Tis the fashion just now, you know, for the ladies to wear their bonnets as big as the starn of a lugger, and what they call Leghorn straws is all the go. Every lady as goes abroad comes home under a roof of thatch big enough to shelter a whole family. She buys it in France, and as the Government don't tax the dress a lady wears, why she escapes the duty. Now, I've heard the duty on every one of these is summat like a pound. So, you see, there's a petticoat captain, a sort of man-milliner, living in the town here, who is making a bouncing fortune by running regular three cargoes of bonnets a-week through the very jaws of the custom-house. The way he does it is this; he hires a parcel of drabs and cinder-wenches, and ships 'em aboard the French steamer, which sails from Dover every other day. He claps on the head of every one of 'em a bran new Leghorn, to be worn on the return voyage. They drop their tiles at his house so soon as they come back, and then they are forwarded to London, to sarve the duchesses. I've understood he pays his hands, or I should say his heads, sixpence a-day and their victuals; and 'tis said, as there is always plenty eager for the employment, that he gives 'em the sack so soon as they get over the sea-sickness and begin to find their appetite."

"And so he escapes the duty, because the articles are worn on the person?"

"Just so. He don't go in the *Margaret* (that's the English steamer) because the fare is double, and that would spoil his profits."

"What is the fare across?"

"Ten shillings by the English boat, five shillings by the Frenchman. But that is not all; if the tide don't serve, you have to pay four shillings a-head for being put on board by a boat."

This information set me a-musing on the state of my finances, and I resolved, if possible, to get across the Channel without the help of either steamer. We walked down to the harbor, and witnessed the landing of the passengers, together with the bonnet regiment, whose appearance fully justified the description of my friend.

I rose with the lark the next morning, and hastened down to the harbor in search of a cheaper means of transit than was presented by the *Margaret*, with her ten-shilling fare for a distance of nineteen miles. There was nothing but an old cockleshell of a boat, belonging to two French fishermen, which was going to sail at the same time as the steamer.

As I stood looking at the rents in her sides, an old weather-beaten figure that sat in her stern munching purple eggs boiled hard, ejaculated, as he spat away the shells, "Go to Calay for von shilly."

I pointed to a hole larger than my fist in the side of the boat.

"Oh, noting," said he. "Dis boat nevare sink; me sail many time, very—twenty year—not sink vonce."

I thought I would venture it, and told him I would go if he kept his time. Having breakfasted, and lifted my boxes on the shoulders of a porter, he carried them down to the boat, and was going to put them on board, when he was ordered to take them to the Custom-house, which stood close by, for examination. This ceremony, which took me by surprise, was rigidly gone through; every shirt was unfolded, the stockings turned inside out, the pockets of my clothes ditto—the old fiddle was shaken and scrutinized through the S holes—and when all was gone over, the tumbled heap was returned to me to re-arrange as I could. When at length I got back to the boat, I found it crowded with such a set of miserable, famished looking creatures as I had never set eyes on before. It was not without reluctance that I stepped on board, but the steamer was already on the move, and, as our wretched craft blocked the way, I was bundled in, and our moorings were loose before there was time to demur. The noise of the paddle-wheels behind us, accompanied by a volley of curses from the look-out on board the *Margaret*, put our aged Tritons upon their mettle. The ragged sail was set in a twinkling; and, under the influence of a fair wind blowing a lively breeze, we bounded over the billows, and soon left the white cliffs of Kent far in the rear.

CHAPTER III.

The Straits of Dover, and of Nottingham weavers—The virtues of bread and butter—Unanimity among the passengers—A cheap voyage—Calais touters—I mount a knapsack, and start for Paris on foot—Last view of Old England—How the gens-d'armes turn a penny—I make an acquaintance—A French country wagon and team—My first lesson in the language—French farming—Triumphant and distressing entry into Abbeville—Road-side inn and its inmates—Supper and song—Singular sleeping quarters—Primitive price of accommodation—We proceed on our way—I find myself in possession of a wagon and five horses—Grandvilliers—Beauvais—I lose my only friend—I arrive in the Palais Royal—An English home in Paris—I commence the study of the language—How I managed it—A scoundrelly Parisian shark feeds me with false hopes, with the view of plundering me—Odd sort of dramatico-gastronomical entertainment—I scent the designs of the shark, and escape his fangs—One of his victims—Am introduced by M. Galignani to Count D——, who gives me employment.

THE two old fishermen constituted the whole of the crew of the crazy little craft in which I had embarked; but it was so filled with passengers that it was difficult to count them; and it was not till we had proceeded a mile or two, and all had at length contrived some sort of accommodation, that I found myself seated in the midst of eighteen of the most woe-begone countenances I had ever had the misfortune to be acquainted with. They were of all ages, from twenty to sixty; but every face bore the unmistakeable traits of misery and destitution. Long fellowship with want and discomfort had made them insensible to the attacks of the weather; and while I was regretting that I had not unpacked a great coat to shield me from the fresh breeze that seemed to cut my ears off, they one and all bore the blast, which pierced through every rent in their tattered suits, without shrinking. I soon gathered from their conversation that they were a party of Nottingham weavers, who, having been starved out of their native place through want of employment, were going over to Calais in search of it. Most of them had left wives and families behind, others had left their parents. The entire luggage of each was packed up in a cotton handkerchief, and some had not even that. One, who was otherwise unprovided, boasted that he had on three new pairs of woollen drawers, which would fetch a good price in France. He reckoned without his host, however; for I saw him stipped of all three at the Custom-house, in Calais, by the French *douaniers*.

We parted company with the steamer soon after leaving Dover, she running east, past the South Foreland, in order to come into Calais on the back of the tide, which was near the turn. As our tub—it did not deserve the name of a boat—drew scarce a foot of water, we had no need to take any such precaution, but shot straight across. Our old steersman, who persisted in navigating by compass all the way, notwithstanding both coasts were continually in sight, fired off a few harmless jokes relative to the fine specimens of the John Bull family whom he had on board. Understanding, however, that with the exception of myself, not one of them had breakfasted, he produced a couple of loaves, near a yard long each, from a locker upon which he sat, and calling upon his companion for the butter, which was cooling in a small crib under the prow, he helped every one liberally to as much as he chose to eat, observing to me in a whisper, " Dat it not good to be sick ven dere is noting in de stomyack, and dey all vill sick before ve make Calay."

His prognostication was true enough. Before we got into mid-channel we began to roll and pitch in a manner so tremendous that I momentarily expected to see half our wretched live cargo spilt in the brine.

The captain roared out, as they were thrown one against the other with a violence which threatened the old planks with disruption, "Hole fast de von de todare. Ven you fall ovare you nevare come again!"

They took his advice, and, linking elbows all round, sat it out as well as they could, with a rueful resolution, which provoked my laughter in spite of all I could do to restrain it. Fortunately, perhaps, for us all, this violent commotion did not last very long. The boat altered her course a little, and we got into smoother water; but the effects of the troublous visitation we had experienced soon became visible in the increased yellowness of my companions' faces. They glared grimly at each other, and looked for some time unutterable things. There was no sophistication among them. Not a soul was fine gentleman enough to think of concealing his sensations, yet they all maintained a rigid and ghastly quiet, as if convinced that the first that broke it would be the herald of calamity to the whole. At length one turned his head over the side, and his example was instantly followed by the whole company, who were soon unanimously engaged in what Sir Francis Head calls "casting up solid ejaculations to the fishes."

Pending the settlement of the account, I had some conversation with the steersman, who assured me, "Dey vill all be vell again in no time—butter-bread fine ting for sick," a prophecy I did not find so true as the former one. Some of them, indeed, got well enough before we landed, but the major part of them were too ill to walk, and had to be helped ashore. We reached Calais in about three hours from the time we started, and just two minutes before the steamer . and as we were in their way on leaving the Dover harbor, so we stood in their way between the piers of Calais, but we met with much more civil treatment than we had experienced on the other side. The old boatmen were now in no hurry to move out of the way, but deliberately landed their passengers on the lowest step of a muddy ladder, while those from the steamboat were crowding across the gangway to the wharf above. A full half of the poor fellows on board our boat had not strength to mount the ladder, so much were they shaken by sea-sickness, and were obliged to be hauled up by a rope. They paid sixpence each for their passage, bread-and-butter included.

No sooner were we landed than off we were marched, in the rear of our baggage, which was unceremoniously seized by a set of nondescript bipeds, who laid hold of it as a matter of right, to the Custom-house. Here, the number of arrivals by the steamer having been unusually large, a strange hubbub and confusion prevailed. Packages and trunks, bundles and boxes, of all shapes and sizes, were piled in heaps on the floor; and there was a general struggle among the owners, most of whom wanted to recover some box or bag charged with articles in immediate requisition. The place was so crowded that I could not squeeze into it; and, after several vain attempts, had to make up my mind to wait the issue patiently. Among the crowd were a number of touters of both sexes, all vociferous in praise of the accommodations and good fare their patrons had to offer. One praised his fine feather beds, another his strong English beer; a third her roast beef and plum pudding; and a fourth boasted every thing comfortable, and a fine view of the sea from the window. All were clamorous for custom, and all thrust their cards of address in our faces, and each abused the rest, and asserted roundly that the house he or she represented was the only respectable house in Calais.

The sea-air had aroused my appetite, and the mention of roast beef had sharpened its edge, and I longed for the sight of the dinner-table; therefore, accosting a youth of about nineteen, who though active and earnest as the rest in his occupation of touter, yet could not refrain from laughing heartily at the fun, I asked him what was the use of inviting us to dinner if we were to be kept prisoners there all day. He said, if I would dine at his house, he would get me through at once, and clear my luggage for me afterwards. I consented, and he was as good as his word. I followed him to a dull, quiet street of tall houses in the rear of the town, and soon commenced operations with the knife and fork, in company with about a dozen other guests

After dinner I set out with the young touter, or, as he called himself, *commissaire*, to procure my passport and to view the town. The passport business was soon settled at the cost of four francs; and then the young Frenchman, who spoke English as well as myself—his business for the day being over, as no other boats were expected in—proffered his company and guidance. I found him an amusing companion. He talked incessantly, and told me his whole history without being asked or it; and enlarged upon his future intentions, which were nothing less than to earn a thousand pounds by teaching French in London, and to double it by marrying an English heiress. By the time he had shown me what was to be seen out of doors, it began to grow dark, and he led me into a cafe where I found some of my fellow-voyagers of the morning carousing with a party of the same trade who had long been in Calais, and by whose invitation they had come over. They were much improved in appearance since the morning. Their old comrades had shared their wardrobes with them, and were then treating them to grog, and instructing them in the game of billiards. I understood, upon inquiry, that there was no fear of their not finding employment, and that none of them expected to have to proceed further in search of it.

We now returned to our hotel; I made up a sort of knapsack of a few necessaries, corded and directed my boxes to the Rue Montmartre, Paris, "to be left till called for," and sent them to the office of the diligence to be forwarded in due course, resolving to trudge the whole distance on foot, for the sake of gratifying my curiosity on the route, as well as for the sake of economy. After an early supper and one or two songs from a couple of peasant girls, who sang sweetly, and accompanied themselves cleverly on the guitar, I called for my account, which was extremely moderate, paid it, and retired to rest, informing my landlord that I should be off with the dawn.

Before the sun had risen next morning I was up and breakfasting, wishing to get to Boulogne in sufficient time to have a good view of its neighborhood ere dark. I left Calais soon after sun-rise, with my knapsack on my shoulder, and a stout staff, the present of Jean Baptiste, the aspiring commissaire, in my hand I dined and rested for an hour at a village about half-way, and arrived at Boulogne between three and four o'clock in the afternoon, not having set eyes on above a dozen persons during a walk of twenty-seven miles. The town appeared to be full of English, and many of the shops bore English inscriptions. My first care was to engage a lodging, where, having deposited my knapsack, by way of taking possession, I sauntered leisurely through the town and environs, and before the sun went down took a last look at the dim grey streak on the other side of the Channel which indicated the coast of Kent.

The next day saw me marching on the interminable road, with its rough pavement in the middle and its rows of trees on either side, which leads to the capital of France. It took me two good hours to get out of sight of the tall pillar which Napoleon raised to commemorate an invasion that never happened; and this had hardly been accomplished when, entering upon the precincts of a miserable assemblage of huts, I was assailed by a gens-d'arme, who, barring my passage with his halbert, demanded my passport Snatching it from my hands, he motioned for me to follow him; and then entering a wretched cabin upon the door of which were rudely painted a bottle and glass, he called for brandy, gave me a small portion, drank the remainder himself, returned the passport without looking at it, and desired me to pay for what had been drunk As I understood no French I had to gather his meaning from his gestures, but these were unmistakeable, and as the demand was only four sous, or two pence, I judged it best to comply. I found this the uniform practice at every little beggarly hamlet or village that I passed through on the whole route. In the larger towns no such ceremony was observed, nor was my passport demanded at all at either of the places where I passed the night. I slept at Montreuil the second night; but as the rain had soaked me to the skin in the course of the afternoon, I was glad to rest my weary limbs, and dry my clothes by a good wood fire, instead of making the circuit of the town.

Refreshed with a long night's rest, I rose to resume my journey on Thursday morning. The sun shining brightly, and a delicious freshness pervading the air, I felt in capital spirits, and put the best foot foremost for Abbeville. When about five miles (English) on my way I was overtaken by an empty wagon on two wheels, driven by, or rather in charge of, a young peasant farmer of about my own age. He hailed me laughingly, wished me good-day, which was all I could comprehend of his greeting, and put several rapid questions, to which he got nothing but a shake of the head for a reply. He stopped his vehicle, and made signs that I should mount and ride with him. To this proposition I was nothing loth, and was soon seated by his side, upon a sack stuffed with fodder for the horses. The machine in which we rode was a perfect novelty to me; four planks not above a foot wide each, but nearly twenty feet long, rudely nailed to cross-pieces about four feet apart, were balanced centrally over the axletree connecting the single pair of wheels. The wheels were nearly six feet in diameter, and that portion of the planking close to which they revolved was fenced by a few stout railings, four or five of which running up aloft, were tied together in the centre, forming an arch over our heads, and sustaining a white canvass covering which yielded effectual shelter from rain or sun. My companion carried a whip, but it had no lash, and, to all appearance, was seldom, if ever, used. He had no reins, but guided the team, which consisted of five hardy horses, two wheelers, and three leaders, solely by his voice. The animals were accoutred in a sort of rope harness, but there was no bearing-rein, and they wore no blinkers, yet they were more playful, docile, and manageable than any horses I ever saw in England out of Astley's. When my new friend wanted to get them into a gallop, all he had to do was to withdraw to the farthest extremity of the wagon and rush suddenly up to the other end, making as much noise as he could with his nailed heels at every step. The creatures took this as a frolic; and lowering their heads almost to the ground, and whisking their long tails in the air, started off at full gallop, at the rate of *six* English miles an hour. As I could not talk to my companion, I pulled a small octave flute from my pocket and played some of the melodies of his country. At the first bar of "C'est l'amour," he leaped to his feet and began both to sing and to dance at the same moment. He footed it with remarkable agility on the long floor of the empty wagon for some time, until my lungs were well-nigh exhausted. In return for my music, he set about teaching me French, and produced several articles from his pockets (among the rest a knife, which when opened, was almost as long as a small sword) and laid them on the floor between us. There were a dozen things altogether, and of these he made me learn the French names, and would not be satisfied till I was perfect in my lesson, and could name any one of them as it was pointed out. He possessed admirable patience, and would have made an excellent teacher.

Soon after one o'clock we came in sight of Abbeville, and stopped to dine at a road-side house, where we had a plentiful dinner of soup, meat, vegetables, pudding, sour wine, and brandy, at a cost of twelve sous a-piece. We stayed here for a couple of hours, and rambled about the farm at the back of the house while the horses were resting The whole was as complete a contrast to the neat and thrifty homesteads of Devonshire as could well be imagined. The cattle were wretchedly small and ill-conditioned ; the sheep, dirty and matted, I mistook at first, and should have asked my companion, had I been able, what animals they were ; and the pigs, long-legged, melancholy misanthropes, seemed made up entirely of bone and bristles. Nearly the whole of the business of the farm appeared to be managed by women. I saw but one man, and he was engaged in the house, of which apparently he had the sole charge. I was not a sufficient judge of the crops as they then stood to be able to pronounce upon the prospects of harvest; but the absence of anything like a decent fence, and the substitution of a trench about a foot wide for a hedge, gave me a dreary and uncomfortable notion of French farming.

When all was ready for starting we mounted the wagon, and paced gently on towards Abbeville; but no sooner did we come within a stone's throw of the gate of the town, than my new friend seized the whip, which I had not seen him use hitherto, and commenced a course of action which made me think for the moment that he was verily gone frantic. He lashed the two wheelers with all his might, and with a rapidity scarcely conceivable. He stamped furiously with his feet; he *sacréed* and yelled at the leaders, whom he called severally by name; he hallooed and screamed till he was well-nigh black in the face, and kicked, and sprawled, and swore, and played such mad antics, that I began to rue the day that ever made us acquainted. I would have given a guinea to have got out, but that was impossible. The horses, goaded to fury, dashed in a wild gallop through the gates of the town, and along the abominably paved streets at such a rate, now jolting over a huge stone, now sinking in a deep rut, that it was only by holding on to the railing with both hands that I could save myself from being bruised to a mummy.

While I was speculating as to how this was to end, and wishing myself well out of it, we pulled up suddenly at the door of a house at no great distance from the gate of the town at which we were to make our exit. Here were assembled a group of the young farmer's friends evidently on the look out for him, and who had doubtless been brought to the door by the uproar by which he had thought fit to announce his arrival. An old gentleman shook him heartily by the hand, and he, having kissed the party all round, invited me to alight. We were ushered into a neat room, which was nearly dark from the black hue of the wainscoating, and he introduced me as a friend, and pretended to talk to me in English, a piece of vanity which I could do no less than countenance I spoke my own tongue, and he jabbered an imitation which gave him the credit of understanding it. While we drank a few glasses of tolerable wine, several bales of goods were hoisted into the wagon, and we set off again after a stay of half an hour.

Having now above a ton weight to lug along, our career was much more slow and circumspect than it had been. We got over about a dozen miles by sun-down, and put up for the night at one of the roadside hostelries with which that part of the country abounds. We found a pretty large company already arrived, and I noticed five or six vehicles of a similar construction to the one driven by my companion. A capital fire was blazing in the common room, and a side-table was set for us two near the hearth. A wrinkled grandam, the very counterpart of Willie's Femme de Normandie, broke a score of eggs into the frying-pan; to them she added several feet in length of sliced bacon, and soon produced a dish which left us nothing further to desire. The pale sour wine of the country, in clear glass bottles of half-gallon capacity, was furnished plentifully as water; and I was perfectly amazed at the quantity of it which my companion, and indeed the whole party, imbibed. To me a mixture of home-made vinegar and water would have been preferable then, though I learned to like it well enough in after-times. After we had appeased our hunger the tables were removed to the back of the large room, and upon a small settle in front of the fire three flagons newly filled with the sour beverage so much in request were deposited for general use. A great deal of conversation ensued, which, unlike that of such assemblies in England, was conducted on the principle of one speaker at a time. When it had continued for an hour a young girl of about thirteen stepped into

A PRIMITIVE DORMITORY.

the circle, and, with the aid of a very fat guitar, sang a couple of songs, and immediately disappeared, without any appeal to the company for payment.

Before the wine was half consumed many of the party dropped off; and while it was yet within a few minutes of nine o'clock, my companion made signs to me that he would show me to my bed. I followed him through a long passage on the same floor, and we entered a large room more than thirty feet square, and containing nearly twenty beds, each one concealed within a recess in the wall. He led me to one, the curtains of which were not drawn, and pointed to my hat and knapsack, lying on the coverlet, as a sign that it had been allotted to me, and then wishing me good night, left me to my repose. When he was gone I began to take a survey of my quarters. The only light was from a small oil-lamp that hung suspended from the middle of the ceiling, and out of my reach. If I were to judge from the number of the beds the curtains of which were drawn close, and from certain nasal demonstrations that greeted my ears, there were at least a dozen occupants already in the chamber, yet there was not a vestige of anything like a garment to be seen. I took the hint, and as I undressed laid my own clothes upon the further side of the bed. Seeing that there was no flooring to the room beyond the native mud of the district, I had some fears on the subject of damp sheets; but these were effectually quieted by the discovery I soon made that there were no sheets at all. Any further discoveries were prevented by a sound sleep which took possession of me almost the moment I lay down, and from which I was only aroused by a rather rough shaking from my companion at five o'clock the next morning. I rose and dressed, and followed him to a spring of clear water in the yard at the back of the house, where we washed and made our toilet. We then visited the stable, and gave the horses, who all manifested the greatest joy at the sight of my friend, a few handfuls of corn and a piece of bread each. While thus occupied the old woman called us to breakfast, which, consisting of rye-bread, butter, cream, coffee, and an omelet, was smoking on the table. After a hearty meal, finishing with the smallest glass of brandy, the old lady demanded payment. When the young farmer had settled his bill, including the charge for his team, she came to me, and I gave her a five-franc piece; to my amazement she gave me back four francs, besides some nondescript beggarly-looking coppers, of whose value I could form no notion—thus receiving less than tenpence for my supper, bed, and breakfast; the two meals, to say nothing of the bed, were abundant and excellent of their kind.

Soon after six we were plodding steadily along upon the road to Paris, walking by the side of the horses, with whom my friend constantly kept up a kind of conversation. We had hardly proceeded above three miles when he discovered that he had left his huge knife behind him; and putting the whip into my hand, and speaking to the horses, who immediately fell into a slower walk, started off at full speed back to the inn, in search of his weapon. When he was gone my position struck me as rather comical; and I could not help laughing at finding myself driving a noble team belonging to somebody whose name I had never heard, and going I did not know whither. Just then the diligence from Paris appeared in sight, and the horses I was driving turned of their own accord from the *pavé* to let it pass. As it rattled by I was saluted with the first words of English that had greeted my ears since leaving the coast. "Where did you steal that wagon and horses?" roared a gent. who was sitting beside the driver. "Where did you learn manners?" I asked in return. I did not hear his reply owing to the noise my own team made in grappling with the smooth-worn stones to get again upon the *pavé*, which they very much preferred to the soft mud of the sideways

My friend did not make his appearance again till more than two hours had elapsed, and then he was in a desponding mood, for he had returned without the object of his search. I pressed upon his acceptance a small two-bladed Sheffield knife, with which, when he had snapped off the top of the pen-blade, and thus assured himself of the good temper of the metal, he was highly pleased, and re-assumed his spirits and vivacity. We stopped at Grandvilliers to deliver the goods brought from Abbeville, and there we remained full three hours, our steeds requiring rest. I was pleased with the aspect of the town. Though small, it appeared busy and thriving; the streets were wider and better paved than any we had yet passed through; and I might almost have taken it for an English market-town, but for the costume of the inhabitants, and their to me unintelligible jargon.

We started again about four o'clock for Beauvais, galloping through the market-place like mad creatures; but without exciting much attention from the natives, who seemed too much used to such noisy demonstrations to care anything about them. The sun was setting when we came in sight of Beauvais, and I gathered from the operations of my companion as we approached this fine town, that here we were about to part company. As a sailor puts his vessel in trim before he sails into port, so did he, slackening our pace, proceed to put the whole equipage in the neatest condition it was capable of assuming. He reefed up the awning, which had hitherto been allowed to flutter in the wind, and tied it neatly over the centre. He swept the flooring, and folded the now empty bags. He produced a comb from his pocket, and plied it well on the manes and tails of the beasts; and with the knife I had given him trimmed the harness, cutting off the dangling shreds and frayings; and finished all by fastening a sprig of hawthorn upon the heads of each of the three leaders. Thus refitted and garnished, we entered the maiden city in gallant style. My passport was demanded by an official at the entrance, and returned after the glance of a moment, and we drove up to an inn of modest appearance, when my companion signed to me to alight.

Here he took leave of me, after recommending me to the care of the good woman of the house, to whom he seemed well known, and with whom he gossipped merrily, with, as was evident, often-repeated allusions to myself. She produced a tankard of good, rough wine ; we clinked glasses together, and drank a parting health; after which he mounted his vehicle, and, as old Bunyan says, " I saw him no more."

The next day, first devoting a couple of hours to a glance at the town and the fine old cathedral, I resumed my journey, and got easily as far as Beaumont before dusk, without fatigue. I should have done it much earlier but for the frequent stoppages at the several small towns and villages through which my road led me, occasioned by the demand for my passport and the indispensable ceremony of performing, at my cost, a libation of wine or brandy pending its examination. There being nothing very remarkable at Beaumont, I did not feel tempted to remain there during the Sunday ; and the following morning, which shone bright and fair as a Sunday should, I started at sunrise, in the hope of entering Paris by mid-day. As I drew near the capital, however, the towns and villages on my route were much more frequent, and my delays in proportion; so that it was not until near four o'clock in the afternoon that I found myself in the Palais Royal, in the centre of life and gaiety—myself a weary, and dusty wayfarer, among a crowd of well-dressed holiday-makers, all apparently enjoying themselves to the utmost. As I had no friend, or even acquaintance, in the whole city, my first care was to look out for an Englishman to whom I might make my wants known. This was no very difficult task ; and I soon obtained directions from one of a group of fellow-countrymen to an English house in the Rue St. Honore, where he said I should find reasonable accommodation, and meet with others from whom I could get any information I might want. Hearing that I spoke no French, he called a boy who was playing near us, who bargained to conduct me to the spot for a couple of sous. When we got there I found that the house was full, and every bed engaged, but Mrs. G., the landlady, taking compassion upon my weariness and dusty condition, said she would contrive to house me for the night, and, when her lodgers came home, would endeavor to make some permanent arrangement in my behalf. She brought me some cold meat and bottled ale, and left me to the enjoyment of the meal and my own reflections until evening. These were not of a very enlivening description. When I considered that I had wandered thus far from home for the mere chance of obtaining employment, without which I must soon become destitute, I began to doubt, now it was too late, the propriety of the step I had taken. I felt, moreover, especially mortified at my ignorance of the language spoken by all around me, and made a vehement resolution to supply that desideratum with all the energy and perseverance that Heaven had thought fit to endow me with.

I met with a hearty welcome and the kindest treatment from my countrymen, when they returned home in the evening, and to my inexpressible satisfaction I found that one among them was a printer, in the employ of M. Galignani. He gave me every encouragement, assured me that I had done right in giving London the slip, and that I should not be long out of work in Paris. Unfortunately I did not find his prediction in this particular so true as I could have wished it. I called on M. Galignani myself the next day, and obtained a promise of speedy employment; but this promise was reiterated so often before the performance came, that I began to lose heart and hope. It was the beginning of May when I arrived in Paris— it was near the end of it before I had earned a franc. I had found an employment, however, which enabled me to bear the delay much better than I could have done in a state of idleness; this was learning French, which I set about immediately, in the full spirit of the resolution previously formed. Upon one of the interminable book-stalls, or rather book-walls, which display their leafy banners along the quays of the Seine, I picked up a Cobbett's French Grammar for a franc, and a pocket dictionary for another. A fellow-lodger lent me a Testament and a Telemaque; and to these materials I applied doggedly from six in the morning till dinner-time. I read the grammar through first, and then made an abridgment of it on a small pack of plain cards, copying out the ten conjugations of verbs, each upon a single card at one view; and when these were mastered, doing the same with the irregular verbs—the whole of which, by repeated copying, became indelibly fixed in my memory, so that I never lost them afterwards. To each of the other parts of speech I devoted a separate card, into which I crowded all that was really necessary to be committed to memory. Upon others I made a compendious list of adverbs, particles, and connecting words, with their corresponding English terms; and in a small book fitted to the waistcoat-pocket I began a vocabulary, where I entered all the new words which I acquired every day. After my seven hours' study in the morning, I dined and then walked out ' with my mouth open," as Curran said, "to catch the accent." When I found two people talking loudly together, I would stand and listen, to see what I could make of it—a practice which had its inconveniences, inasmuch as I was more than once appealed to as referee upon a debate upon which, though I had heard all, I had understood next to nothing. I derived more instruction from listening to the conversation of children at play than from any other source. Their simple talk was a course of admirable teaching for one in my situation, and I resorted every fine day to the garden of the Tuileries, where they were always playing round the fish-pond, to avail myself of it. The evenings I devoted to reading, translating, and comparing, and to the course of exercises contained in the grammar. By these means, sedulously pursued, I made rapid progress; but finding that living in an English house prevented the necessity of speaking French, I removed to an hotel in the Rue Richelieu, where, for twelve francs a month, I found accommodation "in a parlor next to the sky." In the course of a fortnight I could manage, with the help of a dictionary, to read the advertisements in the French newspapers, which I now began to peruse, not without a hope of finding employment of some other kind, in case the printing should fail.

One day, by dint of an hour's study, I managed to get at the meaning of an advertisement in the *Moniteur*, which ran pretty nearly thus:—' Wanted, by a literary gentleman, the services of a young Englishman, qualified to read aloud the authors of his own country, and to make extracts with correctness and despatch. Attendance six hours a day." This was followed by the delicious announcement, in capitals, "ABONNEMENTS, 250 FRANCS PAR MOIS,' and a direction to apply at a certain address in the Rue du Coq St. Honore. I had no sooner mastered the sense of the paragraph than I became electrified with joy, and silently returned thanks to Providence for throwing it in my way, and for crowning my studies with so much success as to enable me to read it. It was then too late to make application that day; and I got into a perfect fever of anxiety and fear lest some one else had forestalled me. A young Englishman came and sat at the same table, and called for coffee. I was afraid he should see the advertisement, and to prevent his rivalship dropped the paper on the floor, and kicked it with my heels under the bench upon which I sat. I stayed till he was gone, and, indeed, till nearly the whole of the *habitués* of the *restaurant* had departed, and had the satisfaction of leaving the paper undiscovered. All night long I lay awake, restless with anxiety and expectation, building castles in the air, and plotting means for spending my money and employing my leisure. The advertisement stated that application must be made between the hours of ten and four; and, consequently, within five minutes after ten I knocked at the door, and was ushered up-stairs into the bureau of the advertiser. He was a tall and gentlemanly looking personage of about forty, who, upon my making a most villanous attempt to address him in French, told me blandly to speak in my own tongue as he understood it perfectly well I was pleased with this, and immediately acquainted him with the purport of my visit, adding that I hoped the office was not already filled, and that I should have applied yesterday had I seen the advertisement in time. He smiled benevolently, assured me that I was in very good time, and that he was glad, for my sake, that it was so, as he thought the situation would suit me very well; he was pleased, moreover, to compliment me upon my address and the propriety of my diction. "In the meantime," said he, "there are other applicants; but if, as I trust, you can write well and legibly, I do not think you have any cause for fear. Have you brought a specimen of your handwriting?" I confessed that that had not occurred to me, though it should have done so. "Then go home," said he, "and prepare one, and let me have it; bring it yourself before four o'clock. I will forward it to the Marquis with the others this evening, and be assured I will enclose a special recommendation in your favor." Back I started to my lodgings, and occupied myself for four hours in spoiling a quire of paper with extracts from Milton, Shakespeare, and Byron, transcribed from memory. About three o'clock, armed with a couple of the best written of my copies, I was again at the bureau. The gentleman praised my writing exceedingly, and complimented me upon my orthography, which, he gravely assured me, was a most important accomplishment, and one that was by no means too common. He then desired me to call again the day after to-morrow, by which time he would be able to inform me of the issue, which he had not the least doubt would, from the interest he felt and should express to the Marquis in my behalf, be favorable to me. I left his presence as happy as a king; and as I had been living for some days upon very short commons, dining often upon rye-bread and apples for the sake of eking out my funds, I resolved this evening to indulge in a little dissipation upon the strength of my improved prospects. Accordingly, so soon as it grew dark I directed my steps to the Palais Royal, and took my place in a singular establishment then open for the accommodation of the French lieges. It was a theatre and a tavern combined in one immense saloon, but bore little resemblance to places of similar pretensions since started in England. The stage was elevated near a dozen feet above the heads of the audience, and inclined slightly towards the footlights, to allow of the figures in the background being seen. The orchestra was out of sight. The space occupied usually by musicians was crowded with tables and stretchers laden with wine and viands for the use of the spectators. The performance was conducted throughout very much in the manner of a rehearsal—the actors appearing perfectly aware of what was undoubtedly the fact, that not a dozen persons out of the five or six hundred present were paying any attention to what was going on upon the stage. Half of the people assembled sat, in fact, with their backs to the actors, as, indeed, they were compelled to do by the disposition of the long tables, which, having benches on either side, were placed parallel with the front of the stage. The audience talked much more and much louder than the performers, and waiters ran about incessantly, drawing corks, and clattering knives, forks, and dishes, without any apparent consciousness that a dramatic performance was going on. Here I took my seat among the rest, and calling for *patés* and wine, supped merrily, being much amused with the novelty of the scene, and the many curious specimens of Parisian society which it presented to my inexperienced eye; though it must be confessed that I could by no means fathom the philosophy of the entertainment, or enter into the joke of the thing, if a joke were meant.

I thought the following day the longest of my whole life, and passed it in a state of restless anxiety, with alternate hopes and fears. When that had at length arrived which was to crown my hopes with success, it was not without a sentiment of awe that, at the appointed hour, I ascended the stairs and was ushered into the presence of my gracious patron. He received me with his usual kindness, and, in reply to my faltering inquiries, smiled, and said that the affair was not yet *quite* decided, but that he felt assured it was in the right train for me, and that in a day or two, at the farthest, he should have the pleasure of congratulating me upon my appointment. I expressed my gratitude for his kindness to a perfect stranger, and requested to know when I should call again. "Call when you like," said he, "in two or three days at the latest." I bowed, and was retiring, when he called out, ' Stop a moment, my young friend; you have forgotten a trifling matter: you are indebted to the bureau ten francs for services rendered. You know your country's proverb, 'Short reckonings make long friends;' I make a point of observing it religiously;" and he held out his hand. There was something in the manner of his delivery while giving me this remembrancer that put me instantly upon the right scent. I felt my blood rising, and my fist clenched instinctively; still I was sure of nothing, and therefore mastering my emotion, I told him, what was true enough, that I had brought no money with me, but that I pledged my honor that I would pay the debt *the next time I called.* I watched him narrowly while I spoke, and saw that he was a little disconcerted in spite of his admirable self-possession. He replied, however, with all his previous suavity, reminded me that punctuality was the soul of business, and politely bowed me out.

I descended the stairs in a cold sweat, convinced that the fine-spoken gentleman was a rascally humbug, yet harboring still in my mind a lingering doubt upon the subject, which doubt I resolved should be cleared up satisfactorily out of hand. In pursuance of this resolution, I ensconced myself in a snug position about fifty yards from his door, and watched it with the gaze of a lynx for something more than an hour. At the end of that time I saw a young cockney, whom I had frequently encountered in my walks in the Tuileries, advance to the door, knock and enter. In less than a quarter of an hour he re-appeared, and I was soon at his side, with a request that he would show me the way to the Rue Vivienne. He was willing and proud to do so, and as we walked along I easily drew him into conversation. I took him into the reading-room of Galignani's, where I was in the habit of looking over the papers while waiting to see the proprietor; and though he was very shy at first on the subject of the bureau, I succeeded at length in extracting the whole truth from him. The advertising scoundrel of the Rue du Coq St. Honore had been administering to him precisely the same course of treatment with which he had deluded me. The young blockhead had been under his hands six mortal weeks, and had been plundered of near a hundred francs "for services rendered." On comparing notes, we found that the course of treatment was a stereotyped formula, marvellously adapted to all cases of diseased expectation. The same pretended interest and special regard, the same flattering encomiums upon personal address and diction, the same singular orthographical merit, and the same winning assurance of his private recommendation, had been bestowed with equal liberality upon both of us, and most probably upon a dozen or two other greenhorns who had left their native country to learn experience at Paris.

My companion became perfectly savage when at length his eyes were opened, and he saw how villainously he had been duped. He raved and raged, and bit his lips till they bled, and became so furious that I was obliged to take him out of the house. He was determined on revenge, and swore he would have it, come what might. Among other modest proposals, he suggested that we should both call on the rascal together, and that I should hold him down while he smashed his head with a cudgel. Declining to take part in the administration of so gentle an anodyne, I did what I could to mitigate his passion, and suggesting to him to have good advice from some competent person before he proceeded to execute Lynch law, I took my leave of him.

On returning again to the reading-room, I had the good fortune to encounter M. Galignani, who at length rewarded my patience, and dissipated the dismal apprehensions which the low state of my funds, coupled with my late disappointment, had given rise to, by presenting me with a note of introduction to Count D———, who, he informed me, would give me immediate employment upon receiving it; adding, that I should most probably find him at the printing-office at six o'clock that evening. I did not require the admonition of the bureau scoundrel to assure me that punctuality was the soul of business. Long before the hour had struck I was crossing the Pont Neuf, on my way to the Rue du Pont de Lodi, where the office was situated; and while the clocks were yet striking, was, in obedience to the signalling of a wrinkled hag, who did duty as a portress, groping up the dark staircase in search of the counting-house. While I was floundering among the loose boards of the dilapidated stairs, I heard a voice demanding, in French, "Who is there?" I made an abortive attempt at reply in an accent that doubtless betrayed my origin, when the same voice said in English, "What do you want? Come this way." At the same moment a figure in a dirty apron, shirt-sleeves, and paper cap, appeared at a landing place, and beckoned me towards a window at the end of a narrow passage. "What is your business?" he demanded. I requested him to give the note I presented to his master, and to say that the bearer was waiting. He snatched it petulantly from my hand, and to my astonishment tore it open. He was himself the Count. Having read it, he stared at me blankly for a moment, and then rang a bell, telling the messenger, who appeared in an instant, to call Mr. L———, the overseer of the English department. He also made his appearance with marvellous celerity, and was desired to take me up-stairs, appoint me a frame, put copy in my hands in the morning, and report to him on the coming Saturday as to my capacity and conduct. I followed the overseer to the scene of my future labors, took formal possession of my quarters by depositing the implements of my trade, which I had brought with me, upon my frame, and mounted a pair of cases full of new shining type in readiness for the next morning's operations.

A mountain was removed from my mind. I had found employment at last, and I returned to my ninth floor in the Rue Richelieu happy in the anticipation of setting about it on the morrow.

CHAPTER IV.

Paris on a summer's morning—A gratuitous bath, for which I am very near paying too dear—An innocent pickpocket—The Breakfast of the operative Masons—The custom of *faire greve*—A French Printing office in 1826—Pirated editions of Scott's novels—I pay my footing, and am hoaxed according to rule—My English acquaintance in Paris—Gentlemen R———Franks the old Peninsular campaigner—A Duel of a French and English trooper—The man of many tongues—N———, the infidel philosopher and republican—A tippling Cockney and his notions of prudence—A French workman of the old school, and his reminiscences of the Revolution of '89—Olfactory misdemeanors—M———, the type-farmer—I apply for work at press—Vanity of the overseer—Unexpected encounter with the Fish—His past history and present confidences—The Fish in love—I am introduced to his Inamorata—A trip to Versailles—Extraordinary experience in returning to Paris

At the very first glimmering of dawn on the day so long wished-for, that was to present me with the means of earning an independent livelihood, I started from my bed, and, having fervently thanked God for the opportunity of industrious exertion at length open to me, I was soon in the streets, with my face towards the office. The clock struck four as the grumbling *concièrge* pulled the string and let me out of the little door in the great gate of the hotel in which I lodged. The sun had not yet risen, but many of the owners of coffee-shops and restaurants were already up and active, engaged in the quiet gloom of morning twilight, deepened by the shadows of the tall houses, in lighting fires in small iron baskets mounted on tripods of the same metal, and roasting thereon, in metal cylinders, the quantity of coffee necessary for the day's consumption. Wherever I went my nostrils were saluted by the welcome fragrance of the luxurious berry, a fragrance which I never failed to recognize afterwards when drinking the infusion in French houses, but which, it is said, is never perceptible in coffee which has been roasted for a longer period than thirty or forty hours. As I approached the banks of the river, the first rays of the sun fell upon the domes and spires of the tallest buildings. The atmosphere was as clear as perfect crystal; not a figure was visible upon the long lines of quays upon either side of the water; the only sound was the rapid rushing and gurgling of the stream as its surges dashed noisily against the old timbers of the floating wash-houses and charcoal-boats which lined the shore. Instinctively I jumped into a washing-boat moored off the Pont Neuf; and casting off my clothes, dived into the stream with the intention of swimming across, but was carried through the arches of the bridge by the rapidity of the current. I landed again below the Pont des Arts, and had to run for it to regain my clothes, swimming against the stream being out of the question, as I found after several vain attempts. Upon regaining the boat I caught sight of a queer-looking fellow stooping over my clothes, and on the very point of investigating the contents of the pockets. He was sprawling on his back, with my angry grasp at his throat, in far less time than it takes to tell it. He assured me, as far as I could make out, that he was honest; that he thought I was drowned, and that he was only searching my pockets for information, for the purpose of apprising my friends of my fate, after he had delivered up my garments to the authorities. As this seemed likely enough, and was in all probability the truth, I apologised as well as I could, and allowed him to rise. He was very civil, but not altogether disposed to put up with the treatment he had received, without some sort of compensation. He pointed to a bruise on his forehead and a torn striped shirt, and whiningly insinuated that I should give him a *dedommagement*, to the extent, at least, of a breakfast. I told him I would willingly "dis-damage" him to that amount, if he would show me how. He laughed rather doubtingly, and, beckoning me to follow, took his way toward the Place de Grève, which he crossed, and after two or three turns through narrow, filthy-looking alleys, ascended a flight of steps of a dingy-fronted large house, and introduced me into a roomy but grimy and greasy saloon, hung round with torn and blistered representations of the gardens and scenery of St. Cloud and Versailles. Here were above a score of fellows of his own grade in life, mostly laborers attached to the various departments of industry connected with building—plasterers, bricklayers, stone-cutters, &c. Some were sitting at small tables, and occupied in the discussion of hot and savory messes of what appeared to me to be vegetable soup, in which were floating in profusion sliced herbs and roots, among which carrots cut the most conspicuous figure; others were lounging on benches, smoking and jabbering the patois of the south, of which not a word was intelligible to me. My cicerone made up to a woman sitting in a recess at one end of the room, and receiving a lump of bread half as big as his head, motioned to me to pay his scot, amounting to twopence-halfpenny, and then joined one of the eating groups. He set about his breakfast with an air of deliberate satisfaction. First cutting the bread into long strips, which he laid to soak in the liquid two or three at a time, he amused himself with fishing out with the point of his knife the various vegetables most agreeable to his palate, until the bread had imbibed as much of the fluid as it would contain. As each sop was duly soddened it was lifted tenderly to his mouth, open at a level with the ceiling, when it instantly and noiselessly disappeared. I was not long in discovering that the house I was in was a house of call, frequented by laborers and artisans out of employment; and that it was open thus early in the day, as a matter of policy, to enable parties in search of workmen to engage their services previous to the hour of commencing the day's work. I saw several hands engaged by foremen, who came to make their selection while it yet wanted half an hour to six o'clock; indeed, before the hour struck, almost the whole of the party cleared out, my companion and I along with them, and made for the Place de Grève, where other groups were already congregated in hopes of finding a market for their labor. I learned from inquiries subsequently made that this spot—the throne of the revolutionary guillotine—is and has long been the established rendezvous of operative masons and builders seeking employment; and, further, that from this fact the practice of applying for employment is designated among Parisian artisans of all classes by the term *faire grève*.

I left my queer friend chaffering with a patron for the price of his day's labor, and, retracing my steps to the Pont Neuf, crossed it; and, finding the office open in the Rue du Pont de Lodi, was soon at my post, eager to commence operations. None of the English compositors had yet arrived, but two or three French hands and a Spaniard were busily engaged on works in their own languages. The Spaniard spake neither French nor English, but was an excellent workman, lifting his types with that silent and almost motionless celerity, which is the invariable characteristic of a good compositor. The Frenchmen, on the other hand, were wretchedly slow and awkward, never loading themselves with more than a line at a time, which they made a rare clatter in completing and getting rid of ere they commenced another. It had struck seven before a single Englishman had arrived, and was near eight ere the foreman, from whom I was to receive copy made his appearance. From him I received, as my first job, half-a-dozen leaves of Walter Scott's novel of " Woodstock," which had not yet been published in England. It was about the commencement of the third volume, and the copy put into my hands plainly was, as I could see by the reader's marks in the margin, the corrected second proofs, with, as I judged from the pen-and-ink alterations of an expression here and there, the author's corrections transferred Of course, I cannot pretend to say that there was any bribery or breach of faith in the business, all I can state is, that ultimately the work was printed and published in Paris at the price of half-a-crown a volume, within a few days of its publication in London at half-a-guinea a volume.

I commenced my work with a full intention of setting a good example of industry and capacity, as well as of making a good bill; but my first efforts were defeated by the most apparently trifling circumstance. This was nothing more than the practice which prevails in France of placing the nick (a distinctive mark to guide the compositor in arranging the types) upon the back of the letter instead of the front; as with us. The consequence was that half the letters of my first pages were standing the wrong side upwards; and it occasioned me almost as much trouble to get them right, as it would have done to compose new ones. It was some weeks before I had conquered my old habits so far as to be able to work with average rapidity; but notwithstanding that, the work being good, well paid, and type plentiful, I managed to earn nearly forty francs the first six days, and my mind was therefore perfectly at ease on the subject of pecuniary matters. It is true that, being paid but once a fortnight, my funds were completely run out before pay-day came round; but I found no difficulty in obtaining the loan of a sum sufficient for present emergencies from the overseer, who repaid himself from the amount of my bill on the second Saturday night.

After the novel of "Woodstock" was completed, came Cooper's "Last of the Mohicans," and then a pocket edition of the works of Lord Byron, which was followed by other popular works, pirated from English authors and proprietors as fast as they made their appearance. The want of an international law of copyright was the occasion of our prosperity; and the question of printer's piracy, though it was not very profoundly discussed amongst us, was, whenever alluded to, invariably settled on the principle that "whatever is, is right." The whole of my companions agreed on this point, though they were perpetually disputing upon every other. They agreed also upon the subject of a "footing," which I was called upon to provide as soon as I had been there a month, and which consisted of sundry bottles of bad wine, drank in common, until every man had imbibed a sufficient quantity to incapacitate him for effective operations during the rest of the day. They were unanimous, too, in their concurrence in a species of practical wit very much in vogue among the profession, the ingenuity of which consists in the concoction of some gross deceit calculated to result in the inconvenience, pecuniary loss, and mortification of a fellow-workman. Thus, on one occasion, I found in the morning a note lying on my frame, purporting to come from my friend at Galignani's, dated from his lodgings at the other end of the city, and desiring to see me instantly on an affair of the last importance. I set off immediately—lost half the day in a vain attempt to find him out, and only discovered the hoax on inquiring for his real address at the office where he worked. Again, on applying one day for copy, I was informed by the deputy that the overseer was gone to procure some, and that I was to follow and bring it back, as he would not return that day. Following the directions given me with accuracy, I found myself at the Morgue for the first time, in the company of two stark rows of dead bodies, in all stages of corruption. To resent this delectable treatment only makes the matter worse, and would probably result in the victim's being sent to "Coventry," which is often equivalent to loss of employment. The only thing necessary is to bear it patiently—good-humoredly if possible—and to acquiesce in the truth of what it would seem to be their laudable endeavor to impress upon the mind, namely, that whatever their individual characters, they are all liars in the aggregate, and that their word is on no account to be believed. For my own part, I may say that so soon as I had arrived at this conclusion, and acted upon it, all further attempts at such annoyances ceased, and I was received into favor and freedom, as a being equally respectable and enlightened with themselves.

With such trifling and transitory drawbacks my time passed away agreeably enough. For immediate companions I had the silent Spaniard on my left hand, devouring a pocket edition of "Don Quixote," at the rate of fifty or sixty francs a week, and an unfortunate Frenchman on my right, who worked twice as hard for fourteen or fifteen. In front of me stood, singing snatches of Beranger, or else disputing lustily in dispraise of Bonaparte with some angry Parisian, the now talented editor and provincial proprietor of the —— Chronicle, at whose lordly lodgings (so I thought them then) it soon became my pleasant custom to resort, to flute and fiddle it in time to his extemporaneous madcap accompaniments on the piano until near midnight.

The English force was made up of two very distinct classes. The one was composed of men who, like myself, were entirely dependent upon their own exertions for the means of support, and who, if they ever attained to a prosperous condition in life, must achieve it for themselves—the other party were very young men, the sons or protégés of English printers, visiting Paris for a short time with the double object of acquiring the language and improving their knowledge of the business. My musical friend, R——, was of this latter class, and was pre-eminently the gentleman of the corps. He was a good workman, but received too many remittances from home in the shape of five-pound bank of England notes, to permit him to become an industrious one, and was then of too mercurial a temper, and too fond of the dissipations of the theatres and concerts within, and the Chaumières and dancing gardens without the walls of the city, to be very scrupulous in his attendance at the office, where he seldom made an appearance before ten o'clock in the day, and he rarely returned to work after his dinner at four in the afternoon. It need hardly be remarked that the overseer was compelled to confide the greater portion of the copy to those hands whose circumstances obliged them to pay attention to it, as no very great reliance could be placed upon the exertions of the others, who were constantly either in expectation of a supply of funds from home, or engaged in the pleasant occupation of getting rid of what they had received.

The " oldest inhabitant" of the English department was a man of the name of Franks, the history of whose life would have furnished a very different record from that of most members of the profession. He had been apprenticed when a boy to the proprietor of a newspaper in the West of England, from whom, seduced by the charms of a soldier's life, and an unconquerable fancy for the saddle, he had run away, and enlisted in a regiment of dragoons. Before he had been three years on horseback his regiment was ordered to Spain; and, under the command of the Iron Duke, Franks had the satisfaction of assisting at most of the bloody ceremonies called battles, from his first essay at Salamanca to his last at Toulouse. He considered that he had gathered rather more than his share of the compliments of the season, being pretty well scarred about the neck and shoulders, to say nothing of a ball through the left arm. At the last entertainment, however, he received a salute from a sabre, which laid open his cheek, and severed both his lips, and effectually abolished his claim to the appellation of a "pretty man," heretofore accorded him. He recovered in time to reach Paris soon after Napoleon was on his route to Elba. But, here, sick at length of his share of glory, and unprescient of the future, he resolved to desert; and, aided by a Parisian damsel enamored of the *brave Anglois*— aided also by the proceeds of a modicum of private plunder which he had found means to carry on on his own account— he actually lay *perdu* during the perilous "hundred days," the bombardment of Paris by the Allies, and their occupation of the city until the re-establishment of the Bourbons. He described to me, with evident pleasure and exultation, the mortified and wretched appearance of the French cavalry, as their separated and straggling bands found their way into Paris after the rout of Waterloo. "I saw the lot of 'em reviewed by the Emperor," said he, "and there wasn't a man of 'em but thought he was going to nab Old Nosey" (so he termed Wellington) "for his own share. But our fellows soon cracked a goodish lot of their tin kettles for 'em, and a pretty sprinkling of them that came back had left a piece of their muzzles behind 'em. Our chaps, I fancy, had got tired of peppering their crabshells with bullets, and throwing away powder for nothing, and so took to shaving at close quarters." His opinion of Old Nosey, as he called him, was anything but what might have been expected from a soldier who had followed the first military commander of the age through an unparalleled series of successes. He hated him, in fact, with a hatred for which he could find no expression in language, which made me suspect that he had himself suffered personally, at the Duke's order, for some slight breach of military discipline. How likely he was to have incurred punishment in such a way, may be inferred from an occurrence in which he was fatally concerned, and which took place not long previous to my arrival in Paris. One fine Sunday afternoon, being out with a pleasure-party at the suburbs, and having drunk more wine than he could prudently carry, nothing would suit him but he must go to his lodgings, don his old regimentals, and strut about the Boulevards in the uniform of an English dragoon. As might have been reasonably expected, he soon found himself affronted and insulted by some of the French soldiery stationed at the barriers, and whom he took no sort of care to avoid. Their sarcastic language, followed by his contemptuous retorts, soon mounted to a violent quarrel, and Franks received a blow from a grenadier, which he returning with interest, the striker drew his sword, and demanded combat on the spot. The spectators interfered—not to prevent the duel, but to settle the preliminaries, and arrange the affair according to the laws of honor then in force. This process was very summarily got through. A young officer volunteered his services as second to the Englishman, who immediately accepted the offer; and the parties retiring at once to a small garden in the rear of a petty cabaret, in less than ten minutes from the commencement of the fray both combatants stood bareheaded and with swords drawn in front of each other. It was but the affair of a moment. After a few feints, Franks drove his ponderous broadsword sheer through the skull of his antagonist, literally cleaving him to the throat; and having behaved, according to the testimony of the witnesses, in a manner perfectly honorable, was conveyed ceremoniously to his lodgings by the comrades of the man he had slain. The deed had, as it may be imagined, sobered him at once; but he took no advantage of the opportunity afforded him for escape, and was consequently led off to prison on the following day by the gens-d'armes, who came thus late to his quarters with probably no expectation of finding him. At the trial which followed, after some weeks' imprisonment, alleviated by the contributions of the officers who had witnessed the duel, the facts were gone into, and the crime brought home to the delinquent; but, according to regulations made and provided, for the accommodation, it is supposed, of persons of honor, the proceedings were broken off at the critical moment, the trial deferred for an indefinite period, and a day or two after, the prisoner, at the application of one of his friends, suffered to go at large on his own recognisance, and mulcted only in the loss of the seedy regimentals—the worthless *irritamenta malorum*.

E——s was the most accomplished man of the English party, and also the most industrious. He was near forty years of age, and boasted that he had not wasted an hour, unless when he could not avoid it, since he was twenty. He was an " own correspondent" as well as a compositor, and filled up all his intervals of time in the study of some new language, of which he kept a volume and a small manuscript grammar constantly in his pocket. In this way he had acquired sufficient Greek to read any part of the "Iliad;" Latin enough to read Horace, whose Odes he seemed to have by heart, and for the proper scansion of which he was a pedantic stickler; and Lucretius, with whom it was his delight to bother me by crabbed passages picked out for the purpose. He spoke French fluently; was the only man among us who occasionally exchanged a few words with the Spaniard, read Italian readily, and averred that he had learned it without the aid of either grammar, dictionary, or living teacher; and was then working hard at the German, for the attainment of which he had allotted himself twelve months. The example of R——— had excited him to the study of music, of the theory of which he had made himself sufficiently master, though he was deficient in practice from the want of an accurate ear. To all these accomplishments he added the most execrably captious temper and vengeful disposition, which it was no difficult matter to rouse into fury upon the most trifling occasions. He seemed to look upon a request for information upon any subject with which he was acquainted as an attempt to rob him, as though if he imparted it to others he must necessarily lose it himself. Nature had connected this charming disposition with its usual concomitants—a petty figure and powerless frame.

N——, by whose frame stood that of E——s, was a man of an entirely different stamp. Somewhat younger than the other, he was yet old enough to have acquired a profound knowledge of the world, which I had reason to believe had cost him no small share of misery and adversity. Upon first coming to the office, a year previous to my own arrival, he had apologised to his companions for his want of skill in the art he was about to practice, and stated that since the expiration of his apprenticeship, fifteen years before, he had not touched a type. He volunteered no further information respecting himself, but it had leaked out in the course of a twelvemonth's companionship, that he had been a bookseller in a large way of business; that he had failed suddenly through the villany of a pretended friend, and that he had been obliged to fly his country, leaving a wife and family behind him, to avoid overwhelming pecuniary liabilities to which he had been induced to pledge himself. He was the best speaker and the best read man with whom I had ever yet come in contact. With the most ultra violent principles he combined the most modest and unassuming demeanor; and when asked for information on any topic, generally replied *impromptu*, in language at once terse and elegant, delivered in a strain as fluent and unhesitating as though he were reading a passage from some celebrated writer. In politics he was a Republican, and seriously declared that had he been an Hindoo he should have been a Thug. In religion he was an infidel, yet wavering according to his own confession, between atheism and deism, and doubting at times whether the doctrines of the latter were those with which a thorough free-thinker could remain permanently satisfied. In all disputes, whatever the matter under discussion, he was generally appealed to for a judgment, and his dictum, which was never refused, for the most part finally settled the question.

Dick D—— was a cockney of the very first water. Types and tippling were the alpha and omega of his existence. He knew the quality of the liquor retailed in every public-house within the sound of Bow bells, and was unceasing in his search after information of an analogous nature in reference to the wines sold by draught in Paris. Though a slovenly workman, scrambling and shovelling his types together without any regard to the exact mechanical neatness which is an instinct with the good compositor, he would yet, from his astonishing celerity, have earned more money than any of us had he possessed an average share of application and perseverance. But he had been born and bred among the worshippers of Saint Monday, at whose shrine he was a faithful devotee, and upon whose altar he sacrificed the first day of every working week with a pertinacious piety highly honorable to the sincerity of his religious principles. The sacrifice was invariably accompanied with libations to his patron saint, of the liberality and copiousness of which libations the appearance of the votary, dragged by necessity from the ecstasies of his seventh heaven to the drudgery of the working world some time in the afternoon of Tuesday, furnished abundant testimony. He seldom began work in earnest before Wednesday morning, as he usually found his copy in the hands of others, who, having undertaken to finish it, were unwilling to give it back. Though he had been a year in Paris he had made no progress in the language, and had no intention of making any. He knew how to call for a pint of wine or a glass of grog, and could pay his reckoning without the help of French (he said) and should not bother his brains about it. His notions of economy and forethought were on a par with his ideas of sobriety. He considered himself fully provided against every emergency by the possession of a capital silver watch, upon which he could raise two pounds at " his uncle's," whenever he wanted it. " This 'ere ticker," said he to me " cost me but a five-pun' note ven I bort it fust, and I've popped it more than twenty times, and had more than forty poun' on it altogether. It's a garjian haingel to a fellar, is a good votch, ven you're hard up." Upon my representing to him that if he had paid twenty per cent. for the loan more than twenty-times, his watch must have cost him considerably more than he mentioned, he met me with a stare of astonishment, and answered with a tone of ineffable contempt " that he knowed best what he gave for his watch." The calculation, simple as it was, involved an amount of arithmetic of which he had not the remotest idea.

Co-operating with the English hands upon English work were three or four clever Parisian workmen who had adopted our *modus operandi* and the use of similar implements. They fully appreciated the English mode of getting over the ground at a more rapid pace, and as their earnings increased in proportion, their example was speedily followed by others. Thus the importation of London workmen into Paris was by degrees conducive to the improvement and advantage of the natives; and the present race of French compositors are, no doubt mainly owing to this cause, little if anything inferior, either in accuracy or celerity, to those of our own country; though I question much if they are ever required to work the long hours with which the custom of the trade has saddled the London workmen, or could by any means be brought to consent to do so. The French offices, all, at least, in which I wrought, were opened at daylight in the morning, so that the industrious workman might prosecute his labors as soon after sunrise as he chose and was at liberty to earn as much money as he could during the day, with the certainty that he would receive the whole of his earnings when pay-day came round—a certainty by no means guaranteed in London offices, where average mediocrity rules the roast, and condemns superior industry and skill either to descend to its own dead level, or else robs the possessor of those qualifications of the profit and pre-eminence which he ought righteously to derive from the exercise of them.

I considered my station between the silent Spaniard on one side, and the plodding old Frenchman on the other, as particularly fortunate. The Spaniard on the left saved me from noisy disturbances, and with the old Parisian I could carry on an occasional conversation to the extent of my capability, which I found daily improving under the advantage which his deliberate utterance and pains-taking explanations afforded me. He advised me to drop the use of the French and English Dictionary, and to make use of that of Wailly, in which the words were explained in French. I followed his counsel, and soon reaped the benefit of it in a more perfect knowledge of the proper place and power of the terms I wished to employ, as well as in an improved faculty of selection, and a more extended and more simple vocabulary. My old preceptor was an original in his way; he had witnessed all the horrors of the Revolution of '89, had been present at the execution both of Louis XVI. and Marie Antoinette, had looked on at the massacres and bloody gaol-deliveries in which a populace intoxicated with license sought for pastime in the excitement of vengeance and murder, had beheld the slaughter of the Swiss guards and the worship of the Goddess of Reason in the church of Notre Dame, and had been a spectator of most of the terrible and disgusting atrocities of that eventful era. Being the only son of a widow, he had managed to escape the conscription throughout the whole period of the wars of Napoleon, from which his short stature (he was little over five feet) might not otherwise have saved him, and had worked quietly on at his three trades of cutler, saddler, and printer, during the decapitation of aristocrats and the overthrow of dynasties. Of all these events he spoke with the utmost indifference and *nonchalance*, and with a tone of a man discussing the variations of the weather or the chances of a game played by others. He blamed the unfortunate Louis for not putting himself in the outset at the head of the Revolution, or, if he chose to stick by his party, for not dealing with the first mob of insurgents as Napoleon at a later period dealt with the Sectionaries. "Twenty twelve-pounders," said he, "administered in time, would have saved the nobility and the throne." He told me, which turned out true enough, than in less than seven years more we should see another revolution in France, unless it should first please Heaven to relieve the country from the imbecile rule of Charles X., and settle the Government upon a more stable basis.

I reaped considerable advantage from my conversation with this stolid old talker, and should have reaped more but that his propinquity offended my nose even more than it profited my ear. He was enamoured of dirt to a degree which it is impossible to express in decent language. He acknowledged that he never washed or bathed, professing a mortal aversion from the contact of water with his skin. He never used a razor, but ground the beard occasionally from his face with a kind of pumice-stone, which he carried in his pocket. It is my serious belief that he never changed his linen from the day when he put it on new until that when it was too ragged to be worn any longer. He was in other respects filthy beyond the comprehension of an

English nightman; and as the warm weather of July approached, after I had stood near two months by his side, I found myself compelled to apply to Mr. L——, the overseer, for a new location. My application was received with a general chorus of laughter, and a declaration on all sides that they had been expecting it for a month past, but were determined to see how long I could stand it. This was followed by a unanimous order to old A——, my unsavory friend, to decamp with his frame to his old dark corner, whither I assisted in removing him, not without a pang of remorse at being the occasion of a change which must materially diminish his weekly earnings. He bore it, however, with admirable equanimity, and remained perfectly content in his mal-odorous solitude.

Among the number of my former companions there is yet one who demands a place in this desultory chronicle. The hirsute and merry-faced M—— was a constant source of vivacity and good-humor. He was neither compositor nor pressman, but having by some means obtained a footing in the office, made a comfortable living by speculating on the industry of others. Like many of the French compositors, he had picked up what knowledge of the business he possessed without any regular teaching, and was from habit better adapted for the line of action he had beaten out for himself than for settling closely to work at the frame. He made his gains by buying-up, for ready money, any amount of type already composed which the compositors were inclined to sell, taking the labor of making it up into pages, and the trouble and responsibility of correction, upon himself, and charging the whole to the employer as his own work. In this way it would often happen that he had twelve or fifteen pounds to receive at the end of a fortnight, six-sevenths of which he had previously paid out as purchase-money. He was wary in his bargains, never giving too much for careless or ill-punctuated matter—generally declining to have anything to do with that of his own countrymen, which was necessarily incorrect from their ignorance of English, but giving within a fraction of the full price for the composition of those upon whose correctness he could rely. The plan succeeded well with both buyer and sellers. He made an average of thirty or forty francs a week by his commerce, and the best workman were but too willing to get rid of the disagreeable task of correction, together with other minor interruptions in their labor from which they were relieved by disposing summarily of each day's work as it was done. This fortunate fellow had received from nature an inexhaustible stock of cheerfulness and good-humor, which it was beyond the power of misfortune to damp or restrain. At any of those little mishaps to which printers are liable, such as breaking a page or misplacing one in a sheet, and on account of which most journeymen are wont to growl an oath or two, he would burst into a laugh prolonged till the roof rang again. In the course of a couple of years' practice in the office, he had picked up an assortment of the most unaccountable jargon, which he thought was English, and prided himself upon displaying on all occasions. In this he had been maliciously assisted by the whole body of my countrymen, who found good sport in cramming him with absurd and ridiculous blunders, and in encouraging the pompous parade which he made of his acquirements. If you asked him how he did, he was always " plenty well ;" and once when I wished him a good appetite to his dinner, he responded, " And you, I confide you shall play a man with your stomach," bowing at the same time with grave politeness.

He was well-built, and strong as Hercules; could swim easily at a walking pace against the current of the Seine, and when stripped for the exploit, stood apparelled in a natural suit of black hair, which covered every part of his person, with the exception of his broad forehead and the upper part of his face.

I rose every morning with the sun, and made the best of my time while the opportunity served and the work was plentiful. My fortnight's bill often merged upon a hundred francs, and sometimes went beyond it; and before the end of July I had saved and laid by a sum fully equal to that with which I had set out from home. Just at this period, from the simultaneous completion of several English romances, the copy fell short of a sudden, and I found myself standing still for several hours every day. This not being at all to my taste, after lounging about for the best part of a week, I made application to the overseer of the presses on the ground-floor for employment at press. He, knowing that I was a compositor, doubted, or affected to doubt, my capacity as a pressman, but upon my assuring him that I had had good experience in that department, said he would give me a trial. He led the way into a long room, extending, apparently, half the length of the street, where stood arranged in precise line a whole regiment of Columbian presses, of London manufacture, the number of which, as the crowning eagles rose and fell with rapid irregularity, I in vain essayed to count. Having marched me up and down the whole length of the building, to show me, no doubt, true Frenchman as he was, the extent of his dominion, he told me, what he must have known perfectly well before, that he did not see any vacancy there, and bade me follow him to the other side. I obeyed, expressing as we proceeded, my unqualified admiration of the order and cleanliness of his department, and the good working condition of the presses, as evidenced by the impression they produced. The ink used, though of the deepest color, bore an indication of blue rather than of jet-black, and I had noticed some clever but simple contrivances for securing its equal application to the surface of the type which remains to this day a desideratum among English printers. "Now I think of it," said the overseer, "there is a countryman of your own in want of a mate; if you can manage to keep up with him, for he is a fast hand, it may be more agreeable to you to join him than to work with a stranger. Perhaps you may make something of him; I must confess I can't, though he has been with us these six months." I expressed my preference for the companionship of a fellow-countryman, and begged to be introduced to him at once.

Following my guide into a room at the right of the entrance-gate, what was my astonishment upon beholding, in all his stalwart dignity, as in the days of yore, the old friend of my boyhood, the redoubtable "Fish!" There he stood, working single-handed at a super-royal stanhope, and handling it, to all appearance, as easily as a gamester would a dice-box, whistling furiously the while Dibdin's famous air of " Poor Tom Bowling," as though his lungs wanted employment and he was willing to give them a turn. He took no notice of us beyond suddenly checking his strain as we drew near, but when I hailed him with the once familiar salute, " How now, old Fish?" the frisket fell from his hands, and he stood aghast with astonishment. It was some minutes before he could make me out: I had been so silly as to follow the example of some of my companions in cultivating a moustache, which, together with some alteration of costume, prevented his ready recognition of my features. No sooner had he identified them than, exploding my Christian name with a burst of triumph, he was at my side, and clenched both my hands with a grip that made me perspire in every pore. Though restrained by the presence of the overseer, he could not altogether repress the demonstrations of satisfaction which burst forth in an involuntary chuckle even now and then. When the overseer proposed me for his partner, he was overjoyed—swore in a horrible mixture of French and English terms, of which the former understood not a syllable, that I was the best pressman in all England, and bade me strip to work and show my training, that my introducer might see how well he had taught me my business.

The overseer left us together, and as it was then past noon, and I had no intention of working at press in my present garb, the Fish accompanied me to my lodgings, where, having accoutred myself more to my liking, we sat down to a trifling refreshment, and went over the fortunes of both since we had last met. Like myself, he had journeyed to London in search of occupation, but having more strings to his bow than I could boast of, had met with better success. Finding the printing business, as he said, in shoal water, he had found temporary employment in unshipping goods in the river, and had subsequently succeeded in hiring himself, through the recommendation of an old sea-captain with whom he had formerly sailed, as servant to a young gentleman setting out on his travels. He had managed the transit of his master's horses and travelling-equipage as far as Paris, where, finding himself disqualified for the post he had undertaken, "for lack of the lingo," as he termed it, which he had picked up by rote during a short stay in the Mauritius, twenty years before, and hearing, upon inquiry, that he could readily obtain employment as a pressman, he had left his master, and found an engagement in the office where I had so unexpectedly encountered him. He said he was doing very well at his work, and that together we might expect to make, by sticking to it, a good eighty francs a week, if we chose to do our best.

We commenced work the same afternoon; and so little had I been accustomed of late to continued active exercise, that the perspiration streamed from my person for days together during the hours of labor. The Fish, however, was as gentle as he was strong; and moderating his pace to suit mine, insisted upon monopolising all the extra duties requiring only a single hand, to give me time to recruit my strength. Before a week had elapsed I became thoroughly seasoned, and without the aid of stimulants of any kind was able to keep up with the rapid motions of my companion.

We had not been many days at work together before I became aware, from certain hints he let drop, that he had got some important secret upon his mind of which it was his intention to make me the confidant, though, from some motive or other, he was plainly half-ashamed or afraid of disclosing it.

I resolved to pump it out of him, and using all the address of which I was master, at length arrived at the delicate fact, which was nothing more nor less than that he was enamoured of his landlady, or of her comfortable surroundings, I could not make out which with any degree of certainty; that he was determined to have her; and, finally, that he wanted my co-operation in the conduct of the courtship. He looked rather blue while I laughed long and loudly at this comical disclosure, and when I had done asked me rather sharply whether I intended to bear a hand in the business or no. Upon my assuring him that my services were at his command whenever he might require them, and that I would do what I could to realize his project, he became much elated, said he considered the affair as good as settled, and promised to call at my lodgings and introduce me to the lady on the following Sunday afternoon. I asked if he could reconcile it with his conscience to enter into matrimony without giving up his old habits and predilections in favor of strong drinks. He assured me that he was very much reformed in that particular; that French beer was a mere wash, French wine gave him the colic, and that he confined himself to brandy, which he had latterly taken to diluting with coffee, and that a couple of bottles or so lasted him a week. I congratulated him on so near an approach to sobriety, and inquired as to the condition and qualities of the lady upon whom his wishes were centred. He informed me that she was the widow of a hotel-keeper, and mistress of the house in which he lodged, which she managed admirably, and had done so before the loss of her husband, a lazy and bloated sot, who did nothing but smoke cigars, drink grog, and play billiards, and who had died four months ago from sheer idleness and fat.

At the appointed hour on the following Sunday a fiacre drove into the yard of the hotel where I had my quarters, from which descended the Fish, in the costume of a perfect gentleman, his hard horny palms indued with kid gloves, and his raven hair yet glistening from the hands of the *frizeur*. As he entered my little dormitory, where I sat reading, and expecting his presence, he produced from his pocket a handsome figured waistcoat, which he insisted upon my wearing on the occasion, and which he would never afterwards consent to receive back. I had no sooner, in obedience to his commands, "got into it," than he hurried me down stairs, where the object of his admiration sat in the vehicle awaiting our coming. He motioned me to be seated on one side of the lady, and mounting himself on the other, shouted to the jarvey "A Versailles," and away we drove to see the grand exhibition of waterworks in the gardens, which was to come off at four o'clock. The widow was a black-eyed brunette, with long eyelashes and dark orbs, nose a very trifle *retroussé*, and the prettiest mouth imaginable, affording in its rapid play rare but occasional glimpses of a snow-white set of teeth; but three-and-thirty years, or thereabouts, had traced their indelible characters upon these once blooming beauties, and the seams with which the old *edax rerum* delights to furrow the fairest faces were cruelly visible upon hers. I was charmed with the vivacity and frankness of her manners and conversation, and gratified by the playful politeness with which she corrected the numberless blunders I made in maintaining my part of it. I could see plainly enough that up to this time, at least, she had not the slightest idea of any serious intentions on the part of her English suitor; and that having for full twenty years been in the habit of receiving the homage which, in Paris especially, is universally paid to beauty, she had regarded his attentions as nothing more than her due, and, perhaps, might even have been sensible of a degree of condescension in submitting to them. She was dressed with exquisite taste, in a sort of half-mourning drapery, which became her exceedingly, and seemed fully conscious that she was receiving admiration, and was worthy of it.

I enjoyed the excursion amazingly, and, I have no doubt,

chattered an immense deal of bad sense and worse grammar in the course of our perambulations through the gardens among the prodigious crowd which clustered upon every available point of view. The Fish, though he was watchfully attentive in supplying us with refreshments, with which he had taken care to load the cab, was silent, as if he had really been furnished with fins, and swimming in the element we were gazing at. He was gratified, however, at the favor shown to me by the widow, and asked me in a whisper if I should not do well to change my quarters, and swing my hammock alongside of his own berth, where I could speak the lady at any time. As I had long felt annoyed by the scoundrelly *concièrge* at the Rue Rivoli. who gave me a jobation every time he let me in after twelve o'clock, and as I thought, moreover, that I might derive both pleasure and improvement from the conversation of the pretty widow, I fell in with the notion at once, and resolved to carry it into practice if possible. With this view, as soon as the show was ended (which, as it has been witnessed by half the adults of Cockaigne, and is detailed at length in the guide-books, I need not here describe,) I questioned the lady on the subject, and was gratified to hear that she could make room for me on the same terms as I then stood, and would feel a pleasure in so doing. We took an agreeable cup of tea at a coffee house in one of the quiet old streets of Versailles, and about six o'clock, my companion having succeeded in unkennelling the driver, mounted our vehicle to return to Paris.

As this drive home was one of the most singular experiences I have ever undergone, and as its recurrence is now impossible since the construction of a line of railway along the route, I shall describe it briefly for the edification of the reader. The weather had been for several weeks dry and hot, and the first Sunday in August proving remarkably fine, with the somewhat rare accompaniment of a delightful breeze, had tempted forth an unusual number of visitors. While surveying the vast multitude that thronged the gardens, one might have supposed that Paris had completely disgorged itself upon Versailles. As they had been arriving gradually during the day, from the first dawn of morning up to four or later in the afternoon, little or no confusion had arisen during the gathering; but when, the entertainment being concluded, they nearly all pushed homewards at once upon the one grand route leading to Paris, a scene ensued which baffles all power of description. Upon emerging from the comparatively retired street in which we had taken our refreshment, I requested the driver, as he had a good horse, to make the best of his way, as we were anxious to get home. He took no notice of my request beyond a shrug of the shoulders, but turning the corner into the main road, was immediately fast jammed in a crowd of vehicles of every possible and impossible description, without the power of moving beyond the pace of the slowest hack among them. To return was altogether impracticable, as in a few moments we had a crowd pressing in the rear which altogether precluded the attempt. Everything that could by any contrivance be mounted upon wheels, from old lumbering statecoaches and worn-out diligences down to a few planks bound together with ropes, and stuck about with backless chairs and three-legged stools, had been brought into requisition; and everything that had ever worn the shape of a horse, and yet possessed the power of locomotion, had been mercilessly roused from its dying agonies to furnish a further profit to the rascally owner. Add to this that each carriage was clustered over with human bipeds thick as bees upon a honeycomb, and some idea may be formed of the spectacle. As nobody seemed willing to walk, and as there was not half-sufficient accommodation for the whole to ride, there were continual fights and fracas between those on foot for the occupancy of any vacant place which an over-greedy Jehu might contrive to discover. Post-chaises crammed to suffocation within, and fringed around with a circle of legs dangling from their flat tops, and drawn by bony hacks, already bound for Montfaucon, stumbled along at a snail's pace, and occasionally came down with a crash, and blocked the path of those in the rear. Such calamities were hailed with a roar of laughter from all sides; while the disconcerted driver, aided by his dismounted customers, who, according to the order of the day, had all paid their money in advance, set hastily about repairing the disaster by the plentiful application of ropes, the Gallic remedy for coach fracture.

I enjoyed the fun exceedingly so long as it was visible, expecting, too, that we should speedily get out of it, and trot off gaily homewards; but when, after half-an-hour's progress, we had got beyond the precincts of Versailles, within which, but no farther, the roads were regularly watered, the sensation was anything but pleasant. The obscurity from dust alone was greater than that of the densest London fog, though it was not, like the fog, an obscurity of darkness. We breathed dust instead of air, were covered with dust as effectually as if we had rolled in it, and dared not open our lips to speak for fear of being choked with it. It was not till we arrived at Sevres that we were enabled to mend our pace, and, as it was, we were benighted before we reached Paris.

I took leave of the Fish and his charmer at half-past ten o'clock, and must refer the reader to the next chapter for the conclusion of his amour.

CHAPTER V.

The Loves of the Fish—A musical acquaintance—Extraordinary Musical Performance—A trap for the widow—I urge my companion's suit—The friend of the family—The widow not to be caught—The Fish disappears in dudgeon—I grow fond of billiards—The Pool and the Pole—A Duel by moonlight—New resolutions—A new study—Pursuit of knowledge under a blanket—A literary auction—My friend N——and his extempore Homilies on Politics and Religion—Their effect upon me—N—— turns author, and I commence as Professor of English—My first pupil—Difficulties of teaching; the Future tense and the Subjunctive mood—Account of my Patrons.

BEFORE I went to work on the Monday morning, I made known to the porter my intention of removing to the other side of the water at the expiration of my month, to which it wanted but a few days. He was glad enough to get rid of me, and said he would guarantee that no difficulty was thrown in the way of my removal—adding, that he wondered "what the devil I wanted with a lodging at all, seeing that I could not lie in bed like other folks, but must enter after midnight and must be let out before it was light in the morning." I reminded him that I had done so but on very few occasions, and he graciously accepted my apology, conditioned with the assurance that I was really going, and that he was at liberty to let the apartment to another.

With the assistance of the Fish, who was but too glad to secure my services in the promotion of his suit, my goods and chattles were transferred to the establishment of the widow, where I also took up my quarters at the end of the week. Here I found myself much more comfortably accommodated, as, instead of having to ascend an interminable flight of stairs to my dormitory, I was provided with a snug little cabinet which opened on the landing of the first floor. My window looked into the court-yard of a neighboring establishment crowded with the ponderous and unwieldy vehicles, built very much on the model of an English stage-coach, but twice as large and five times as heavy, in which travelling families are, or were, accustomed to make the tour of the South of France or the passage of the Alps. Together with these were the nondescript fish-wagons, shaped like colossal hearses, in which live sturgeon, carp, and other luckless finny victims, were hauled from the Lake of Geneva, or the shores of the Mediterranean, or the agricultural fish-warrens in the Valley of the Saone, as well as from the nearer coasts of the northern departments. Some of these equipages were either coming in or preparing to start continually; and it was a constant source of interest and amusement, when nothing better offered, to watch the proceedings of the couriers and abigails, the ladies' men and ladies' maids, and to mark the disinterested care which each one took in providing for his or her individual satisfaction on the route.

The widow's establishment, denominated an hotel, according to universal custom, combined within itself the convenience of a coffee-house, lodging-house, and billiard-rooms. It was in excellent order, and subjected to a constant and vigilant administration, the lady herself being the guiding and animating spirit. She was up in the morning before the lark, securing by her presence the attention of her domestics to their duty. She made all purchases herself, kept the keys, and administered the stores with her own hands—having one confidential female assistant, who received money and doled out to each customer his modicum of lump sugar. I suspect that the mistress took a nap of an hour or two regularly after dinner, as she was peculiarly animated and lively of an evening, and had no objection to indoctrinate me in the science of billiards, which she played admirably, after the guests had withdrawn and the house was closed for the night. On these occasions the Fish acted as marker, with extraordinary demonstrations of politeness and assiduity towards the fair object of his devotion. His suit, however, was not by any means progressing as fast as he wished, or even fancied. I found my position as interpreter of his advances too equivocal to be altogether pleasant, particularly as I was not long in making the discovery of what I had indeed suspected from the first, that the lady was unaware of the existence of any serious designs on his part, and might probably be disposed to resent them should they become too apparent to be mistaken. In acting as his dragoman I found myself constantly compelled to modify the words and phrases he put into my mouth, he knew enough of the language to be sensible that he was not literally translated, but was often undecided whether he ought to be grateful or affronted on account of the liberties I thought fit to take.

Convinced myself of the true state of the case, I endeavored, one day, while we were at work together, to open his eyes, and to put him in possession of the facts as they really stood. He heard my statement to the end, and then, dropping the roller on the ink-table, folded his arms, looked me sternly in the face, and demanded whether I thought him a " sea-calf or a thundering fool."

"By no means," said I; "I think the choice you have made a very sensible one, but wiser men than you have been mistaken in such matters; and you must take into account that you have not to do with an English lass, with whom such attentions as you have shown would be naturally enough construed as so many advances towards matrimony. Madame ——, on the contrary, is too much accustomed to the admiration of her neighbors to regard yours as anything extraordinary, and take my word for it, has no idea that you have any matrimonial designs against her."

This seemed to stagger him. He resumed his work and said nothing for some time, and when, at length, he did speak, it was upon another subject. I saw through his assumed indifference, and felt that he was making up his mind to some decisive course; and therefore was not surprised when, during our walk home in the evening, he asked me if I had any objection to break the business to the widow at the first opportunity that offered, and to pop the question for him, as he was determined to bring the matter to an upshot one way or the other. This I volunteered to do, stipulating only that the mode of doing it, as well as the selection of a fit opportunity, were to be left to my own discretion.

On the opposite side of the landing upon which the door of my little cabinet opened, lodged a Genevese, a musician possessed of marvellous talent on the violin. I had been made aware of his proximity on the morning after my arrival, when, while unpacking my boxes, I had stumbled upon my old fiddle, and, urged by the whim of the moment, and a sort of longing to hear again the notes of one of our old home tunes, I had screwed up the strings and commenced a bar or two of "With Verdure clad." Stopping for a moment to look for the resin, I heard the strain taken up by another instrument in so masterly a manner, with such expression and tenderness, that I could not help throwing open my door to listen. The performer came forth from his room to apologise for having interfered with my melody, and thus we became acquainted. He was engaged in the orchestra of the Odeon Theatre, situated in the district, and having to play there every night in the week, Sundays not excepted, we who were absent during the day saw but little of him. I was usually off to work before he commenced practice in the morning, which he generally did for three or four hours in bed, after which he rose and went to the rehearsal; but on Sunday mornings I had the full benefit of the superior strains he drew from his instrument, and not unfrequently sat by his bedside well pleased to watch "his flying fingers kiss the strings," and drink in the delicious witchery of his music. He was a dark but handsome fellow of about thirty, spoke a little English, and was anxious to speak it well, and seized every opportunity of talking it with me for the sake of improvement. He possessed one peculiar talent, perfectly unique in itself, so far, at least, as I have ever heard, productive of the most exquisitely pleasurable emotions, and yet

A MUSICAL PHENOMENON.

utterly useless both to himself and others. I know not whether I shall succeed in describing it, though its effect is present in my memory, and often haunts my senses in the vigils of the night. One Sunday afternoon, during a pause in a rain-storm which had lasted for six or seven hours, and during which the Genevese and I had been fiddling, and talking, and reading, and dining together, he took occasion to remark upon my fondness for music, and said he could gratify it in an extraordinary way if he thought fit. I begged him to explain himself. He was in no hurry to do so, but, after some coquetting and delay, rose from his seat, and taking a large cloak from a peg in the wall, laid it open upon the bed, and then locking the door and closing the window-shutters, to exclude, as he said, even the slightest sound, seated me upon the cloak, sat himself down as close to me as possible, and pulled the hood over both our heads. Then placing his lips close to my ear, he said, " You must not speak—you must hardly breathe. Listen !" I held my breath and listened curiously for the best part of a minute before I was aware of any sound, and was just going to break the silence, when a small but piercingly shrill strain seemed to traverse the very innermost chambers of my brain. I was not aware of the precise moment when it commenced, but I perceived instantly that it was accompanied by another note harmonising with it, produced by different mechanical means, and a twelfth lower. The shrill treble ran dancing with inconceivable rapidity up and down a comprehensive gamut, in a kind of fantastic variations upon some popular air, which I could identify, while the accompanying bass, which might be compared for continuity to the drone of a bagpipe, but which, unlike that, was " musical as is Apollo's lute," though limited apparently to five or six notes, gave the successive intonations with all the precision and certainty of an instrument. The longer I listened the more rapturous was the music, or, which is more probable, the more sensitive my perceptions became, and the better was I qualified to appreciate it. The notation of the treble, which at first hearing had seemed to glide up and down, because by degrees distinct and articulate as that of a flageolet, to which, however, it bore no sort of resemblance, and the sustained notes of the bass assumed a triumphant, pealing tone which thrilled me with delight. When at length the strain suddenly ceased, and the Genevese, throwing off the cloak, sprung up and opened the window-shutters, it was some time before I could recollect where I was. He laughed at my embarrassment, and upon my complimenting him upon the beauty and delicacy of the performance I had heard, asked me whether I could show him how to turn it to account. As he confessed that without the precautions we had taken the music would have been inaudible, and that the hum of the smallest fly would have drowned the whole, I was forced to acknowledge that I could see no mode of making such a species of harmony marketable.

Now this musician of silence had frequently offered me tickets for the theatre where he performed, which hitherto I had as often refused; but having concocted a plan for settling the Fish's affair with his landlady, I asked him the morning after I had accepted that delicate commission to be so kind as to oblige me with a couple of tickets at his first convenience. They were not long in forthcoming, and accordingly, in pursuance of the plan I had formed, I made an engagement with the lady to accompany her to the Odeon, where it was my determination, between the intervals of the performance, to urge my client's interest. I made my fellow-workman acquainted with my intention, which he approved, and accompanying us to the theatre, left us to a *tête-à-tête* in a box, seeking a place for himself in another part of the house.

The play was a rattling French comedy, and at first I was so enchanted with the astonishingly natural acting—if acting it ought to be called—of the lady and gentlemen performers, that for an hour I lost sight of the main object for which I had come. I was reminded of it however, by an incident in the drama enacting before me, and at the close of the third act took occasion to make a comparison between the heroine on the stage, who seemed to be much embarrassed with the various claims of her rival suitors, and the widow herself, whom I pretended to suppose in a condition of equal perplexity. This made her very merry, and she talked so fast and so freely that I was emboldened to reply in the same strain. But she was more than a match for my total inexperience in such matters, and would certainly have got at my secret, if I had had any, without betraying a particle of her own. As she denied having any lovers at all, I seized upon this denial, asserting warmly that she could not possibly be ignorant of the sentiments of my friend in regard to her, and of his honorable intentions. It was not without a deal of fencing on both sides, and a renewal of the charge on my part several times in the course of the evening, that I at length succeeded in bringing the matter before her in a serious point of view, and when this was at length accomplished, her manner entirely changed, her face assumed an expression of business-like consideration, and, after a silence of two or three minutes, she desired me to defer any further conversation on the subject until the following evening, when she would talk to me at home. She enjoyed the pleasures of the performance just as much after my communication as before, and seemed to have forgotten all about it by the time it was concluded.

I reported progress to my companion next day at the office, and perceived that his expectations were considerably modified by the complexion which my narration threw upon the business. Still he would go through with it, and know his fate. In the evening, as I had been led to expect, I was invited to a conference with the lady in her private sitting-room, where I must confess I was rather taken aback by the presence of a third party in the shape of a grizzly-pated, seedy-looking hunks of a fellow, whom I had occasionally remarked slumbering on the benches of the billiard-room, or lounging about the *salon* with his hands in his pockets. The sight of this apparition, furnished with pen, ink, and paper, and seated magisterially at the table, prepared me for the ceremony which shortly ensued. The widow introduced him to me as a "friend of the family," and me to him as a person making a proposal of marriage on behalf of another. A series of questions ensued on the subject of Monsieur Cotton's family, connexions, and status in England; his havings, and gettings, and prospects in reversion, &c., &c., to all of which I was requested to return categorical answers. I made the best I could of the business, extolled the charming disposition of the Fish, said what I could for the respectability of his connexions at home, professed ignorance on the score of his family, and made some sensation by the announcement of his annuity, which, though only twenty pounds a year, had a respectable sound under the designation of five hundred francs of rent. I added that he was an admirable workman, and could earn a good salary, a recommendation which did not appear to carry much weight with it. The "friend of the family," reduced all my replies to writing, and when they were finished, added up the sum total with an ominous shrug of the shoulders and an elevation of the eye-brows, which but too faithfully foreboded the result of the investigation. The lady, when appealed to, left everything in the hands of her grizzly counsellor, who decided at once, without any further consideration, that the match would be imprudent on the part of the widow, and was therefore unadvisable. I was requested to impart their conjoint ultimatum to the unsuccessful suitor, coupled with an assurance from the lady that she was fully sensible of the value of his friendship, and hoped that she should have the happiness to retain it.

Thus ended the Fish's amour, and with it, to my great annoyance at the time, ended my companionship with him. He could not be brought to look upon the affair in the same light with the lady, nor would he willingly look her in the face again. He left me to work single handed, while he tramped about to the different offices to procure his passport and get it *viséed*; and in less than a week from the eve of the conference fatal to his hopes, I bade adieu to him on the top of a diligence at St. Denis, having accompanied him thus far on his road homewards. Although I did not much feel the loss of his society, for there was not much to be got out of him, yet I reaped the disadvantage of his absence in another way. Having no companion to stroll about with of an evening, I began by degrees to devote too many hours to the billiard-table, and became, as my skill with the cue increased, so fond of the game, that every leisure moment was engrossed in its pursuit. There was one table on the ground-floor appropriated by a party of pool-players, who assembled every evening at dusk, and sometimes before, and continued their game till midnight. Long years of continued practice had made them so expert, that any stranger who happened to join the party was infallibly victimized. A constant attendant was a jeweller of the neighborhood, who was pointed out to me as the least expert of the number, who had yet paid for the skill he did possess by the loss of a large sum of money, and the ruin of a fine business through neglect, consequent upon his infatuation for billiards. Another was a tall Pole, with a black moustached muzzle, who was unrivalled in the use of the cue, by which it was said he gained his living, and who departed a winner nearly every night in the week. He was considered to have been the chief depository of the jeweller's losses.

One evening, having made ready a form about seven o'clock, and not feeling inclined to begin a short number, which yet I could not finish that night, my fingers itching, too, for the grasp of the cue, I put on my coat and went home. As I entered I heard the noise of an altercation in the pool-room, and ran thither to see what was going on. Here I found the jeweller in a violent rage, frantically swearing and gesticulating in the centre of a noisy group, and insisting upon the exclusion of the Pole from a party of players, which he had arranged before the arrival of the other. The Pole stood as cool as a post, but, in reply to some scurrilous abuse, made use of an expression which incensed the passionate man to such a degree that he sprang upon him like a cat, and fell with him to the ground. They were parted, and rose immediately, when the Pole, making for the door, beckoned the other with a commanding gesture to follow him. In a minute the billiard-room was empty, and all, even the old grizzled family friend and counsellor of Madame ———, were bustling on by the shortest cut to the Barrier d'Enfer. I made up to my old questioner, and asked him what they were going to do.

"Do?" said he, "fight, to be sure; there is nothing else to be done now."

"And what will come of it?" I asked.

"What always comes of it when these two are antagonists. The jeweller will bleed again, that's all. Bah!"

It grew dark as we hurried through the streets, and as we approached the barrier the group fell into a slow walking pace, and, in a careless, sauntering manner, made for the Maison de Santé, which stands, or then stood, at no great distance beyond the gate. The full moon was rising broad and bright, and threw her peaceful light upon the spot. I could track the tall figure of the Pole as he walked arm-in-arm with a companion, and several times came up with him; and, urged by curiosity to see how a man looked who was going to fight a duel, fastened my eyes upon him as well as the deepening twilight would allow. His pale face looked no paler than usual; but I remarked one thing which assured me the fellow was a bit of a knave, and most probably an old hand at the duello. He kept his eyes shut. I could not be mistaken, for I looked at him a dozen times, and observed that the long lids were firmly closed over the pupils. His object doubtless was to avoid the dazzling glare of the lamps in the streets he had to traverse, and thus to secure the advantage of a clear view of his antagonist when they came upon the ground.

A retired spot was selected not far beyond the Maison de Santé; but, as the friend of the family observed to me, the pleasures of anticipation were reserved to us, there being as yet no weapons; the man despatched to secure them not having made his appearance. He arrived, however, before ten minutes had elapsed (without any attempt being made at a reconciliation), bearing a couple of rapiers, the choice of which the Pole, whose property they were, tendered to his antagonist Both combatants threw off their coats, and in the light of the full moon, partly obscured by the foliage of an old stag-headed elm, prepared to carve each other—certainly not for the gods. The Pole assuming a gracefully defensive posture, held out his cold iron as motionless as an icicle, and awaited the onset. The Frenchman, on the other hand, attitudinized with astonishing activity, and after whirring his weapon around him, as though to admonish us all to keep at a respectful distance, advanced upon his enemy with a display of grace and valor which impressed me with the idea, which I really believe to be the true one, that he enjoyed, upon the whole, the business he was about. Without much previous ceremony he made a fierce lunge at the breast of his adversary, which the latter put by with a slight turn of his wrist and allowed him to recover his position.

"Do you see how he fools him?" said the old fellow at my side "It is really a cruel thing for the Pole. If he kills his man he loses his best customer. Bah!'

The Pole evidently managed his opponent as he chose for some time; but the latter not appreciating the lenity shown him, or perhaps from vanity, not being aware of it, only grew the more reckless in his attacks, and at length received a thrust through the shoulder, the pain of which effectually quieted his antics, and sent him groaning to the arms of his second. The affair thus finished *secundum artem*, the wounded man was consigned to the accommodation of a carriage and a surgeon, both of which, by some natural instinct, had found their way to the spot; and the rest of the party, adjourning first to a wine-shop in the neighborhood for a temporary refreshment, returned quietly to their old avocations and pleasures.

The scene of which I had been a witness kept me awake all

night; and the vigil led to a review of the life I had been leading for the last few months, which my conscience not altogether approving, I set about forming new resolutions with a view to its amendment. Among other things, I resolved to have nothing more to do henceforth with billiards—not because I feared being drawn into any quarrel such as I had witnessed, but on account of the loss of time and money it entailed; and in order that I might not be tempted to play, I determined to get upon some new hobby, and to ride it with the natural impetuosity of my disposition.

I remained working at the Rue du Pont de Lodi until the latter end of autumn, sometimes at press, and sometimes at case. As an employment for my leisure hours, I took up with the study of the Italian tongue, in which, from my previous knowledge, such as it was, of the Latin and French, I found no difficulty worth mentioning until, after a few weeks, I had mastered the modern dialect, and began to turn my attention to the older poets. To these I found an admirable key in the two volumes of Ferrajo, containing translations of the most difficult passages of the works of Dante, Petrarch, &c., into modern Italian. With the help of this key I worked away doggedly at the "Inferno," in which I became tolerably proficient, and could read whole pages of it into French before twelve months had elapsed from my commencing the language

About the end of October, I left the Rue du Pont de Lodi, and went again to work as a compositor in the Rue Montmorency, but without changing my lodging; as, notwithstanding the distance, I was unwilling to give up the society of the Genevese and the merry widow. Here I again encountered N——, of whom I have made mention in the preceding chapter. He had now a somewhat better position, and seemed in far better spirits than when I last parted with him He had the management of an English volume in his own hands, and from him I received a portion of the copy. He was appointed reader and press reviser as well of the English department, and made the proposal to me that he and I should work in pocket, as by reading each other's proofs we should insure greater correctness, and get the work out in a more creditable manner. Though slow, I knew him to be a remarkably clean compositor, and I closed with his proposal at once, which was advantageous to both of us, and to me in particular. Since I had last seen him, N—— had sent home for his wife and children, and they had joined him in Paris. He introduced me to his little domestic circle, and I ceased to marvel at the improvement in his spirits and temper when I saw and conversed with his charming and amiable wife and lovely children. She was a diminutive creature, but a perfect model of English elegance and quiet good-breeding; and though brought up in the usages of comfort, and perhaps luxury, had yet the good sense and tact to accommodate herself to their altered circumstances, without evincing the slightest consciousness of degradation

I wrought with N—— through the whole of the winter of 1826-7, and did very well in a pecuniary point of view, but suffered an immense amount of discomfort from the severity of the weather, and the abominably deficient means of providing against it. The precious modicum of wood allowed us for fuel was generally burnt out by twelve or one o'clock, husband it as we might, after which we endeavored to treasure up the warmth it had engendered by closing the doors fast for the remainder of the day, in spite of which precaution we had sometimes to thaw our frozen type by burning paper upon the face of it, previous to the nightly ceremony of distribution. At home it was still worse. The coffee and billiard-rooms were too much thronged to allow of study there; and, in order to pursue my Italian campaign, I used to tumble into bed as soon as I got home, and, with my nose emerging from a pile of clothes, pore for two or three hours over the pages of Tasso or Dante by the light of a single candle placed upon the chair at my side. I stuck to my resolution to abandon the billiard-table—a resolution which my fair landlady gave me credit for adopting. I may mention, too, that the jeweller had had enough of the game; and though he speedily recovered of his wound, returned no more to the all-engrossing pool, but devoted himself to the re-establishment of his business.

Calling one morning at the Rue du Pont de Lodi for a "galley" I had left there, I found my old companions all assembled at a sale of the perquisite copies of the works recently turned out, which took place in one of the press-rooms. The singular sale, to which there is nothing analogous in English printing-offices, is a periodical auction of complete copies of every work printed on the premises, one or more of which, according to the number of the impression, by an old custom of the trade, become the *vails*, or perquisites, of the workmen employed in their production. The oldest pressman was acting as auctioneer, and, mounted upon his "bank," discoursed eloquently upon the merits of the different books as he put them up, desirous, of course, of getting the best price he could, to increase his own moiety of the proceeds, which were to be divided among the workmen of a certain standing. As I was invited to bid, I did so, and bought several of Scott's and Cooper's novels, together with a one-volume edition of La Fontaine, and another of Byron, all in sheets, for something under twenty francs. There was a warm competition for a copy of a volume of satirical verses, by some anonymous writer, which there was a talk of suppressing; and the competition was so artfully nursed by him of the hammer, who kept continually quoting some piquant passage amid roars of laughter, followed each time by an advance of a few centimes, that the work was finally knocked down for double its publishing price, and delivered, with many mock congratulations, to the buyer, who had only bid, as he said, "to keep the game alive," and immediately had it sold again for a third of the price he paid.

I enjoyed my association with N—— at the office. His opinions upon most subjects, always admirably expressed, came upon me with all the force of originality, and insensibly led to more agreement on my part than a strict examination might have warranted. He was fond of speculating on the present constitution of society, which he averred to be what it is from the inevitable result of circumstances. "It is the law of nature," he would say, ' that the strong should prey upon the weak; and the force and beauty of that law we do not fail to recognize in its working among all the countless tribes of unreasoning creatures. It saves the vast majority of them from a dire amount of suffering, by reducing the unavoidable penalty of death to a momentary pang; and it makes arrangements for an incalculably greater amount of joyous existence than could possibly be provided for under a different system Now, the same law prevails among human creatures, though in a different way. The strong prey upon the weak, or, which is the same thing, the knowing subdue the simple; for knowledge in any shape, however objectionable, be it art or science, skill or sagacity, cunning or dexterity, or even the myriad forms and phases of roguery and fraud, is still power and strength, and will, as such, find out and subdue its subjects and victims. To counteract the mischievous operations of evil qualities we are furnished with a moral law, of which, however, unfortunately for mankind, the actual provisions and obligations have never yet been discovered, much less actually defined From the clashing of these two principles human laws and governments have had their origin. These have been framed with the avowed intent of enforcing the obligations of morality, which has always been their ostensible purpose; but they have invariably been constructed on a principle calculated to insure a very different result, owing to the inherent vices of governors, sovereigns, and law-givers, upon whom their constitution has devolved. Selfishness was the first parent of legislation. The power that was first strong enough to seize and accumulate wealth, next obtained sufficient influence to make laws and regulations for its preservation. But the laws being made by men who had everything to lose, very naturally became the barriers and safeguards of property and power—not of justice and of rights. Hence the poor, in time, became the serfs of the rich, and, from having nothing to lose, became by degrees incapable of possessing anything, and made bulwarks of their bodies to defend the pretensions of their worst enemies. Wealth converted Poverty into the material of aggression, and paternal Governments marshalled their legions of blockheads by line and rule to cut each other's throats according to military science, for the sake of determining a question which ought never to have arisen, and which never would have arisen, but for the fundamental depravity of the Government of one or other of the quarrelling parties, or of both. This is the history of all nations, and will continue to be their history until one of two things takes place. Either Governments, under some miraculous influence, must reform themselves, and frame and administer wise laws, constructed on the basis of morality, instead of a selfish expediency, or, which is far more likely, the peoples of the earth must work out their own emancipation, by effecting their own improvement, and thus making themselves worthy of it. The spread of information, and the spread of something, too, worthy the name of education among the masses, will prove superior in the end to the power of fire and sword. I look upon it that none but fools fight for other people, and that therefore, when the press has done its work, and the multitude are wiser, princes and potentates must either take to blowing one another's brains out, according to some new system of etiquette to be devised for the emergency, or else dispense with that sort of entertainment altogether. With the prevalence of some approach to equality in that species of common-sense knowledge on subjects political, commercial, and domestic, which is attainable by all, we shall soon see as much equality in our social condition as it is desirable to have—an equality, to wit, of rights and privileges; for more than that no man of sense and honesty would contend. The natural law that the strong should prey upon the weak will still maintain its force and integrity; but under the influence of a more widely-diffused intelligence and a purer morality, embodied in new codes of law and justice, its operation will be only what it was intended to be, that is, will secure to superior habits and qualities of mind and character that influence above the common herd which we ought to possess, and must possess for the sake of the general good. Intelligence, then, and not property, will be the basis of the franchise, and by means of a representative system thus reasonably constructed, which is the only real guarantee for good government, social abuses and grievances will be reformed and removed. With the elevation of the lower ranks there will be a corresponding reduction of the higher. Thrones will topple down with all their barbaric tinsel and trumpery; aristocracies of title, blood, and descent will dissolve, and crumble into neglect and forgetfulness before the true nobility of intellect and character, which alone are worthy of the sane man's admiration. This is the only millennium I look for. Its advent is inevitable in the very nature of things. I hold the germ of it in these infernal types which are freezing in my fingers; but its completion neither you nor I shall live to witness."

Into such a style of homilies my companion would occasionally launch out as he was filling his case of an evening in preparation for the next day's "dig." His notions on the subject of religion were equally heterodox and still more violent, though never violently expressed. He held that all the forms and ceremonies of all religions that had ever flourished were but the multiplied materials and contrivances which priestcraft had invented to maintain an influence established to govern and plunder mankind, through the medium of their superstitious feelings and fears. To all the hackneyed objections of Paine and other infidel writers against Christianity he added new ones of his own, which seemed to arise instinctively in his mind whenever any particular doctrine set forth in the sacred writings came accidentally into discussion. I made as manful a stand for the truth of the Bible record as my limited reading and (I am ashamed to say) still more limited thinking on the subject permitted. But the tirades of my companion Martin still clung to my recollection, and, in spite of all my care, warped my judgment; and I often found myself assenting, before the close of a dispute, to dogmas which, in the outset, I had resolutely determined to refute.

N—— was fond of vindicating those characters in Scripture history whom the sacred writers condemn. He had taken Esau under his especial protection, and converted him into a model of manhood and disinterestedness, while he loaded the cunning Jacob with all the opprobrium of fraud, knavery, and theft. He defended Balaam as one who had acted (supposing the narrative to be true, which he did not) with the utmost caution and prudence in a difficult business. He censured in the strongest terms the conduct of Peter in the affair of Ananias and his wife, who, so far from having merited death for not having contributed the whole of their possessions to the common cause, were plainly entitled to thanks for bestowing anything, and contended that the very last man upon the face of the earth to punish them for want of truth was Peter himself, who not very long before had been guilty of a much worse offence in first telling lies and then swearing to them, at the instigation only of his own cowardice. He was the ingenious apologist of Judas, who came out of his hands not a traitor and a thief, but an over-zealous and miscalculating partizan, who had delivered his master into the hands of his enemies from the secret assurance that in so doing he should only accelerate his triumph over them. He found, in short, a subject of admiration wherever the Scriptures held forth an example for warning and condemnation; and, by a corresponding instinct, had a fund of vituperation at his disposal for the characters exhibited in the Bible for our imitation. He never expressed the slightest desire to bring me over to his own way of thinking, often declaring that to make a proselyte is in many instances nothing more than to discover a fool, but he advised me to examine the matter thoroughly for myself, and to put a candid face upon the conclusions I should arrive at. "Ninety-nine hundredths," said he, "of the individuals professing Christianity throughout Europe, whatever they may imagine that they believe, are practically infidels to the faith of it; and I put it to you whether it be not infinitely more creditable to the true manliness of man to disown a faith which he cannot find grounds for practically accepting, than, avowing it, to give the lie to its efficacy by a life of total indifference to its claims."

It could hardly be otherwise than that such animadversions should have their effect upon my own mind. I never confessed, or, indeed, considered, that his arguments carried sufficient weight to overturn my faith in the truth of Christianity, but they yet secretly undermined it, and exercised an influence which, though I never willingly acknowledged it even to myself, I could not fail to recognize in the different perceptions which I began gradually to entertain in reference to subjects which I had been taught from my childhood to consider sacred. I mention these things here because the principles of infidelity have of late years taken refuge among the working-classes, among whom alone they are openly avowed and defended; and it is therefore incumbent upon those upon whom their education devolves that the young operatives of our offices and workshops should be well instructed in the grounds of their faith, and armed with sufficient arguments to defend them.

I must hasten now more rapidly over the history of my residence in Paris. The life of a working-man employed in the daily pursuit of his avocation presents but little interesting to the general reader. I found employment at different times in most of the printing-offices of Paris, in the capacity either of pressman or compositor, and I often experienced what is peculiarly the curse of the printing-business, namely, a sudden deprivation of employment, and the misery of forced and uncompensated idleness. It was fortunate for N——. who had more demands upon his industry, that he also possessed better qualifications for the market, than I had. By the middle of the year 1827, he had made himself so good a French scholar as to be able, with the aid of a young Parisian, who for a trifling compensation revised his manuscripts, to write articles on French and English politics for one of the popular journals. For these he was well paid; and they were, as they deserved to be, so well received, that he subsequently contracted an engagement with the proprietors of the journal, which enabled him to lay down the composing-stick, and, with the help of a little proof-reading as a make-weight, to devote himself to literary pursuits. Let me record it to his honor that he was not unmindful of his old companion in the time of his prosperity. He sent for me at a time when he knew I was out of employment, and introduced me to a gentleman, a young journalist, as a person well qualified to teach him English. It was well for me that my pupil knew much better how to learn than I did how to teach. He agreed to pay me five francs per lesson of two hours, on the condition that I should instruct him on his own plan, and not on mine. As I had no plan at all, having never had experience in teaching, this suited me exactly. His plan was to make use of me as a talking dictionary and grammar, confining my teachings exclusively to the answering of such questions as he thought fit to put. Having made this arrangement, he produced a copy of the "Vicar of Wakefield," and, commencing at the title-page, read it after me, looking to me for a translation as he went along. In this way we got through four or five pages in the course of the first hour. The second was devoted to conversation, with the help of a book of phrases in both languages, during which we invariably drank a glass of wine together to the success of his studies. These lessons took place three times a week, and yielded me a regular income of fifteen francs, which for a good portion of the spring of 1828 was unfortunately the whole extent of my earnings. My pupil studdied Cobbett's "Maitre d'Anglais' to good purpose during the intervals between the lessons, and made a rapid and satisfactory progress. It is true he never mastered the pronunciation, nor ran any risk, as he flattered himself he did, of being taken for an Englishman; but in the course of nine or ten months he could express himself with perfect propriety in every other respect, and politely sent me my *congé* in an epistle of some length, with the perfect grammatical purity of which I could find no fault, however much I was aggrieved by its contents

Encouraged by the result of my efforts in this direction, and by the warm recommendations of my first pupil, I started in a small way as a professor of the English language, and printed and privately circulated cards and prospectuses with the view of obtaining pupils. I found it by no means so easy a business as I had imagined Anybody who knows a language thoroughly may easily teach it to another knowing the principles of grammar; but to impart a correct knowledge of a foreign tongue to a man who does not know his own is just one of the impossible things which none of the "wondrous new machines of modern spinning" have been found competent to effect. The two great stumbling-blocks in the way, as well of myself as my pupils, were the Future Tense and the Subjunctive Mood. The distinction between *shall* and *will*, as the tense stands arranged in our plan of conjugation, no Frenchman could or would understand; they seemed to have taken an unanimous oath against it. Revolving the matter one day in my mind, and impressed with a vague recollection of something I had seen on the subject in a volume of Dean Swift in my father's library, I resolved to split the Future Tense into two moods, and try if I could cram my pupils with it in that shape. With this view I arranged the bisected tense on a card thus:—

THE FUTURE TENSE COMPRISES

THE MOOD OF VOLITION *and* THE MOOD OF DETERMINATION

Sin. I shall	*Sin.* I will
Thou wilt	Thou shalt
He will	He shall

Plur. We shall	*Plur.* We will
You will	You shall
They will	They shall.

The reader will perceive that by this arrangement the ambiguity of the "shall or will," so puzzling to foreigners, as it stands in our English grammar-books, is done away, and that a learner who had made himself master of this simple scheme would only have to reflect for an instant whether he wished to express a mere volition or a positive determination, to know which to use.

I promised myself great things from the use of this contrivance, and printed a couple of packs of the cards, and distributed them among such of my pupils as I thought had brains or industry enough to make use of them. It may appear an odd thing to relate, but it is an absolute fact—and as it is one that tells of my own failure and mortification, I shall hardly be suspected of sophisticating it—that not a single individual among nearly thirty adults, most of them of more than average intelligence, reaped a grain of practical advantage by my plan. It is true that many, indeed most of them, understood the scheme, and committed it to memory; but even with the cards in their hands they would select the wrong term as often as the right, to my unspeakable amazement and indignation. But useless as it was to me or to my pupils, the plan was considered worth stealing. One of my cards got into the hands of an Irish professor of English, engaged in initiating the gentry of St. Germain in the mysteries of the brogue—which sagacious professor, with the modesty peculiar to his nation, stole the contrivance and published it as an important discovery of his own, in his Franco-Anglo Hibernian grammar of the English tongue, of the fifth edition of which it formed the only new feature. I had my revenge in the reflection that I had seduced him to the committal of a gross plagiarism, when he only intended to be guilty of robbery.

With regard to the other great grammatical difficulty, the

Subjunctive Mood, after a long counsel with myself on the subject, and after reading over all that I could lay hands on respecting it—one octavo volume in particular, by an English member of the French Institute—I came to the convenient conclusion that there was really no such thing as a subjunctive mood to the English verb, and boldly abolished it altogether. I assured my pupils that such forms of expression were nothing more than colloquial licences, to be admitted or rejected at pleasure; and when confronted, as I was sometimes, with the learned work of the professor of the Institute, I referred the dissentients to a hundred passages which I was prepared to pounce upon, all demonstrating plainly enough that, whatever he found it prudent to establish as the irrefragable law, he by no means considered binding upon himself, using, in paragraphs perfectly parallel in their construction either the indicative or so-called subjunctive mood, without the habit, because without the necessity, of discrimination.

The reader may probably think I was perfectly right when I inform him that I never had sufficient confidence in my capabilities as a teacher of language to abandon my trade in favor of the practice of tuition. "Between two stools," says the proverb, "a man falls to the ground;" the truth of which was brought home to me more than once, since I lost several chances of employment at my business through looking after pupils. But, on the other hand, I oftener reaped the benefit of having "two strings to my bow," and sometimes managed to maintain myself for months together, during periods of depression in the printing business, when, but for the little connexion I had picked up as a teacher, I might have been reduced to dismal straits.

This connexion was of a rather curious description, and embraced men, and women too, of various ranks and classes. One of my pupils was a monk of forty years of age, who always gave me his blessing in addition to the twenty sous which he paid for his lesson, and tried hard to wean me from heresy, and bring me over to the bosom of the true Church. Our lessons consisted almost entirely of conversations, which he generally contrived to divert into a religious channel; and he sometimes plied me so vigorously with arguments in favor of Roman Catholicism, that I was fain to find a refuge from their assaults in the correction of the wretched syntax in which they were couched. Upon these occasions it was amusing to mark the evident conflict in his mind between his penchant for proselytizing and his abhorrence of false grammar. He would drop the controversy to pick up a concord, and return again to the argument with unwearied pertinacity, though it cost him half an hour to clear the way to it. He was a man without guile, and, I believe, sought my conversion from a sincere and profound sense of Christian charity and duty. Another pupil was a *danseuse* and widow of a *figurant* of one of the theatres, who took lessons of a morning before she rose from bed, and who made it a condition of the contract that I should tune the violin of her son, a dirty little urchin of six years old, who walked about the room in his night-gown scraping away at the gamut, while his mother toiled painfully at the elements of English grammar. Among the number were a couple of milliners, who clubbed together, receiving lessons alternately, and each imparting instruction to the other, thus securing tuition at half-price. I had a dozen or more of artizans and operatives of different trades, some of whom, by the way, made good and rapid progress, and, by cultivating the acquaintance of Englishmen, learned to speak the language with boldness and fluency. My best customer was a *restaurateur*, who gave me solid pudding for empty conjugations, paying for lessons, which he took three times a week, with tickets for dinner at thirty sous a-piece.

My new vocation, while it gave me some insight into the domestic habits of a not very comfortable class of the Parisian public, also afforded me much more leisure than had heretofore been at my command. But I cannot say that I ever thoroughly enjoyed this leisure. The instinct "to be doing," the result of the habits of my life, twelve hours a day of which had been passed in constant labor fiom my childhood, drove me continually to some manual occupation; and I tried my hands at all sorts of contrivances—such as cobbling my boots and clothes, binding my books, and manufacturing musical instruments, with little better result than quieting the reproaches of my handicraft conscience, which would not suffer me to rest without the attempt, at least, at producing something real and tangible. As for study and mental improvement, I am sure it is a fact that I bestowed far less time upon them than I had done when fully employed at my trade.

CHAPTER VI

Thoughts of home—Reminiscences of Parson C——, the gambling Divine—Death of a Country Squire—Weak resolutions—The Sampford Ghost—An apology for Gaming—Interior of a Gaming house—Interview with C——His suicide—Charles X and his advisers—The Ordonnances—N—— joins the Republicans and I take care of myself—Barricades, Bullets, and Dragoon pepper—First and second days of the Revolution—Cockney mettle—Night of the 28th—Victory of the Republicans on the 29th—Lafayette and the Duke of Orleans—The Chances of War—A sudden stop to my professorship—I start for home with half a passport—A fond Irish husband—A capsized Diligence—An affectionate re-union—I arrive at home

OCCUPIED alternately at my trade and profession—now a compositor lifting types at the rate of sixpence a thousand, and now a professor of English giving lessons with a grave face and with a dogmatic assumption of authority for which my youth and inexperience may be tendered in apology—now picking up a page of type for tenpence, and now explaining a page to a pupil for a like amount—the months and years rolled over my head.

A factitious kind of gaiety and frivolity not at all natural to my temperament stole over me by degrees, and was the result doubtless of associations which engendered habits both of thinking and acting altogether contrary to my true disposition, and which, while I now review them at the distance of nearly a quarter of a century, I can hardly recognize as having ever formed part of my own personal history. I became gradually thoughtless, *insouciant*, and regardless of the future as the veriest Frenchman of my acquaintance; and though my funds and prospects were at times at the lowest possible ebb, the melancholy forebodings which under such circumstances would a few years before have taken entire possession of my faculties were now unknown, or, if the recollection of them recurred at all, it was only to be laughed at. Certainly, if happiness consists, as some philosophers pretend, in freedom from care and exemption from want, these were the happiest years of my life, seeing that my cares were fewer and my wants less than they have been at any subsequent period. I maintained an occasional correspondence with home, which the expense of postage precluded me from indulging very largely : and my thoughts often reverted, especially during the wretched season of winter in Paris, to the family fireside of my parents. Many a time and oft my imagination dwelt with affectionate yearnings on that central point of all my desires, and home I should have gone twenty times but for one unfortunate consideration—the collapsed condition of my purse, to wit, which at such times, and at such times only, gave me cause for uneasiness. I stayed in Paris until the Revolution of the Three Days of July—which released the French nation from the government of a jesuitical tool, who was both a coward and a blockhead, and afforded them an opportunity of trying a new experiment in monarchy under the sway of a man who, whatever his failings, was the very antithesis of both—deprived me of all prospect, at least for some time to come, of employment, and sent me, as well as hundreds of others, to the right-about, in search of it elsewhere.

Before I proceed to give my history of the Revolution of 1830, which, being the experience of one who had little or nothing but a whole skin to take care of, and economised that to the best of his ability, will be found rather different from most authentic accounts, I shall devote a few moments to my reminiscences of a character remarkable for the extent and profundity of his talents, the various mutations of fortune, self entailed, which he underwent, and for his inordinate addiction to a vice of all others the most degrading and destructive to intellectual strength—who was yet great in intellect and purpose amidst all the strange vicissitudes of which he was the self-constituted victim, and beneath the pressure of moral and physical degradation which he would never have undergone but for the influence of one fatal and overwhelming passion.

One of the very first objects of my boyish reverence and veneration was, as might be expected with a child religiously educated, the parson of the parish in the market town where I was brought up. Parson C——, who, I believe, held the benefice of St. Peter's in my native place, was a man whom, having once known, it was not very easy to forget. I could have been hardly six years of age when I first saw him without his canonical garb, on which occasion he was playing a trout on the end of his line under one of the weirs in the river Exe. At that time the town was pretty well stocked with French prisoners. The gaols were crammed with the miserable soldiery of Napoleon's generals captured in the Peninsular war, then raging, and numbers of French officers on parole were installed with the housekeepers of the place in the capacity of lodgers. With these our all-accomplished divine was almost the only man in the place who could hold converse. A part of my father's house was occupied by a couple of Gallic strangers to whom the parson's visits were many and frequent. As they dined at the common table, their society, together with that of the reverend gentleman, was shared by the whole family, and we thus became more intimate with him than we otherwise should. It is said that familiarity breeds contempt. Certain it is that my father's veneration for the character of his and our spiritual guide and instructor suffered considerable declension from his closer acquaintance. Still what he lost in reverence he perhaps gained in another way. The parson's kind, agreeable, and social manners won the admiration and good-will of the whole family, and though he had a good many enemies in the town, we could not be of the number. He was a man of eccentric manners and fine genius, and, though then but young, had given proofs of talents of no mean order. He had published a rather bulky poem on the subject of Hypocrisy, a subject with which his detractors were not slow to observe he ought to be very well acquainted. But he was not really a hypocrite in the true sense of the word, if indeed, as may be questioned, he deserved the imputation at all. He was rather the subject of ever-varying impulses, under the instigation of which, were they good or bad, he would instinctively proceed to act without consideration and without restraint. He would be eloquent as Demosthenes in the pulpit in praise of the Christian virtues, and would work himself into a passion of tears on behalf of some benevolent or charitable purpose, the claims of which he would enforce with the most irresistible appeals to the conscience; and the next day he would gallop after the fox with a pack of hounds, fish, shoot, or fight a main, in company with sporting blacklegs, bruisers, dicers, *et hoc genus omne*. But he never made any personal pretensions to religious sentiment, that I am aware of, except on one occasion, which, as it tends greatly to illustrate the true character of the man, I shall relate.

Among the companions of his sporting pursuits was a country squire of the neighborhood, a dissolute and drunken specimen of a class of men of which, fortunately for humanity, the present generation knows but little. He had ruined his fortune and nearly beggared his family by extravagance and intemperance, when, after a long course of uninterruped and abused health and vigor, he was laid by the heels upon a sick bed, from which the doctors had no hopes of ever releasing him. In this dilemma he sent for Parson C——, who appeared forthwith in the chamber of the sick man, and was beginning to mutter over the service for the visitation of the sick, when the latter, belching forth a volley of oaths and curses, swore that he did not send for him for any such purpose; that what he wanted was an acknowledgment from the parson's own lips of the fact, which all parsons' lives declared—that their religion, and all religion, was a lie. This was an admission which C—— declined to make. A horrible scene ensued, of impotent rage and blasphemy on one part, and shame and confusion on the other. It ended in the death of the frantic and despairing drunkard, in the very presence of his ghostly adviser, whom he cursed with his last breath. This deplorable climax to such a scene of horror, it may be readily imagined, had a powerful effect upon the impulsive and excitable nature of poor C——. He left the chamber of such a death an altered man, and, proceeding homewards, shut himself up in his closet

On the following Sunday morning he took occasion to preach impressively, from the most solemn text he could select, upon the uncertainty of life. In the course of his sermon, he called upon all present to prepare for the doom which none could escape—which, inexorable to all, might be immediate to any, and therefore demanded instant and energetic preparation. He wound up his discourse with the extraordinary declaration that he, for one, had made up his mind upon the subject; that he had seen the error of his ways, and determined to abandon them, and that he was resolved thenceforth, with God's help, to devote the rest of his remaining life to his own preparation, and theirs, for the dreaded hour. He then called upon his auditors to bear witness to the resolution he had expressed, and to aid him in carrying it out. There was something like a commotion even in the church when this announcement was concluded; and the sensation and excitement it occasioned in the town, for some time after, only subsided as the parson's resolution waned in strength, and its effects became less and less observable.

For some months he held fast to his purpose with the most laudable tenacity. It was in the spring of the year that he made his public declaration, and though the old friends of his follies laughed at it, and laid heavy wagers against his perseverance, he held on his way steadily. He began a course of pastoral visitation—sought out and relieved the poor and afflicted—parted with his fishing-tackle, and commenced an enthusiastic canvas for a dispensary for the poor. Of his old friends among the "ungodly," and his old enemies among the pious, few knew what to make of it. The Parson C—— of old time was no more; but, in his place, a new man with the same face was everywhere active in the cause of charity and

Christian benevolence. Those who knew him best doubted most of his stability; and among these, I remember my father's expressing his conviction that the reformation was " too hot to hold." So it turned out in the end. Three, four, five months of exemplary conduct, and then came the first symptom of declension, in the shape of the parson's grey horse harnessed to a dog-cart, with his gun and brace of pointers, in charge of a groom, the whole " turn-out" ready for starting, and waiting at the entrance of the churchyard on Sunday evening, the last night of August, to carry the parson so soon as service was over, to a celebrated shooting ground, five-and-twenty miles off, that he might be on the spot ready by dawn for the irresistible first of September. Those who prophesied from this demonstration a return to old habits had speedy occasion to pride themselves upon their augury.

The Sampford Ghost soon after came upon the stage, with his mysterious knockings and poundings; and defied all objurgations and exorcisms, save and except those of Parson C——, at the sound of whose classical Greek, or gibberish, as it might happen, he absconded to the bottom of the Red Sea, as in duty bound. Here was food for wonder and gaping superstition, to which the reverend divine condescended to pander, by the publication of a pamphlet supporting the supernatural view of the subject, which, being on a marvellous topic, sold marvellously well, and brought grist to the clerical mill.

Of the subsequent career of this eccentric genius, from the time I ceased to reside in Devonshire to that when I encountered him in Paris, I have no personal knowledge. I only know that he afterwards obtained a benefice in the neighborhood of London; that in the year 1820 he published a work which has run through many editions, is in high repute with a certain class of readers, and is said by competent judges to manifest a profound practical acquaintance with the philosophy of the mind, and to contain more original views in relation to that science than any other work of equal dimensions.

I have already hinted that my vocation as a teacher of English introduced me to a new order of French humanity. Among the various pupils who sought my cheap assistance in the promotion of their studies was one Maubert, a young fellow of four or five and twenty, who was contemplating a removal to London in the exercise of his profession, which was neither more nor less than a gambler. He had a relative in one of the hells at St. James's, who had offered him a lucrative engagement so soon as he was sufficiently master of English to be enabled to undertake it. I was astonished to find a person of such mild, meek, and almost effeminate manners engaged in such a pursuit, and still more to hear that he had been brought up to it from boyhood, and was but following in the steps of his father, who was employed in the same establishment in a situation of great trust and responsibility. In the course of our bilingual conversations, I made no scruple of expressing my perfect horror of gambling, at which he appeared to be heartily amused, and attributed the feeling I manifested not so much to moral principle as to constitutional peculiarity. It soon became apparent to me that he had not himself the slightest idea of disgrace or discredit as attachable to the profession of a gambler, so long as it was carried on upon principles of honesty and fair play. "What is gambling," said he, "after all, but a species of exchange, skill for skill, or chance for chance? It is true, there is no solid merchandise in question; but, since you are determined to consider it in a moral point of view, what, let me ask, does the merchant or the shopkeeper care for the goods that pass through his hands? Is not his sole object to profit by the transfer? Does he not speculate to gain? and is not all speculation, morally considered, gambling? Now, all the professed gamester does is to get rid of the lumbering medium of trading speculations—to clear the game which all men are willing to play of the cumbrous machinery that clogs its movements when played upon commercial principles, and to bring it to a crisis and a close at once. You talk of the misery and ruin entailed upon families by gambling; but depend upon it the same men who ruin themselves and families by play would do precisely the same thing were there no such thing as play. For one Frenchman ruined by hazard, ten Englishmen are ruined by commerce. In fact, as a people, you gamble much more than we do, though in a different way; and when you choose to gamble *as* we do, you do it to much greater extent, and with a recklessness to which our habits in that respect afford no parallel. There is an Englishman now in Paris who has repeatedly won and lost ten thousand francs at a sitting, and whom you may see, if you choose to come with me, any evening you like."

"What is his name?" I demanded.

"Colton. He is a priest, too, I have heard, and of course, when at home, a preacher of morality."

"Well," said I, "with your permission, I shall be glad to have a look at him."

"Very well; you shall dine with me to-morrow at the Salon Francais. Meet me there at six, and then, after dinner, I will accompany you."

"Agreed."

And so it came to pass, that, about nine o'clock on the following evening—for we had dined at most gentlemanly leisure, and followed up the dinner with a complete debauch of sugared water—I entered, for the first time, one of the saloons devoted to gambling on the first floor of the Palais Royal. There was not so great and gorgeous a display of taste and expenditure as I had expected to see; though everything was substantial and elegant, nothing was pretentious or superb. Tables arranged with a view to convenience rather than order or regularity, and covered with the means and materials of gaming, were surrounded, on three sides, by persons already engaged at the sport. We passed through several rooms thus furnished, and more or less tumultuously filled. Hazard appeared to be the most favorite game ; as I noticed during my stay that the tables where that was played were first in full occupation, and throughout the evening were more crowded than others. Maubert led me to a room, which must have been the fifth or sixth we entered, and, pointing to a table at the further end, upon the centre of which rose a brazen dragon, with a pair of emerald eyes, a yawning, cavernous jaw, and a ridgy tail, whose voluminous folds coiled round a column of polished steel—told me that there I should find my man in the course of the evening, though I should have to wait for him, as he had not yet arrived. He informed me that I could act as I chose, without being questioned; and then took his leave, as his services were wanted in his own department.

I amused myself for nearly a couple of hours in contemplating *en philosophe,* the scene before me. I had heard and read much of gamblers and gambling, and here they were in multitudes to test the truth or falsity of my impressions I noticed particularly that, while the younger players acted throughout as though gaming were a frolic, and welcomed both their gains and losses with a joke or a laugh, the older hands maintained a perfect silence, and accepted the decrees of fortune without betraying the least emotion. The table near which I stood was appropriated to the following purpose : A ball, or rather solid polygon, of near a hundred sides, each side colored blue, red, or black, was dropped into the mouth of the dragon ; and, while it was rolling audibly through the long folds of its tail, the players placed what sums they chose upon red, blue, or black-colored spaces on the table. Whatever color the ball, upon emerging from the tail and finally resting, showed uppermost, was the winning color ; the rest lost. The first operation of the manager, after each throw, was to rake into the bank in front of him the several amounts placed on the losing colors, after which he paid the winners, doubling the stake for black, trebling it for red, and multiplying it by five for the blue. Most of the young players began upon the black : but whether they won or lost, and the chance was equal for either fate, they invariably migrated to the other colors; or, in other words, doubled or quintupled their stakes as their passion became heated by play. The old ones, on the contrary, kept mostly to one color; and, in pursuance of some cunningly-concocted plan, frequently consulted pricked or penciled cards, upon which they had perhaps made previous calculations, or chronicled the course of play as it went on. The physiognomy of these old stagers certainly afforded a rich variety of exceedingly ugly faces. Disappointment, however, was not the prevailing expression; and, from what I observed of the general manifestation of their hardened visages, I was led to the conclusion that your calculating gambler, who has his passions under control, is *not*, in the long-run, a loser, but the contrary; and that the support of the bank, and the whole establishment, is derived from the swarming flights of raw, inexperienced and uncalculating pigeons which every day brings to be plucked. One old fellow walked off with a bag of five-franc pieces, which could not have been worth less than twenty pounds English, accumulated in little more than half an hour; and others pocketed various smaller sums, and then withdrew. An English gentleman lost several five-pound notes in succession on the blue, and, continuing the stake, recovered them all with a profit. An Irishman, who had been playing for silver on the black, attempted to do the same; but his heart failed him, or else his pocket, after the loss of his second note, and, with a guttural oath, he retired in a rage. To win at gaming, it would seem from such examples, requires but a large amount of courage and capital; and it must be from this fact alone that, where the game, whatever it be, is fairly played, the bank which has the courage to challenge all the world, and unlimited capital to support the challenge, is so largely the gainer. The natural advantage of the bank may, however, be met by calculation and cautious adherence to system in playing; and instances are not wanting where the bank, though well stocked, has been broken, and the whole funds carried off through the success of a deep-laid scheme.

While I was indulging in these speculations, in which I have no desire that the reader should place implicit faith, the personage whom my curiosity had led me hither to meet entered the room, and made towards the place where I stood. The long interval that had elapsed since I last saw him had effected such an alteration in his appearance that it is probable that, had I not been expecting him, he would have passed unrecognized. As it was, the first glance assured me of his identity. From added years, or from long-enduring sedentary habits, he had acquired a slight stoop, and the old sprightly elasticity of step had given place to the sober foot-fall of mature age; but the face, though of a somewhat darker hue, and now lined with faint furrows, bore the same contour and much of the same expression as of yore. There was the same classic and intellectual profile, and the same common-place and rather sordid indications in the full face which had formerly given rise to the saying among his flock, that "The parson had two faces, one for Sundays and one for working days." He took his seat at the left-hand of the money-raker, and, presenting a paper, probably a cheque or foreign note, received a pile of gold and silver, which he spread before him. I had intended to watch his game, and perhaps, if occasion offered, to speak to him, but the sight of the very man from whose lips my infant ears had caught the first accents of public worship preparing to take part in the debasing orgies of the Pandemonium in which I stood so revolted my feelings—and his action, as he bent over his pocket-book in search of something he wanted, brought so forcibly to my recollection his old gestures in the pulpit—that I resolved to spare myself the witnessing of his degradation, and accordingly walked away, and out of the accursed den, to the side of the fountain in the quadrangle, in the cool spray of which I sat for an hour, *not* enjoying my reflections upon the past.

I learnt from Maubert subsequently, that, though C—— played the boldest game, he was far from being a welcome guest at some of the tables he chose to patronize. He won, occasionally, large sums; and if he lost them again, as from his known difficulties at certain seasons it is pretty sure he did, he did not lose them at the public tables, but at some of the private gaming-houses of the nobility which he was known to frequent. That he was occasionally reduced to unpleasant straits I have reason to think; because, long after the encounter above related, I met him at a place whither I had resorted for a cheap dinner, and where we dined together on a deal table from soup and *bouilli*, for a sum not to be mentioned in connexion with the repast of a gentleman. On this occasion, I somewhat alarmed him by inquiring, in a broad Devonshire accent, if he could inform me of the address of M. V——, naming one of the French prisoners with whom the parson had been especially intimate in the time of the war. He stared at me fixedly for a minute, and then, with a voice like one apostrophizing a spirit, said, "You are ——, the son of Thomas ——. I know you from your likeness to your father. Do not know me here. Let me have your address; I should like to talk to you. M. V—— is dead—dead! And your father, is he yet living?"

I was going to reply to his queries, but, snatching the card I presented, he bade me hastily adieu, and disappeared.

It was rumored about that he won a large sum of money previous to the breaking out of the Revolution, and that, having accomplished his object, he withdrew from the gaming-table. But he had played the game of life too fast, and, in desperately acquiring the means of expenditure, had lost those of enjoyment. In the published work to which allusion has been made is the following sentence: "The gamester, if he die a martyr to his profession, is doubly ruined. He adds his soul to every other loss, and, by the act of suicide, renounces earth to forfeit heaven." It is wretched to think that the writer put an end to his own existence, after a life devoted to the very vice he so powerfully deprecated. He blew out his brains at Fontainbleau, in 1832—it was said, to escape the pain of a surgical operation from which no danger could be apprehended.

The popularity of Charles X., great in the beginning, more from the personal contrast he exhibited to his predecessor, the gouty and gormandizing Louis *des huitres*, as the people sneeringly styled him, than from any other cause, had been waning rapidly from his first accession to the throne. He had given mortal offence by his partiality to the Jesuits, and excited contempt by the debasing superstition into which he had plunged headlong by way of atonement for a long course of luxury and debauch. He had committed the ridiculous blunder, among a thousand others, of legislating upon the subject of the pleasures and recreations of his subjects, which he was past the power of participating, and had excited disgust in the general mind by the repeated parade of religious ceremonies in the public ways. Through the medium of his slave and willing tool, M. de Villéle, he had made abortive attempts upon the integrity of the laws dearest to the passions of the French nation, and carried the exercise of the royal prerogative to its utmost stretch. Before the succession of M. Martignac to office the seeds of revolution were sown; and the only hope of that gentleman was, to use his own expression, " that he should be able to conduct the monarchy quietly down stairs, which would else be thrown out of the window." But even this could only have been done by concession; and concession, however liberally it was promised, could not be associated in the minds of the people with the name of Polignac, who soon came into office. It was in vain that that obstinate worthy promised, and indeed executed, liberal measures. The whole French world knew that they were but so many temporary expedients, and therefore would have nothing, would hear of nothing, from him, but his withdrawal.

The elements of discontent and revolt had been for a long time visibly at work; and the forthcoming storm, dimly discerned by the men of the old generation, had been announced without hesitation, and discussed without reserve, as a consummation inevitable, and not far off. Still, years were expected to elapse before the crisis came, which, however, was brought to a head at once by the publication of the famous Ordonnances—decrees which, perhaps, astonished by their impudence, quite as much as they alarmed by their tenor, the exasperated Parisians. These Ordonnances, which would have clapped an extinguisher on the press, and have modified the mode of election in a manner to pack the representation with the creatures of the aristocracy, settled the question of revolt, converted the prophesied revolution into a present fact, and transformed every able-bodied man into a rebel at one and the same moment. Anything short of these measures might have provoked further discussion, and given rise to a vast amount of seditious speechifying and club oratory; but now the only discussion was, as to the readiest means of aggression against authority, and the long tirades of orators were condensed to the significant syllables, "Aux armes!—aux armes!"

The Ordonnances were only published on the 26th, and before the evening of the 27th, under the auspices of those perpetual plagues to unconstitutional rule, the students of the Polytechnique, the battle of liberty had begun—begun, be it remembered, at the instigation of the press, whose very existence was threatened.

I am not going to repeat the history of the three glorious days of July. French revolutions are so plentiful in the recollection of modern readers, that I shall be readily spared the recital of events which all who care to recur to at this time of day know well enough where to look for. What I have to state in relation to them is just what concerns myself and those of my old comrades with whose conduct on the occasion I am acquainted. For my own part, I must confess that, notwithstanding all the warnings received, the Revolution burst upon me like a thunder-clap, and overthrew all my previous ideas of Parisian society.

The first indication I had of what was going on was on the evening of the 27th, when, returning homewards from the Rue du Temple, I was turned back from a short cut I wanted to make, and advised to continue my route in another direction, as a barricade was forming in my path. I had never heard of barricades, since so familiar in French story, and was some time before I could comprehend what was going on. On reaching the Pont Neuf (I then lodged on the Quai des Augustins,) I had some difficulty from the crowd in crossing the bridge, from the centre of which I witnessed a slight fracas between the populace and the troops in the broad road leading to the Tuileries; the soldiers did not fire, however, but, advancing slowly with level bayonets, turned the mob in another direction.

When I got at length to my lodgings, I encountered N——, who was uneasily pacing my room, where he had been waiting an age, he said, to see me. All his republican blood was on fire, and every interest in life had vanished, save the interest of the French Revolution, which he declared had begun, and would prove the dawn of a new era of liberty for the world. I was amazed at his frantic enthusiasm, and he not less so at my almost perfect indifference. His object in calling on me was to induce me to assist him in gathering a body of our countrymen, whom he said we might collect together in the course of the night, and who might signalize themselves and render good service in the cause of freedom. I declined having anything to do with such an unprofitable speculation, and when asked my reason, frankly avowed my decided aversion to close intimacy with cold steel or hot lead, especially when nothing was to be got by it. I spoke with the utmost sincerity, as I really felt the full force of the reasoning of Shakespeare's fop, who, "but for those vile guns, would himself have been a soldier." "Were it a bout of fists or staves," said I, "I should have less objection; but I really have no inclination, notwithstanding my regard for you, to set myself up as a target for the benefit of the French republic—if it is to be a republic, of which I am not at all certain."

He assured me that it must be a republic—that nothing else could follow the triumph of the people, which was inevitable; and that France, once a republic on a settled and stable foundation, would draw all the nations of Europe after her, Britain not excepted. In the hope of diverting his attention from a subject on which I saw he was too much excited to reason calmly, I inquired for his wife and children. He said he had taken them to a place of safety, and bidden them farewell—perhaps for ever. The interests of the cause he had embraced were, if not dearer to him than they, of more importance to humanity than they to him or he to them, and to those interests he had devoted himself. When he found that I would take no active part, he asked if I would oblige him in another way, and, upon my assenting, said perhaps he would put me to the test; then taking the addresses of such of our old companions as I could remember, he took his leave. I saw that, though angry at my determination, he had foreseen it, and was not greatly disappointed.

I walked out in the cool of the evening, and endeavored to get to the Palais Royal, where there had been fighting in the afternoon, but was prevented by the builders of a barricade in the Rue St. Honore, who compelled me to assist in the labor of digging up the paving-stones and cramming them into a water-cart, one end of which had been staved in. I worked at this employment for an hour; and then, fearing another similar engagement, returned home. That desperate measures were resolved on was too plain to be doubted; and I retired to my domicile with the conviction that something tremendous was at hand. Here I found a note from N——, requesting to see me immediately at the Rue Git le Cour. I went to the address indicated—there being no impediments—and found him, with a number of others, (some old acquaintances,) employed in melting lead, casting bullets, and cutting slugs "three picas thick" for want of sufficient bullet-moulds I was requested to lend a hand in the good work; and not thinking it proper to object to this department of war, I remained till dawn casting and trimming musket-balls for the use of the patriots.

I went to bed early on the morning of the 28th, to dream of "battle, and murder, and sudden death," and awoke at a late hour with the opportunity of witnessing the verification of my dream if I chose. My landlord had not opened his shop, but had disappeared early in the day. I had to get my own breakfast the garçon, too, having vanished; after which, not being able to rest at home, I was about to sally out in the direction of the distant shouting and rattle of musket-shots, when I heard the measured tread of soldiers in the rear of my dwelling I ran up stairs and mounted to the top of the house, where, much to my astonishment, I found the missing garçon, surrounded by a store of bricks, stones, broken bottles, and other condiments of the sort, with which he was prepared to pepper the soldiery as soon as they came within shot. As it happened, to my intense satisfaction, he had no use for them. The advancing column crossed the Pont Neuf, and were immediately received on the other side with a volley of similar collectanea, liberally administered from every roof and window. A few shots were fired, whether by them in return I could not make out They plainly took more care to avoid the compliments they were met with than to resent them. They proceeded to the Hotel de Ville, and after a few minutes' fighting, which I could hear distinctly enough, though I could see nothing, they drove out the insurgents.

I passed a miserable and anxious day. Wretched within doors, where, from restlessness, I could neither act nor reflect, and apprehensive and bewildered without; a thousand times I wished myself a Frenchman, or that I was a hundred miles away. The noise of the firing, and the distant roar of a sea of angry sounds, continued almost without intermission the whole day. The tricolor flag was hoisted in various quarters, and waved gallantly from the summit of Notre Dame, while the tocsin pealed incessantly. Late in the afternoon the troops took up a position on the quay between the Pont Neuf and the Pont des Arts, where, being backed by buildings belonging to the Government, they were exempt from the contributions of lumbering sundries, everywhere rained upon their heads by the citizens. No serious attempt was made by the populace to dislodge them; but in the course of the night they retired into the Louvre. The fighting seemed to have ceased, as by common consent, about sunset; and the tumultuous outcries had sunk to a subdued and ominous murmur—an unintermitting roar of dull, portentous sound, without a pause. As it grew dark I shut myself up in my room, and, having tasted nothing since the morning, began rummaging my cupboard for provisions. I had just laid some bread and preserves, sour cheese and a bottle of beer on the table, when in bounced N—— in a bath of perspiration, swathed in a blue blouse, and black as Erebus with dust, dirt, and gunpowder. He had been fighting all the morning in the Rue St Antoine, in company with a lot of brave fellows, he said, who held life as nothing in the cause of liberty. They had defeated the French general, and repulsed a heavy column of troops by an incessant and deadly fire, with but a comparatively trifling loss to the patriots. "I am come to you," said he, "for refreshment. There has been little eating and drinking among us to-day; and I would not touch what our starving band wanted more than I did."

I pointed to the viands, which he attacked with a true republican appetite.

"Think of that infernal braggart, E——s!" said he. "I found him, by your direction, last night, and he mouthed and talked big, and promised to meet us at the rendezvous, and I gave him the pass; but the scoundrel never came. I called again to-night on my way to you. Nobody had seen him all day. I mounted *au troisième*, and knocked at his door. Not a sound in return. I peeped through the key-hole; the key is in the lock! The beggarly skunk has locked himself in in the dark! The window-shutters are closed; the wretch is in bed, shaking with fear: I heard him turn and gasp with affright! Faugh!"

"You forget," said I, "that he is seven men in one! You surely can't expect the proprietor of seven languages, and of a world of accomplishments besides, to expose the casket of such precious treasures to the chances of war?"

"Bah!" he returned, "this is no time for joking. Let him rot. I would break in and unkennel him; but the hours are too precious. By the way, have you seen anything of Dick D——? There's the mettle of a man in that boozy little blockhead, after all. He has been out at the work, but missed us somehow. I could not teach the dolt to pronounce the pass, and so consigned him to the care of Franks. I fancy both found the means of guzzling somewhere, for Franks showed without him, and was not sober enough to give any account of his companion. That scarred old trump has not opened his lips the whole day save to admit a cartridge. The young fellows are infatuated with his ugliness and nonchalance. But I must be up and doing: there is no time to lose.'

"Won't you rest? An hour or two's sleep—"

"Not a wink till the work is done. If you choose to come with me you shall see something worth looking at. What say you?"

"I have no objection, if I may rely on your safe-conduct."

"That you may, and shall have it. Come."

I doffed my coat in obedience to his instructions, and put on a blouse in which I had been used to work at case. We descended the stairs, and proceeding along the quay to the secret dépôt of the night before, were admitted at a signal given by my companion. It was a sort of cellar, hot as an oven, and crammed with fellows naked, like the bakers of Paris, to the waist, making bread, as they termed it, for military digestions, or, in other words, casting bullets for the next day's operations.

N—— was enthusiastically received, and introduced me as a friend to the cause. We made but a brief stay ; and each charging himself with a couple of bags of shot, slung over the shoulders with straps beneath the blouse, set off to consign these indispensable provisions to the caterers for the banquet of the morrow.

The night was glorious—clear, starry, and splendid beyond description ; and a light refreshing breeze displayed the flag of freedom as it curled and undulated gracefully in the quiet sky. We crossed the narrow bridge to the church of Notre Dame, and leaving that to the right, passed over the Pont d'Arcole to the Quai de la Greve, and thence through sundry tortuous windings to the Rue St. Antoine, to the spot where the victorious stand had been made against the troops of the line. Everywhere barricades met the eye, either completed or in course of construction, and at every barricade we were challenged by sentinels who, with arms in hand, kept scrupulous watch. We had but to show our burdens to be received with a very significant welcome, and assisted over the ungainly obstacles in our path. Upon arriving at the spot where the affray had been hottest, at the rear of a barricade near the Place de la Bastille, the sight of many lying dead, and the dismal groans of wounded men, in a great measure cowed the enthusiasm I was beginning to feel. Some of the supposed dead men, however, began to move and stretch their limbs ; they relieved my mind considerably by their yawning, and gave me reason to hope that the casualties had not been so numerous as I feared. From the writhings and groans of two poor fellows who lay on a pallet in an open doorway, I made up my mind that, it was better to be killed than badly wounded in affairs of the sort, and further came to the conclusion that I had done right in declining the risk of either. N—— relieved me of my burden of bullets, which, as it weighed near a quarter of a hundredweight, I was nothing loth to lose, and proposed that, if I did not choose to remain, which he would not press, he should conduct me home again by a different route. I asked him what was his candid opinion of the prospects of the patriots "Four hours ago," said he, " I had some doubts of the issue; now I have none. The work, in fact, is already done. The troops are disheartened and disgusted, there are many of them who have not fired and will not fire a shot against us. They have abandoned the advantages they had won; and, ensconced in three or four central positions, wait only to be driven out by our combined attack. There are some thousands of barricades already up, and thousands more will be finished in the morning; and, you will see, there will hardly be occasion for a dozen of them." I offered to leave him with his warlike comrades, and to return by myself, as I could see no danger in so doing; but he preferred accompanying me, and we set off together in a north-westerly direction, making very slow progress, however, from the frequent challenges we encountered, and the barricades, most of which we had to surmount.

It was altogether a novel, curious, and ominous scene. For the greatest part of our route the whole adult population seemed to have assembled in the narrow inclosures formed by the barricades. The utmost silence compatible with the utmost activity prevailed. Men and women, haggard age and robust youth, wrought together at their strange employment with a vehemence and celerity that seemed to monopolize every faculty of mind and body. Under the direction of the grim and grizzled old soldiers of the Empire, and animated by the example of the students and well-dressed youth of the capital, they dug and hewed, and sawed and hammered, and piled and built in decorous order by the light of flaming torches without parley or questioning. Here a group assembled round a flambeau blazing over a blacksmith's anvil were seen repairing muskets and carbines; and there a little squad of grinning *gamins*, who had got possession of an antique rusty bayonet of a century of two's date, were mounting it upon a shaft yet green from the country-side. Wherever we went, the scene, though differing in detail, was the same in character. The swelling murmur that, like the distant roar of angry ocean, never for an instant ceased, challenged the ear to recognize its utmost limits, and "gave dreadful note of preparation" for a strife plainly destined to be decisive.

After something more than an hour's walking and scrambling we found ourselves in the vicinity of the Marche des Innocens, at a spot where the troops had suffered severely from the tempest of tiles, stones, and heavy masses hurled upon them from the roofs of a lofty and narrow thoroughfare. Several crushed and lifeless bodies lay heaped together in the shadow of a tall building, and three badly-bruised and wounded men lay languishing on rude couches under the care of women— the wives and mothers of their antagonists. Thence we made our way to the Pont au Change, where I took leave of my companion, and, crossing both bridges, returned to my lodging, and, with my mind made up as to the results of the coming conflict, to bed, and at last to sleep.

All the world knows how the bloody game was played out and won on the 29th; how the third day of the Revolution rewarded the gigantic exertions of the second, and avenged the insulting aggressions which characterized the first. The day of popular vengeance had come, and, what rendered its triumph terribly sure, every patriot knew it, and was eager to inflict his share. Along the same routes followed by the troops of yesterday poured the angry masses of to-day. Headed by the students of law and physic, on came the multitudinous bodies of successful combatants against an army of hireling opponents, who individually bore them no ill-will, and who, famished and worn out with fatigue, promised but a feeble resistance. The multitude that, abandoning their cherished barricades, swarmed over the bridges and through a thousand avenues upon the Louvre and the Tuileries, by mere momentum alone might have driven their antagonists from the city. They were received by a smart firing, but the reception they met with was the cold and formal effort of duty and discipline, hardly of determined hostility, much less of enthusiastic valor. The Louvre was first carried, the sudden abandonment of which originated a panic among the defenders of the Tuileries. Confusion, almost amounting to a perfect rout, speedily followed, which might have ended in a massacre of the troops but for the valor and coolness of the Swiss in the gardens, who effectually covered the retreat. The people, having, in the consciousness of their irresistible strength, refused an armistice and disdained a parley, were, before the close of the day, conquerors on all sides; and now it remained to see what they had got by it.

Nobody, however, yet knew that the business of fighting was over. It was thought that the king, who during the Three Days had been amusing himself with cards and masses—short rubbers and long prayers—at St Cloud, might at length wake up, and, by marching troops and artillery upon the capital, endeavor to re-erect his shattered throne. There was now on all sides as much talking as there had been fighting before. The friends of a republic were loudest in their declamations, but they had not an atom of real influence. The Ordonnances were repealed on the 30th, but it was too late; the monarchy *had* been thrown out of the window, and it was no use now to think of walking down stairs.

The populace shouted for Lafayette, and the republicans (those, at least, who knew nothing of state plots and intrigue) bellowed with all their might " Vive Lafayette!" Lafayette came, in a shower of blossoms and perfume, and brought in his hand—not a republic, but the Duke of Orleans, who, as lieutenant-general, assumed the government. This was on the last day of July. The 1st of August was a day of rejoicing; on the second, the old priest-ridden king abdicated, and a very short time after, the very next day, if I recollect right, the scurvy rabble of Paris, with the natural instinct of the *canaille* of all countries and times—the instinct of the mongrel cur who mauls and mutilates the vermin which the mastiff slays—launched their ragged tribes upon Rambouillet, whither he had retired from the tumult he was too senseless and feeble to cope with, and brutally drummed and terrified him out of that last refuge, to seek an exile's home—where his successor sought it with far less ceremony seventeen years afterwards—in the land of his hereditary foes.

The barricades all disappeared, and the shops opened in astonishingly quick time after the accession of the new monarch, for such he became within a few days. I now began to hunt up my old friends, pupils, and employers, to learn what was become of them, and what chance remained of yet obtaining a living in Paris. I called on N—— on the evening of the abdication, and found him calm and quiet as a philosopher, and surrounded by his family in his old lodgings. But I could see that his composure was assumed. He was already aware that, so far as a republic was concerned, he had bestowed all his enthusiasm to no purpose, and was secretly savage with the patriots for throwing away their advantage, and with himself for the part he had taken. He told me that poor Dick D—— was in one of the temporary hospitals in the Louvre, delirious with a broken head; that it appeared the poor fellow had joined the wrong party after all. Mystified with drinking to the good cause, he had wandered into the track of the routed soldiery, whom he mistook for the patriots, and had received a salute on the *os frontis* from a bottle intended for a grenadier. "But I am told," he added, "that there are good hopes of his recovering. It was nothing extraordinary that Dick's head should come in contact with a bottle—a case of magnetic attraction, perhaps; 'tis not the first time, at any rate. It may be a warning to him. But let me tell you about E——s. He has been here half-a dozen times, pumping me on the subject of the Three Days for his correspondence with the —— newspaper. I have crammed him full of lies and long details of events that never took place, in return for his poltroonery. The best of it is, he does not know that I am aware of his cowardice, and he regales me with particulars equally credible with those I furnish him with, of what took place in other quarters of the town *under his own eye* I have no doubt he has despatched an interminable yarn to London, in which he has represented himself as present wherever it was possible for one person to be in the course of the Three Days."

On leaving N—— I repaired to the printing office where I had last wrought. The doors were open, but not a soul save a superannuated warehouse-man was to be seen. Forms half worked-off lay upon the presses, and the ink had dried upon the hardening rollers. The composing-rooms were composed as death; and I could learn nothing as to the resumption of operations. I pursued my search at other houses in various parts of the city with equal ill-success, and began at length to think of turning my face homewards. Not to be precipitate, or lose a chance that might yet remain, I called successively upon all my pupils, and found but one out of the whole twenty-two who was willing to resume the course of instruction immediately. This decided my resolution, and I directly set about putting my affairs in order for a retreat I had bought an old piano-forte, which, no purchaser appearing, I was on the point of abandoning for the benefit of my successor in the lodging, when it occurred to me to pawn it Though no one would buy, I found no difficulty in pledging it for a tolerably fair sum, as it was doubtless expected that I should redeem it again when the long winter evenings set in With the proceeds I bought a selection of new romances in sheets, which I knew would pay me well for the trouble of importation. I now set out to procure my passport, a business which I found it next to impossible to accomplish, from the throng of Englishmen and other foreigners with which all the offices were beset Hour after hour I waited for my turn; and when at length I made my demand was referred to another and another functionary, each of whom I found besieged by a crowd of solicitous expectants, frightened at France, and eager to get away. I managed to get hold of a printed form at length, with the signature of one official I was sick of the pestilent catchpenny ceremonies, and borrowing the passport of a countryman who, after days of attendance, had succeeded in obtaining one, filled up what was wanting in my own with counterfeit scribbling, and resolved to put a bold face on it and take my chance.

I wrote to such of my old comrades as I thought fit to apprise of my return, and gave them a supper and a song on the very day that Louis Philippe accepted the crown of France. After the rest of my guests had departed, N—— remained till the night was far advanced, and we had a long and confidential conversation together. He was miserably disappointed at the result of all the heroism of the French populace, which he declared was utterly thrown away; praised my superior penetration (!) in abstaining from meddling with it, and upbraided himself for a fool in having perilled his life and the destiny of his helpless family for the sake of effecting an exchange which would perhaps turn out in the end, like that of the frogs in the fable, a King Stork instead of a King Log. " I shall return to England before long," said he, " whence it is possible I may sail for America. In less than a year the Statute of Limitations will free me from responsibilities which are only legally mine, and I can come back in safety. If you come in contact with any of my friends, make use of my name if it be of any service to you; but, remember, don't say what a calf I have been "

It was the 10th of August, the day after the proclamation of the new monarch amidst the pealing of bells and the thundering of cannon, that at seven in the morning I found myself on the top of the Diligence, by the side of a squab-faced Irishman, clattering over the rough stones of the Rue du Faubourg St. Denis, on my way homeward. My travelling-companion was in a violent rage with something or somebody, and every now and then, as we proceeded along, expectorated an oath or an unmentionable noun-substantive against some absent individual of the feminine gender, the object of his wrath and malediction. It was with some surprise that I learned at length that all this fury was directed against the wife of his bosom, who he swore had run away with a Frenchman, and all for jist nothing at all at all. "Bekase I choose to enjoy a bit of a skrimmage wid the boys, she takes the thantrums, bedad, and wants to ender me from divartin' meself wid the ruffylooshun · and whin I wouldn't lave the fun intirely at her biddin', she praches me a sarmint a yard long, and ses she'll lave me to me fate. 'Divvle may care, me darlint,' ses I, ' an if you lave me I'll brake ivery bone in yer body whin I come home, my dear.' Be the saints, that didn't mollify her! I was onny out one night, an whin I come back the same day she was clane gone, as I'm a sinner. Divvle fetch you, ses I. and I'll be afther you meself. I've been windin' of her this fortnight a'most, and onny catched the —— varmint 'istherdy aftherrnoon"

"Catched her ?—then I suppose she is in the diligence."

"Thrue for you—she *is* in the dilly gins that started afore this. If you'll tell me whin we'll come up wid 'em, I'll feel obleeged."

"It is not likely we shall come up with them at all; they have had more than twelve hours' start."

"But, tare an hounds ! the boat—will there be a boat across afore we git to Calais ? Sure, we'll nab 'em that way illigant."

I could give him no information on that subject, and for some time we pursued our route in silence, with the exception of occasional involuntary ejaculations on the part of the deserted husband We had travelled all day, a day of intolerable heat and dust, when, towards evening, at a sudden turn and steep descent in the road, we came upon an overturned diligence, which a number of workmen were engaged in repairing. "There," said I to the Irishman, "is probably the coach that your wife was in."

"Och, the blessed Vargin ;" he roared aloud, "I'm bail the darlint is kilt intirely !" With that, as the coach drew up, he leaped with one bound to the ground.

The passengers of the capsized vehicle, none of whom were seriously hurt, came flocking towards us from a cabin on the road-side, where they had taken temporary refuge. Among the rest was the Irishman's wife, a smart young Englishwoman of the abigail genus, with a spirit quite a match for that of her fiery mate. The Frenchman she had run away with was the creation of the latter's jealous brain. They flew into each other's arms with all the ecstasy of lovers, and she was immediately mounted between me and him; and a happier couple, to all appearance, it was impossible to imagine. She spoke French admirably, an accomplishment in which her lord and master was altogether deficient; and he was terribly afraid lest I should tell her all the fine things he had *not* said in her praise. I could not help tormenting him in return for the savage resentment he had betrayed at her escapade. I kept her chattering the best part of the journey, and found out, without much questioning, that, with all his wrath, the "grey mare was the better horse," and that it was well it was so, as much on his account as hers.

We arrived at Calais, my passport having escaped all challenge, in the afternoon of the 11th, and crossed the Channel in the evening in the steamer, which, there being not water enough on the bar to float us into the harbor, dropped anchor about a stone's throw from the shore. We had above a hundred passengers, which the boats took off and landed, plundering each of four shillings for a passage of fifty yards. With a few others I remained behind, refusing to pay more than sixpence for so trifling a distance. When the *victims* had been marched off to the custom-house, our offer was accepted, and we were landed by the same men, who were not too proud to work for fair wages, though they preferred robbery to labor. I slept at Dover—passed my luggage through the custom-house—paid tenpence a pound duty on my unbound English romances—sold them to a librarian in the town at a profit of two-hundred per cent.—and arrived by coach in London on the afternoon of the 12th. The same night I slept on the outside of the Bristol mail, and, having duly forewarned them of my arrival, descended from its roof in the morning to the warm and welcome embrace of my father and brothers.

CHAPTER VII.

The Pleasures of Home—Prospect of employment—A new Patron and a new engagement—The Doctor, his house, and his hobbies—A funny Compact—A trip to London and back—A private Printing Office—I find myself in clover—And in love—The Doctor and the Methodists—A Primitive Preacher—A Fire in the Village, the Doctor's humanity, and the gratitude of his pensioners—A visit to Bristol—Feeling on the subject of Reform—Arrival of Sir Charles Wetherell—Reading the Riot Act—The Bristol Riots—Plunder of the Mansion House—Burning of the Gaols—Burning of the Mansion House—Conduct of Colonel Brereton—Burning of the Bishop's Palace—Sacking of Queen's Square—Destruction of the Custom House—Conduct of the Mob—Cunning and Cowardice of Mob-leaders

I SHALL not attempt to describe the delicious satisfaction I experienced at finding myself once more beneath the humble roof of my parents. I had been absent between four and five years, years which had wrought a marvellous change in everything around me. The boys and girls had grown into men and women. My eldest sister had married and settled in the immediate neighbourhood; the second, who had been studious from a child, had had the benefit of instruction under good teachers, and was now absent from home, being engaged as a governess in a family in London. Tom had grown into a broad-shouldered, brown-faced foreman, with thirty years on his back and twice thirty men under his command; and Ned, little Ned no longer, but a "lither lad" of five feet ten, was almost on the eve of completing the term of his apprenticeship, and looking forward to the time when he should be his own master, and commence a life of independence. My youngest sister, now just budding into womanhood, fair, delicate, and fragile as the wild-briar rose in the hedge side, was the beautiful pet of the house and the idol of her parents. The garden at the back of the cottage, a piece of stony waste land when we first took it, was now umbrageous with foliage and teeming with ripening fruit, and furnished with a roomy arbor of trellis-work, the handywork of Tom and Ned, round which honeysuckles and flowering evergreens hung in plethoric luxuriance. Everything appeared new and foreign to my delighted eyes, which somehow would be dropping moisture, though my heart was laughing with pleasure. Everything was new but the placid, happy, and love-beaming faces of my father and mother, upon whom Time had foreborne to lay his withering finger, and who yet retained, as I assured them, the only family features that I should have recognized had I met them in my wanderings. I was pleased to see that the cottage itself bore evidence of thrift and comfort. The boys, my father said, had almost entirely refurnished it by working at home in their leisure hours, and he had not been wanting himself in supplying his quota of solid mahogany to the general stock. Altogether, I was proud of the superiority of my English home—the home of a family who owed all that they enjoyed to the labor of their hands—to anything I had seen among a similar class in my experience abroad.

I spent the first few days of my leisure at home, in the cottage and in the garden, talking to Patty (my youngest sister), who of course was not to be satisfied with anything short of my entire history, and consulting with my mother as to future proceedings. My father and brothers were generally off to work before I rose, and I did not see them till evening. I learned from my mother that it was the general wish that I should not, if it could be otherwise managed, return again to London; and therefore, with Patty hanging on my arm. I set out before I had been at home a week to see what chance there might be of obtaining employment among the printers of Bristol. We found, on calling at the old office, that Mr. Cousins had given up business, disposed of the stock-in-trade and the printing materials to another, and withdrawn to enjoy the sweets of retirement in a snug retreat which he had purchased in the vicinity of Kingsweston. I called consequently at all the offices in the town, and though at one or two places I was promised an occasional job if I would leave my address, it was plain that there was no likelihood of obtaining permanent employment anywhere, the trade being unusually dull, with no prospect of immediate revival. I reported progress at home, but still my father would not hear of my going again to London—at least, until it should be evident that no other chance remained.

One morning, as we were sitting at breakfast, about nine o'clock, in the trellised arbor in the garden, the postman, who had been knocking at the door without making us hear, peeped over the wall and flung a paid letter on the path. Patty picked it up—it was directed to my father, and my mother opened it. Seeing a thin, close-written sheet in my own handwriting fall out, I was curious to know how it came there. My mother put a half-sheet into my hand from Dr. D——e, of Prospect Villa, near F——d. "There," said she, "is something which I hope will prevent your going to London—read it." The note was an acknowledgment from the Doctor of the pleasure he had derived from the perusal of the inclosure, which he returned to my father, with an intimation that if, as he imagined probable, the revolution in Paris should drive me home again, I would make a point of seeing him before entering upon a new engagement. The inclosure was one of my long narrative letters written about six months before, and giving a rather queer account of my professorship and other goings-on; but how it came into the possession of the Doctor, or who he was, my mother had never been informed. The mystery was cleared up in the evening, and my father was not a little pleased that he had been the means of opening a connexion which he had great hopes would be of service to me. He had been sent by his employer to manage the fitting-up of a library in the villa near F——d, to which the Doctor had lately removed; while there he had beguiled the dinner-hour in reading my dutiful epistle, and had left it with the Doctor, at his request, after some conversation relative to me and my probable future fortunes.

This was on a Friday night, and I wrote off to the Doctor the next morning to inform him that I should have the pleasure of paying my respects to him as early on the following Monday as the sixteen or seventeen miles which lay between us, and which I should have to walk, would allow. In the meantime I resolved, if possible, to hunt up the Fish, who I had every reason to think must be in Bristol or the neighborhood. I called at all the printing-offices and made inquiries to no purpose, and looked in at his old resorts, where, though I recognized some of his ancient pot-companions, I could find no trace of him. I visited the quays and wharves, and went on board the vessels in the basin; and after continuing the search the whole day was forced at last to the conclusion that he was not in Bristol, and had never returned thither on quitting Paris.

Monday morning saw me, after an early breakfast, plodding onwards on the turnpike road to Bath, before reaching which I ascended a steep winding lane to the right, which brought me to Old Down; crossing that, through sundry villages and hamlets of rough free-stone, I got down into the valley of the Avon above the reach of navigation, and before the clock had struck eleven was knocking at the Doctor's door. Three minutes after, *tête-à-tête* with the good man in his well-furnished library, I was paying my devoirs to a substantial luncheon, for which my walk through dusty roads and stubble-fields had given me a rustic appetite. The Doctor plied me with a thousand questions on all subjects but the one I was most interested in—that of employment. When I had rested an hour, he led me out for a quiet ramble in the neighborhood of his house, and talked, and talked, and talked—and introduced me to a complete panorama of picturesque natural beauties by which he was surrounded. Then we returned and had a spell at the books in his library, among which were certain copies of rare and obsolete works of great price, and which I valued, much to his amusement, at fewer pence than they had cost pounds. The clock struck four, and still nothing had been said about the object of my visit. Wishing to get home again by daylight, I took my hat and bade him good day. "No, no," said he, "you are going to dine with me. Your father will not expect you home to-night—I have written to say you will stay a day or two. Besides, I have business to propose which we will talk about after dinner."

Soon after, the dinner-bell rang; and we entered the dining-room, where, at the head of the table, sat the Doctor's wife, and at the foot a young lass of about twenty, whose cheerful face and active vivacious manners were in fine contrast to the frigid formality of the mistress of the house, and made me feel at home at once. After a plain cold dinner, the relics of yesterday's hot one, the lady and the lassie withdrew; and then the Doctor, pouring me out a glass of wine, began to open the business which he had long had upon his mind, he said, and which I should execute for him if I chose. "I have often been upon the brink of publishing," said he, "but there are so many disagreeable things connected with an appearance in print, that I have never yet been able to muster courage enough to do it—at least, in the usual way. You know, perhaps, that the Rev. Mr. —— printed his own compositions with his own hands. I am not qualified to do that; I know nothing of the art, and have not the inclination at my time of life to learn, or the industry to prosecute it even if I knew how. Now, as I am led to understand that you are thoroughly acquainted with the necessary processes, I am ready, if it meet your views, to confide my manuscripts to you, to be printed at your leisure under my own eye."

This proposition rather startled me, and I possibly betrayed some surprise at it. Upon thinking it over, however, I confessed that, beyond the first outlay for types and a press, I could see no practical objection. He requested me to make a calculation of what would be necessary to provide materials. I suggested that as a small volume would not require a full-sized press, he should print his divinity in post-octavo, to which he consented; and upon my informing him that fifty pounds would cover the whole outfit, declared himself more than satisfied on that score. Then came the question of remuneration to me, which was settled at ten pounds a quarter, with board and lodging at his expense. It was agreed that my engagement should commence next day; that a room should be cleared for the reception of the press and types; that I should go to London to procure them in the ensuing week; and that in the interim I should employ my time in making a catalogue of the books in the library. The preliminaries thus arranged, I began to feel comfortable and to look around me in my new home.

The villa was delightfully situated on the crest of a hill, overlooking the village at a distance of half a mile. The river poured its dark, green flood, rushingly, in ceaseless murmurings, and foamed and swirled beneath the planks of a rustic bridge. The high land on the opposite bank, covered with noble trees in full foliage, and dotted here and there with white-washed cottages, peeping modestly forth from their green coverts, shut in the landscape on that side, and formed a picture of peaceful and romantic seclusion which a hermit might have coveted; while, on the other side, from the summit of the hill on which the house was built, the view was only bounded by the ridge of Salisbury Plain, twelve or fifteen miles distance. The Doctor led me round to the various points of view, which afforded the most delightful prospects, and then showed me his garden and orchard, where both fruit and flowers enjoyed a full share of his attention. He then took me to a kind of lumber-room, which overlooked the garden, where, from the presence of at least a dozen fishing-rods and reels, creels, bait-boxes, &c., I became aware that angling was one, if not the favorite one, of the Doctor's hobbies. This room was destined for the printing-office, and as it had a good light, and looked out upon the roses, geraniums, and carnations, then in full flower, I was mightily pleased with the locality. While we were talking over the new arrangements to be made, the old gardener made his appearance, and asked the Doctor if he did not mean to fish to-night, adding that "they would be sure to bite just now." The old gentleman looked at me, and as I immediately expressed a fondness for the sport, he pointed to the tackle standing all ready to drop into the water, bade me shoulder a couple of rods, and, taking as many himself, followed the old gardener down the hill

Crossing the road that led to the village at the foot of the slope, the gardener unlocked the door of a kitchen-garden which abutted upon the river, upon the banks of which were a couple of long benches for the accommodation of anglers. We took our seats, and baiting our hooks with boiled malt-corns, the sharp ends of which were first snipped off with a pair of scissors, cast in our lines to the depth of ten or twelve feet. The old gardener was right in his prognostication; the fish seemed savagely hungry, and bit as fast as the line was let down. Roach, chub, and dace came up walloping to the surface, one after the other, until the Doctor was well-nigh tired of the labor, notwithstanding that the gardener dipped them out with a landing-net, and renewed his master's bait. I killed my own share, too; though, from want of experience in that novel kind of fishing, I lost the heaviest of my customers through their breaking away from the hook. I asked the Doctor how they came there in such quantities, and whether the other parts of the river were equally well-stocked.

"Oh, dear no!" said he, "we feed them all the year round, and they feed us in return, when we want them."

The fish, in fact, were drawn to the spot, where they flourished and grew fat upon a continual supply of brewer's grains, liberally sunk, at the Doctor's expense, two or three times a week. In the course of a couple of hours we had caught as many as we could have eaten in a fortnight; and it being now past sunset, we left the tackle and fish to the care of the gardener, and returned to the house. Here we found the tea-urn singing on the table, and, upon our report of the execution we had done upon the finny race, the young lassie claimed the disposal of our whole catch, unless we should choose to reserve any for the morrow's table, an idea which the elder lady did not seem greatly to relish. A brace only of the largest chubs were selected for home-consumption, and the rest, part by Ellen May (so was the lassie called) and part by the old gardener, were carried to sundry laboring families in the neighborhood, who, having plenty of mouths to provide for knew very well what to do with them without Harvey's sauce.

The next day I commenced operations in the library, arranging nearly 5000 volumes, with the help of the gardener, according to a plan which the Doctor had laid down, and then proceeding to catalogue them. This ceremony took me much longer than I had anticipated, especially as the Docter would not hear of my working after dinner, though he had no objection to my beginning as early as I chose in the morning. The catalogue was nearly a fortnight in hand, and when it was completed in fair foolscap, I set out homewards; and, spending a Sunday with my parents, mounted the London coach, and, armed with a cheque upon a city banker, proceeded to the purchase of my materials. I stayed but two days in London. I bought a small iron press, as good as new, large enough for eight pages on a post sheet, for twenty pounds, and type more than enough for the purpose, both for text and notes, for twenty more. I purchased new glazed-boards for pressing, rollers, ink, chases, and other indispensables; and, without expending the whole sum committed to my trust, provided everything save paper, which we could procure equally well in the neighborhood. Before returning to F——d, I called upon my sister in Sloane-street, who was overjoyed to see me, and who, in answer to my inquiries, informed me that she was perfectly satisfied with her position, having made up her mind beforehand not to think it a paradise; that she was kindly treated by her employer, and in great favor with her pupils. She had a neat little room for her exclusive use, and prompt attendance when she required it, as a proof of which she rang the bell, and told the footman who appeared at the summons to bring refreshment for me. A decanter of sherry and a cold fowl, with the etceteras, were instantly brought in upon a tray, with an intimation from the lady of the house that I could be accommodated for the night if it suited my convenience. What a pity that these good looking facts deprive me of the opportunity of venting a little readable sarcasm against the governess-paying gentry, who gave my sister Polly, in return for her good temper and accomplishments, but twenty pounds a-year!

Before a week had elapsed after the purchase, the types and press were safe landed at the villa, without the privity of any of the neighboring inhabitants, as the publication was intended to be strictly private. The gardener and I managed to put the press together with some difficulty; and to prevent the disclosure of our proceedings, I became carpenter for the nonce, and made a pair of frames, a bank for the press, an ink-table, and various other matters of general utility. I had but two fonts of type, a small pica for the text and a brevier for the notes. Paper was sent in from a mill a few miles off; but we consumed no great quantity, as three quires, or about seventy copies, was to be the whole impression. I had purchased glazed-boards for pressing the sheets; and, it lieu of a standing-press, we contrived to swing a large stone in a shed by means of a pulley, which, giving a pressure of nearly half a ton, answered well enough for a small number. When all things were ready to begin, the Doctor produced his manuscripts. These were mostly in the shape of sermons, enveloped in black shining covers. They had been written, and no doubt preached, as sermons; but they had been digested into somewhat lengthy essays, or disquisitions, by means of liberal erasures and interlineations, and comprised altogether, the good man informed me, a complete exposition of the fundamental doctrines of Christianity, and a vindication of the creed and practice of the Church of England. The thought of at length seeing his lucubrations in print was, I could see, a source of no small pleasure and excitement to the Doctor. He stood by my side, in the simplicity of his heart, quivering with delight as I lifted the first types into my "stick," and could hardly believe his eyes when, in less than an hour, during which he had greedily watched every motion, the introductory paragraph, about a page in length, stood on the "galley," and I read it over to him from the metal. He was amazed at the celerity of the operation, which he imagined to be infinitely tedious, and brought the ladies down-stairs to witness my manipulations Next day I presented him with a proof of the first eight pages as we sat down to dinner, the sight of which actually spoiled his appetite, and diverted his attention from everything else. He forebore his fishing that evening, and remained for hours engrossed in the contemplation of his first proof-sheet. Pleased as he was, however, with the new complexion of his literary labors, he was in no hurry to issue the final *imprimatur*, but weighed well every phrase and sentence, and corrected, and polished, and altered again and again, so that I had the second eight pages composed, and nearly all the type exhausted, before the first was ordered to be printed. When I represented to him that if he did not use more despatch with the proofs I should not be able to earn my wages, he urged me on no account to let that trouble me, said he hoped I could find amusement to fill up my leisure, and that he thought sixteen pages a-week would be quite as much as we ought to get through, and that less than that would content him. Of course, I made no further objection; but, taking care to have every type worked up as fast as it was freed from the press, found myself in possession of abundance of spare time.

The weeks and months rolled pleasantly away. I counted myself the luckiest of all journeymen printers, and began to renew the relish for country customs and a country life which had been the instinct of my childhood. I explored the romantic scenery of the district, borrowed the Doctor's whipping-tackle, and drew the speckled trouts from the brawling brooks that fed the river within a mile of the dwelling. These were an acceptable addition to the dinner-table, and procured me favor with madam, who made me a present of a box of water-colors, which set my brains at work in a new direction. I knew the theory of perspective perfectly well, but found it of little use in the attempts I began to make to imitate the woody landscapes around me; but I daubed and splashed away with the vigor of a new-born enthusiasm, having no other copy than the grey stone cottages, the sandy banks, the rocky ravines through which the brooks rushed headlong, and the waving woods now brown with the hues of October. Strange pictures I made, but I thought them very fine, and stuck them round the walls of the little office that I might see them while at work. It pleased me not a little to find that the views were all recognized, vile as they certainly were; and I resolved that better should be forthcoming before long. Suddenly the weather changed almost at once to winter. The wind veered from the south to the north-east early in November, and a degree of cold set in that centred all our sympathies round the fireside. The library, into which opened the Doctor's study, was, from its sheltered aspect, the winter quarters of the family, and thither the work-table was removed. Now came the long evenings of winter, when, assembled round the blazing hearth, we whiled away the hours with such amusements as were suggested by our various whims and likings. The Doctor, who possessed in perfection the old-fashioned canonical accomplishment of backgammon, which Sir Roger de Coverley, be it remembered, considered a *sine qua non* among clerical qualifications, taught me the game. In return, I gave him lessons on the fiddle, which, considering that he was sixty years of age before he knew the gamut, I have always looked upon as a remarkable proof of the juvenility of his mind. Sometimes I played chess with madam—sometimes read aloud from some work of history or theology selected by the Doctor. At others I practised drawing in sepia, or ground the choruses of Handel on an old-fashioned piano ; and before the arrival of Christmas, had commenced, at my employer's request, giving Ellen a methodical course of instruction in the French language.

What other things I might have attempted, had not this last-named employment set my head a wool-gathering, I cannot at the present moment say. The reader may by this time have come to the conclusion, which is the true one, that I am not of a very inflammable temperament, and never was. On the other hand, I never was or could be insensible to female charms, or dead to the influence of laughing bright eyes and truly feminine manners—being moulded not exactly from stone, or iron, or brass, though the last-named commodity may not be altogether wanting. So it came to pass that when Ellen, with her eyes glued to the pages of Chambaud, began conjugating the verb *aimer* under my superintendence, I began somehow to attach a significance to that universal verb which is not to be met with in the grammar, and to wish by degrees that she could be brought to favor me with the first person of the present tense, indicative mood, with myself as the objective case. Now I am come to a very ticklish crisis in my history, and must mind my P's and Q's, lest I be called to account. Were this a fiction I might readily scribble off the course of love and courtship according to the long-established formula provided for such climaxes of romance ; but the very tolerable fact is, that Ellen has now been my wife for some fifteen years, and having grown, through certain ugly turns with which that jade Fortune has thought fit to visit us, much more matter-of-fact than she was in her younger days, won't stand any romantic nonsense on the subject.

I began to wish, as I said before ; but before I allowed this feeling to gain the mastery of my mind, I resolved to know more of Ellen than I yet knew, for her sake as well as my own. With this view, being always for plain dealing, I asked the

Doctor on his next appearing in the little office, where he passed an hour or two every morning, to oblige me with the particulars of her history. "Everybody has a history," said I, "and if you will tell me hers I shall feel obliged; I have a reason for asking for it." "You shall have it," said he, "in a few words, and perhaps I can guess your reason for desiring to know it. She is the only child of a curate who once officiated for me. Her mother died at her birth—her father five years afterwards. He was a poor scholar, without friends; he confided the child to my care on his death-bed. I promised to bring her up in a domestic way, and I have done so. That is all." "Not a word in her praise," thought I. "You have guessed my reason true enough, and intend that things shall take their course."

I proceeded in my lessons, and my pupil made very tolerable progress. Under pretence of imparting colloquial instruction, I accompanied her frequently in her walks to the village church on Sundays, and in her visits to the cottages of the Doctor's poor pensioners, to whom she was the bearer of a weekly dole. We came, in course of time, to a perfect understanding on the subject of our reciprocal feelings, and were both of us the happier and the better, I have no doubt, for the contract existing between us, though years passed away before its fulfilment.

By the middle of March, 1831, I had completed the first volume, amounting to above four hundred pages, of the Doctor's book. So far as I was capable of judging, it was an admirable work, profound in thought, simple in style, and full of matter, though somewhat disfigured by virulent remarks upon Methodism and Dissent in all forms. Methodism, in fact, was the one plague of the good man's life, the continual thorn disturbing his easy existence. He had long left off preaching himself, having resigned his living in Hampshire in favor of his eldest son, but was more anxious than ever that the pulpits of the land should be occupied by staunch Churchmen; and he groaned for the erection of churches, still more churches, till the conventicles should be blotted from the face of nature. His charities, like all the rest of his actions, leaned to the side of orthodoxy; I am sure he would not have refused his assistance to a starving Methodist family, but as sure as he gave it he would have accompanied it with a biting homily upon the subject of their defection from the national Church.

There was a mill-owner in the village, a follower of John Wesley, who early in the spring set apart a lower room in his mill for the use of the local preachers of that persuasion, who came twice a week to enlighten the benighted villagers of F——d. The Doctor was offended and mortified beyond measure at the step; and, desirous of knowing the extent of the mischief to be anticipated, sent me one evening to reconnoitre and report what was going on. I found an ungainly fellow of about fifty standing behind a small table, with a greasy pocket Bible in his hand, and holding forth with a violence of gesticulation that covered him with perspiration, in the following strain; " Et be a-all vurry wull, tellee, 'slong as 'e beant voun out But how's look then, 'swhat hi want to knaw, whan yer zins do viney out? Tellee how tha 'slook; jess vur a-all th' wordle like thee veather Hadd'm when a'd yett th' vorbidd'n vroot, an' went and hid hisself i' th' boosh. Than Goddamighty come down an' zed to un, ' Hadd'm, whor bist? Why 's'n come out? Has't tha yett th' vroot I towld tha tha shoulds'n yett?'— ' 'Tworn't hi,' zed Hadd'm, ' 'twor th' ooman gied it to hi.'— ' Tellee what 'tis, than,' zed Goddamighty to un. ' Hi doan't kear which onny 'twor,' " &c. &c. &c., of the same sort. I could not preserve a grave face, and was compelled, for decency's sake, to leave the assembly. When I made my report to the Doctor he was far from participating in my risible emotions, and expressed his deep regret that the fold of the Church should be invaded by the ignorant dispensers of such wretched husks of doctrine. I excused my laughter on the ground that I could not help it, hoped that the husks that offended him might yet contain some grains of truth, and suggested that perhaps the best way for the Church to preserve her flocks from the invasion of ignorance would be to educate them up to her own standard.

Though a High Churchman, the Doctor was decidedly a Liberal in politics, and desirous for a re-modelling of the representation and an enlargement of the constituency—it being a part of his theory that political disability was the most fruitful parent of religious heresy. When, during the winter, the whole neighborhood was in a state of alarm on the rumored approach of the mysterious fire-fiend, Captain Swing, whose blazing sacrifices we sometimes witnessed from the back-windows of the house, he had even gone so far as to express an opinion that such demonstrations, being the stern utterances of an oppressed class who had no other means of giving them a voice, were to be regarded as having a use and a signification which the Legislature would do well to ponder. And he looked on with a composure quite philosophical as the lurid fires gleamed far away in the distance like harmless meteors fitfully reflected upon the snowy plain; but when the invisible captain, as there was shrewd reason to suspect, brought, in the latter end of March, the incendiary torch into the neighboring village, and, in burning a wheat-stack, set fire also to the Methodist's mill, his philosophy gave place to the natural feelings of his heart in a manner wonderfully characteristic. He awoke me with a sturdy shake, about an hour after midnight, and bidding me dress and meet him on the lawn, hurried to the gardener's cottage to arouse the old man. We were not long in arriving at the scene of destruction, which, notwithstanding all our endeavors, we could do nothing to retard, much less to prevent. Though there was a river running beneath the flames, there were no means of bringing a drop of water to bear upon them. The Doctor's garden engine, which would have sent a small stream to the first floor, was rendered useless in the awkward hands of the rustics who undertook to manage it; and we were compelled to remain idle and unwilling spectators of the destruction of the entire property. Several small cottages attached to the mill were either burned along with it or smashed to pieces by the fall of the roof and walls ; and for every inhabitant of these a new shelter was immediately provided, either in the Doctor's own house, or in the houses of his tenants at his expense. For weeks after, his sole occupation was the comfortable re-instalment of the poor laborers who had suffered by the fire, every one of them members of the little Methodist Bethel, who piously believed their benefactor to be "a vessel of wrath fitted for destruction," and who, after they were again decently clad, housed, and employed through his charitable exertions, showed their gratitude in the only way they could, by praying at a special meeting that " the light of grace might shine into his benighted heart!"

The general election, which came off at the end of April, brought the turmoil of politics into our quiet district. The Doctor, of course, gave his vote to the Liberal candidate, and looked forward to the speedy passing of the Reform Bill as the grand panacea for all public grievances. Peacefully employed in my little office, or rambling over the fields or among the brooks with my fishing-rod or sketch-book, I passed through the spring and summer of 1831 a total stranger to the general excitement of the season, only too happy in the enjoyment of my present good fortune, and unwilling to mar it by anticipating its close. I had corresponded regularly with my friends, and paid several visits to my father's house. By the time the harvest was reaped and carried, I had finished the second volume of the Doctor's work ; when hearing from my sister in London that she was on the point of quitting her situation, not choosing to go abroad with the family, who were leaving England, I applied for a holiday, to have the pleasure of meeting her in the society of home. The entire month of October, which the Doctor intended to spend at the sea-side, was placed at my own disposal, and the old gardener, his wife, and Ellen and the maid were left in possession of the villa.

I got to Bristol, and took up my quarters with my parents the day before Polly came down in the London coach. Once more we were all assembled together, and the dear old cottage resounded with our merriment and fun. We got up pic-nic excursions, and rambled and ran over the Downs and among the rocks of Clifton; made sailing-parties down the river, took a three-days' trip to Chepstow and Tintern Abbey; rowed in the Wye, and steamed in the Channel; and, passing our days like careless birds in the sunshine, were as happy, perhaps, as God and nature intended that we should be. After we had enjoyed ourselves thus for a fortnight, a sudden accession of showery weather compelled us to limit our excursions to shorter distances, or to confine ourselves altogether to the cottage.

At this time I became first acquainted with the real state of public feeling in Bristol on the subject of Reform, for which the main body of the population were impatiently clamorous; while a small but determined Conservative party were as violently opposed to it. Both parties were equally active in the support of their principles; but the activity of the Tories, assuming, as it too frequently does, the form, acquired the character of persecution, while that of the Reformers wore the aspect, which everybody was willing to concede to it, of sturdy patriotism. The rejection of the Bill by the House of Lords, and the part the bishops had taken in that rejection, had kindled the hatred of the lower orders against both lords and bishops, the latter especially, to a degree which it was impossible to control. But the feeling of the lower orders was also that of an immense proportion of the middle classes and of no small section also of those above them. Day by day the feeling grew stronger, and the fear or the hope, as it might be, of some popular outbreak, appeared likely to be verified. During my rambles about the town in the third week of October I became perfectly intimate with the disposition of the populace, and was by no means surprised when the Bishop of Bristol, who came down to consecrate a new church, was received with general hootings and insult, and a shower of stones. Still I thought that, though the public spirit might continue for some time to effervesce in such time-honored demonstrations as shrieks, yells and brickbats, it would subside at length, seeing that the Bill was inevitably fated to become the law of the land. My father was of the same opinion, and had no apprehension of fatal violence or bloodshed. We were both egregiously deceived.

As the time drew near for my return to F——d, I was anxious to introduce Ellen, of whom, perhaps, I had talked a great deal, to my parents; so, on the afternoon of the 28th, I borrowed a horse from my brother-in-law, hired a small four-wheel phæton, and putting Polly and Patty into it, drove over to the villa, where we passed the night agreeably enough, and the next morning, after an early breakfast, set out with Ellen at my side to return home. The weather not being altogether as fair as could be wished, and the girls having no shelter in an open carriage, I drove on at a pretty smart pace, and soon after ten o'clock was in sight of the churches and chimneys looming mistily over the smoky bed of Bristol. When we were within a mile of the city we were passed by a chariot and four greys, driven at a spanking rate. It was still in sight when it stopped among a dense crowd of people about a couple of furlongs from the town, and a gentleman alighted and got into the carriage of the sheriff, which was there in waiting. This gentleman, though I did not know it at the moment, was Sir Charles Wetherell, recorder of the city, a personage particularly obnoxious to the Liberal party in the place, from the violence of his opposition to the Reform measures. He was received with such a storm of yells, hootings, and execrations as I had never till then imagined possible from human throats; and would, beyond a doubt, have been massacred and torn to pieces on the spot but for a strong guard of horsemen both in front and rear of the carriage, and a posse of constables armed with staves. Now and then a volley of stones afforded a more substantial expression of the dislike of the sovereign people to the messenger of justice. As the *cortége* entered the muddy thoroughfares, the crowd increased to an immense mob. Shoals of draggle-tailed women of the very lowest class swarmed forth from the stinking purlieus of Temple-street, and added their melodious voices to the general chorus; while from the windows aloft, dishevelled heads and dirty faces hooted a discordant greeting to the man who was *not* of the people. I was too glad, for the sake of my timid companions, to keep at a respectable distance, and took the advantage of the first practical thoroughfare to get out of hearing as fast as I could.

Ellen, welcomed as a daughter and sister by my parents and family, was delighted with them all. I told my father, who had come home to dinner on purpose to meet her, of the Recorder's reception. He now expressed a fear that something worse would come of it, as it was known that soldiers had been brought into the town in a clandestine manner, and suggested that I should call at the workshop on the Quay where Ned pursued his labors, and see that he got into no mischief on his way home. Accordingly, I encountered Master Ned at the turn-out from the workshop, just as he was starting off with a brace of comrades to see the fun. To this I had no great objection myself, and proceeded with them to the front of the Mansion house, where we arrived while the Mayor, mounted on a chair, was reading or endeavoring to read the Riot Act, occasionally dodging his head to avoid the flying commentaries of his auditors. The mob, who had made a vain attempt to upset the Recorder in the street on his passage to the Mansion-house, and who in the course of the afternoon had suffered a defeat at the hands of the special constables, were now rapidly increasing in numbers, from the accession of large hordes of laborers and hangers-on from the docks and storehouses (a full half of them vagabond Irish,) and, irritated beyond measure at their defeat, were plainly determined upon having revenge upon somebody. They stormed the Mansion-house with brickbats, stones, and heads of iron-railings, knocked off for the purpose. Glass, wood, window-frames, shutters and doors disappeared in an unaccountably short time before the crushing masses that were hurled against them. The constables, in their turn, numbers of whom were private gentlemen sworn in for the occasion, had to fly for shelter, and barricaded themselves in the building with the beds and costly furniture. Through the hollow, gaping windows poured a continued stream of ponderous missiles till the floors were literally heaped with rubbish—and loud cries and yells for the Recorder, the —— Recorder, mingled with the strains of the national anthem furiously chanted by the mob in the rear of the assaulting gangs. A party of desperate blackguards, headed by a lanky north countryman whose Northumbrian burr betrayed his origin, endeavored to gain possession of the building, but they emerged after a few minutes from the attempt with such an undeniable crop of broken heads and red-streaming viages as effectually lulled their ardor for a time at least. They now began collecting straw, and clamored for a light, with the intention of firing the edifice, when a party of dragoons, accompanied by a magistrate, made their appearance.

If the authorities had now made known the important fact—as they had good opportunity of doing in the comparative calm that ensued upon the arrival of the soldiery—the fact, namely, that the gallant knight, Sir Charles Wetherell, panic-struck by a vision of brick-bats, had clambered, by the help of a woman, over the roofs of the outhouses in the rear, dashed through a stable window, doffed his judicial attire, and indued his knightly limbs in the leather-leggings and worsted hose, surmounted by the red waistcoat and greasy cap, of a groom, and, under the self-imposed appellation of Bill Scroggins, had managed to save his precious trembling carcase, and was by this time the Lord knew where—such an announcement would at that stage of the outbreak in all probability have turned the thoughts of the mob in the direction of an achieved triumph, and wound up the business in a general roar of laughter.

But they missed this golden opportunity; and, confiding the care of the city to the courage and policy of a man who possessed neither, paid dearly for their confidence.

Knowing that the Riot Act had been read, and expecting that decisive measures would be immediately put in force to disperse the crowd, I urged Ned to make for home, whither we were wending our way as fast as the multitude would let us, when on crossing the bridge I was touched on the shoulder by my brother Tom. "I have been looking for you," said he, "and am glad we have met. Ned must be off home at once, and warn the lasses and mother not to expect us till they see us. They need not sit up; I have the key.' We saw Ned clear of the crowd, and then returned to the Council-house, where Tom, who had been sworn in as a special constable, procured a couple of staves, tendering me one, and proposing that I should take the oath. This I declined on the ground of being a visitor only, but volunteered my services, which were accepted. Between seven and eight o'clock, with about twelve or fifteen other recruits, we entered the Mansion-house, at the back of it in Little King-street. It was a complete spectacle of ruin and disorder, which was in some sort repaired during the course of the night by a number of workmen, who boarded up the windows and doors which had been beaten in by the mob. The soldiers, however, to my astonishment, did little or nothing towards dispersing the crowd and clearing the square. They certainly countenanced the removal by the constables of an awkwardly-piled barricade; but beyond sauntering their horses up and down among the rioters, and dangling their sheathed swords in their hands, made no attempt towards the restoration of order. Some of the troop were brought in wounded by the mob, whom, notwithstanding, the commanding officer persisted in treating as good-humored fellows whom he could persuade by kindness. About midnight, finding the Mansion-house too well guarded, the blackguards moved off to the Council-house, and commenced an attack upon the windows, which they were demolishing, when a troop of soldiers arrived, whose leader not having the same singular idea of good-humor entertained by Colonel Brereton, charged the rabble at the sword's point, and having cut down some half-score, and shot one who showed fight, saved the building from certain destruction. For this piece of good service he and his troop were contemptuously ordered out of town next day by the Colonel, who did not choose that the good-humor of the mob should be interrupted. This wholesome administration of severity had, however, one good effect. The mob, who preferred plunder to fighting, slunk away by degrees, and by an hour after midnight but a few straggling groups remained; and my brother and I returned home between two and three in the morning, in the hopes that our services would be no more required.

In this we were altogether out of our reckoning. We had scarcely sat down to breakfast at eight o'clock, when a messenger arrived, citing my brother to join his comrades at the Mansion-house, where the rioting had recommenced. Tom, who had dressed in his best, thinking to go to church with the family, did not half relish the call, especially as it was raining pretty fast; and asked me if I intended to lend a hand. I did not like to refuse him, and bolting a hasty breakfast, we both marched off to the scene of action as fast as possible. We got there too late to be of much service. The building was already in possession of the rebels, who were plundering the cellars and getting drunk as fast as they could. Some of the rooms were sacked and the furniture lying about the square. The soldiers, who had been withdrawn to leave a fair field for good-humor, arrived again upon the spot, and the drunken bands of spoilers were cudgelled from the cellars by the constables, who resumed possession. A magistrate read the Riot Act three times in the presence of the troops and their commander; but not a soul offered to stir from the spot, and not a finger did the soldiers move in vindication of the law. The plunder and the drunkenness went on with very little molestation on the part of the military, who seemed more concerned to shield themselves from the soaking rain than anything else, during the whole of the morning. About noon Colonel Brereton announced, in the hearing of several of us, to the drunken rabble, that he had packed off the 14th (the troop which had dared to intermeddle with the rioters the night before) out of the city. They gave him three cheers, exulting in what they must have felt to be the truth, that by that act the town was virtually surrendered to them.

Notwithstanding the pelting rain, which lasted nearly the whole day, there were always present a very considerable number of the respectable middle-class inhabitants, who, by their countenance and non-interference, sanctioned the proceedings of the rioters. The feeling of this class, who had been offended by the opposition of the Mayor to the Reform movement, was plainly against the authorities, and they evidently viewed the outrageous violence committed without the least symptom of dissatisfaction. Too many of them learned their mistake when it was too late. By noon on Sunday the mob were aware of the fact that the Recorder had ingloriously absconded; but by this time they had drunk five hundred dozen of wine and tasted the sweets of plunder, and having become aware of their power were determined to exercise it. About one o'clock we were startled in the Mansion-house by a sudden peal of stones and bricks, which again burst in the windows of the long room, and were momentarily expecting the building to be stormed, when suddenly a cry was raised, " To the Bridewell—the Bridewell!" and immediately after a large party marched off to lavish their good-humor upon the various prisons of the Reform King, and to demonstrate their loyalty by incendiarism and rapine. The Bridewell was soon in flames, the keeper, with a solitary blunderbuss, having kept them at bay for a while, and at length yielded for the sake of saving the lives of his family. Thence they proceeded to the New Gaol; and, in order that military sanction might not be wanting to their humorous exploits, the

Colonel despatched a troop, with strict orders to do nothing but look on—orders which were religiously obeyed; while the prisoners were liberated and the gaol set on fire. The plunder and destruction of the toll-houses followed next; and that feat accomplished, they crossed the city to Lawford's Gate Prison, set fire first to the governor's house—roasting the poor man's pigs alive as an exquisite sally of humor—and, releasing the prisoners, committed that prison also to the flames.

By this time night was fast approaching, and the state of affairs began to assume a rather terrific and alarming aspect. The volumes of red flame that arose on all sides in the damp and drizzly air served as beacon-fires to the disaffected in the neighboring towns and villages, and through every avenue to the town hordes of desperate ruffians rushed to augment the gangs of plundering incendiaries, now mad with their unlooked-for success. Half-a-dozen soldiers had been left to guard the Mansion-house, and during the excesses of the afternoon, which drew off numbers to other places, this mere show of military protection enabled the body of specials within to prevent further injury to the edifice. But when darkness had set in, and the mob, which all day had remained in the square in drunken riot and frolic, were increased by the return of the immense gangs who had carried fire and ruin to all quarters of the city, it soon became too plain that the Mansion-house was doomed. The few soldiers present made no attempt to prevent the fire, but looked on complacently while a ruffian deliberately climbed a gas-lamp, lighted his candle, and, carrying it to the cellar, of which the mob had had possession for some hours, effectually fired the building. It was hardly seven o'clock when the reek from the cellars, and the black volumes of smoke ascending heavily from the lower floors, warned us to follow the example of the Recorder, and take care of ourselves. We escaped without much trouble over the roofs in the rear, and following the directions of a gentleman who, in expectation of the coming calamity, had been employed with a companion in cutting the pictures from their frames, and removing them to a place of safety, we made our way as fast as possible to an office in College-green, almost adjoining the Bishop's palace.

Here were assembled the magistrates and the commanding officer, expecting an immediate attack upon the Palace, and consulting upon the means of meeting it. The attack came before any decided plan could be formed. The Colonel met it as he had met the former manifestations of the good-humoured mob, that is, with his avowed sanction and countenance. We were hastily desired to join a division of specials advancing from the Council-house. The Colonel drew up his soldiers in two lines in front of the entrance Between these we entered the building, which was already on fire, and swarming with ruffians occupied in plunder. We succeeded in extinguishing the fire, and plied our heavy staves among the thieves in a manner that surprised a few of them, and strewed the floors with their cowardly carcases—scores of them falling without being touched. A number of them made a rush to escape through the soldiers. Tom, close at the heels of a big scoundrel, burly with spoil crammed beneath his clothes, qualified him for the hospital with a blow that would have split the skull of an ox. As the villain fell beneath the horses, the Colonel, rushing forward, swore, by God, that if the constables struck the mob he would ride them down. I heard the threat. Tom did more— he acted on it. Whirling his staff at the heads of the flying thieves, "There goes my constableship," said he. "I have sworn to keep the peace, and I will keep it henceforth like a soldier." Then taking my staff, he sent it after his own; and pushing me through the premises, with the passages of which he was perfectly intimate, we made our escape through the gardens, and, resigning our office in despair, returned as spectators to the square. I may remark here that the Colonel, having thus openly patronized the work of incendiarism and pillage, shortly after withdrew his force, leaving the luckless constables to fight their way through the rioters as they best could. Some of them got severely mauled and wounded, and only escaped with their lives through the general preference of the mob for plunder to blows In less than half-an-hour the palace was on fire in every part, and an immense volume of clear flame, covered with a canopy of black smoke, greeted by a demon roar from twenty thousand rabble throats, announced the admirable humor of the Colonel's good friends and wellwishers.

By the time we had returned to the square the Mansionhouse was in a state of ruin; the whole front had fallen in bodily, and buried a number of the drunken wretches who had wrought its destruction beneath the wreck. But the large amount of timber employed in its construction, the solid floorings, and the massive furniture with which it was stocked, supplied fuel to the flames for many hours; and it burned fiercely till long after midnight, to the immense satisfaction of the mob, who cheered vigorously as the different masses fell successively to the ground. The whole sky was now in every direction a red and glowing arch, like the fiery vault of Pandemonium, resounding with the frantic yells of fiends in human shape. The rain, as it still drizzled down, fell literally in warm drops upon our faces, as we stood beneath the shelter of a half-leafless tree contemplating the disgusting freaks and orgies of the crowd. About ten o'clock the Colonel arrived at the square with his detachment of automatons, whom, wrapped up snugly in their warm cloaks, he paraded up and down among his drunken, plundering *protéges* for some ten minutes, and then, to leave them unmolested in their further diversions, marched every trooper off the spot, and went home himself to supper and to bed, from which neither the sense of duty (supposing him to have had any,) nor all the messages and remonstrances of the magistrates, now driven to their wit's end, could induce him to stir till the morning. He and his red-jackets had not been long off the ground when the mob, now in admirable humor, and increased by fresh arrivals, commenced a systematic course of destruction and plunder upon private property. Beginning at the east end of the north side of the square, they first plundered and gutted, and then fired successively, every house, the dwelling of reformer or anti-reformer indiscriminately. Infirm old men, women, and half-naked children were driven forth from their houses to seek a shelter from the accumulated horrors of the night at the hospitable hands of strangers. Furious bands of Irish savages burst in the doors and windows, and loading themselves with booty of every sort, piled it in heaps beneath the trees, or round the statue in the centre of the area. Others, eager for drink, rushed to the cellars, and soon, mad with the fumes of wine, raged franticly through the rooms, burning and destroying, and roaring and yelling, till the ascending flames themselves had kindled licked them into the glowing abyss beneath, where they perished miserably. The conflagration now exceeded all that had gone before. Many of the cellars were stocked with bonded spirits, and the fierce rush of the fiery columns that rose through the black shells of some of these houses when the fire had reached the spirit-casks was truly terrific to witness. About midnight, the Custom-house was attacked, the officers, to the number of fifty, summarily turned out, and the building fired at once in twenty places. While the flames were raging, a band of insane miscreants sat down to gorge and guzzle in a lower room, and were buried alive or dead drunk in the midst of their orgies by the falling-in of the roof. Some were seen expiring in agony on the pavement, having leaped from the windows of the flaming houses, one impaled himself on the iron spikes of the railings in front, where he wriggled in torture to the infinite mirth of his fellow-patriots.

Of the detestably brutal scenes enacted in the area of the square during the transaction of these disgraceful atrocities it is hardly possible to give an adequate idea by description alone. Around the statue of King William III. immense quantities of costly furniture, the plunder of the burning houses, were flung in disorderly heaps. But with a view to an hour's luxurious enjoyment, tables were spread and heaped with viands of all sorts, and wine and spirits in plentiful array. The hungry wretches despatched the provisions as fast as they were supplied, and loudly clamored for more. Fiends in feminine form, drunk with wine, and naked to the waist—hideous bacchanals, whose gorgon ugliness, matured in the filth and squalor of Bristol's darkest dens and slums of slime and excrement, was in strict keeping with the seething hell of riot and rapine around—gave voluble and vociferous utterance to language which no pen can transcribe or tongue repeat, and urged and goaded their drunken culls and bullies to more remorseless deeds of ruin and ravage. Here a brawny miscreant, mounted on a table, put up the stolen goods to auction, and sold them too, knocking them down generally to the first bidder, and receiving and pocketing the money. If a bidding could not be obtained, smash went the unsaleable article to the ground, shivered in fragments. In this way a large portion of the plunder was disposed of, and carried off by the villain purchasers in the course of the night. Fellows armed with large hammers or crowbars, drew forth from the piles of goods, trunks, boxes, or writing-decks, and, dashing them open, threw their contents upon the moist and muddy grass, while they rifled them of coin, plate, jewels, or other valuables they might contain. Scores of strong fellows, dead drunk, lay stretched among the spoil, snoring amidst the mud and ooze of the trodden and sodden turf. It was, in a word, the saturnalia of robbery and licence got up under the pretence of liberty and reform. The prime movers of all these atrocities were a set of skulking conspirators, strangers to the town until within the last month—mob-leaders by profession, with a genius for propelling others into mischief and withdrawing themselves from the consequences. Their machinations were plainly distinguishable on the night of the 30th. They acted upon a preconcerted system, by which they contrived to do the greatest amount of damage possible in so short a time; and they disappeared like magic when the damage was done, and the tardy sword of justice was at length unsheathed, leaving their deluded followers to brook the summary vengeance of the law. Of the real ring-leaders of the Bristol riots not one ever faced a jury. The foremost and most active of their willing tools and agents were captured, and numbers were imprisoned, transported, and hanged—the heroic contrivers vanishing as they came, without beat of drum.

Weary with hunger, hard work, and excitement, and disgusted with the infernal spectacle before us, my brother and I, after lending what aid we could in the removal of valuables from one or two of the dwellings, the inmates of which retained sufficient presence of mind to carry off a portion of the property they could not otherwise preserve, left the square at about four in the morning, and returned home. We found the whole family up, and gazing from the windows in horror at the distant conflagration. Their personal fears allayed by our return, we all retired to our rooms, and lay down for a short rest. I was asleep in three minutes, and acting over again in my dreams the horrors of the past twenty hours. Tom was up and off before I awoke, and, returning again to dinner, informed us that the soldiers had at last been induced to act against the mob, who scuttled away in every direction at the first charge, and that now, in consequence of expresses sent off in the night, troops were pouring in from all quarters, and no further mischief was apprehended. Hundreds of the plundering scoundrels had been cut down in the streets, and order had been restored principally by the very troop whom the wretched Colonel had contemptuously dismissed the city, and whom he had been obliged to recall. The rest is well known. The Colonel shot himself, to escape the verdict of a court-martial. An enormous amount of the plunder was recovered from the grasp of the robbers through the rigid and vigorous search of the police; and the inhabitants of Bristol derived a lesson from the events of these inglorious three days which taught them the true value of physical force as an engine of redress, and the real character of the ruffians who wield it.

CHAPTER VIII.

French and English Mobs—I resume work at F——.—Second Journey to London to seek my Fortune—Make my *debut* in a London office—Parson Smart—The art of extempore preaching—How to "dish" the Cash—Admirable management of an Overseer—a Greek compositor—"Writing horse"—I am out-generalled by the Grecian—The Sheep's head Delinquent turned Gentleman—He gives me employment—His clever Tactics—I am out of work and miserable—the Cutler Editor and amateur Printer—How to get up a Country Newspaper—The late County Advertiser—Sketch of a Country Market-town—I am cut by the Cutler—Return to Town—Clever and profitable Dodge of colluding Printers—The Latin language not worth sixpence to a Journeyman Printer—I am enlightened on the subject of the Compositors' System of Protection—Which defrauds me of my labor—An offensive Cockney—I "lick" him, and am chapelled and fined—Resolve to give up my berth—Apply for a situation in a School.

THE reflections which I could not help making on the subject of the riots at Bristol, and the comparison which I naturally drew between the proceedings of the English mob and the conduct of the Parisian patriots in the revolution of the year before, were not very favorable to my own countrymen. In Paris I had witnessed the practice of the greatest disinterestedness and self-denial, and the display of unconquerable courage and perseverance united in furtherance of the common good; and I had, moreover, witnessed the virtues of charity and compassion in full exercise towards the common enemy when that enemy was subdued. At home, in a land where freedom had long triumphed more fully than it has ever yet done upon the soil of France, I had seen outrage and ruffianism tumultuously arrayed against law and order, for the sole object, as it had turned out, of creating an opportunity for destruction, license, and plunder I had seen the grossest cruelty perpetrated upon the helpless and unoffending, and the most revolting cowardice, as it is ever found to do, characterizing the perpetrators. I shall not pretend to philosophize upon the causes of the difference of temper and action between an English and French mob. The sentiment of honor, so powerful among the latter, would appear among the former to be displaced by the sentiment of beer. In times of popular excitement and outbreak, the Frenchman becomes intoxicated with the visionary idea of his winged goddess, Liberty, and the Englishman intoxicates himself in a more literal way by the furious imbibition of unlimited alcohol. Perhaps, after all, the latter is considered by our governing powers to be the less dangerous propensity of the two, and this may be one reason why the *profanum vulgus* is politically left to wallow in the mire of ignorance and filth, and to acquire the brutality that they inevitably engender.

But I must pursue my narrative.

Leaving Ellen to spend a few weeks with my parents in the cottage, where she found a new pleasure in the society of my sisters, I returned to F———d on the 2nd of November, in time to meet the Doctor on his arrival at home. I resumed my operations upon the third volume of his work, and completed that and the fourth in the course of the next twelve months. Were I to chronicle minutely the events of this tranquil year of my life, they would be contained in a very few pages, and those would be devoid of interest to the general reader. The same round of occupation in the little office, and the same complacent pleasures within doors and without, characterized the whole period, which yet wanted some of the elements of enjoyment that I had tasted with unmingled satisfaction during the first year of my residence in this secluded retreat. The fact was, as the reader who has had much experience of human nature has perhaps already anticipated, that my imagination was too much engrossed with the pleasant myths it was constantly creating, in which the endeared figure of Ellen predominated as the presiding genius, and the flickering fire-flashes from a cheerful hearth of my own lighted up her laughing face, to allow me thoroughly to enjoy, as I otherwise might and should have done, the real delights of my present condition. I longed, in short, to be making my own nest; the instinct of pairing-time was upon me, and I wanted to be building my own house, which I knew well enough, however much I might have desired it, could never be established in that quiet spot. As day after day and month after month rolled on, I felt more anxious and eager to make a fresh appeal to fortune among the ever toiling energies and activities in competition with which alone independence was to be won. I did not conceal any of these thoughts and desires from her who was the source and object of them. Ellen approved of the attempt I was at length resolved to make to push my fortunes once more in London; and therefore when, soon after Christmas, 1832, the Doctor, the manuscript of whose fifth volume was not yet in a condition for press, began casting about for some other mode of employing my time, I made known my wishes, and, indeed, my determination, and requested his consent and countenance to my purpose. He made no objection, and, I believe, was expecting my proposition; but he insisted that I should remain for a month or six weeks, until the then severe weather was past, as his guest, and make my appearance in London in the early spring. To this I consented, though had I known that I was sacrificing a good portion of the season when in London employment for printers is most plentiful, I should most certainly have refused, and started off at once. This kind of knowledge came with experience.

Among the many causes which operate to drive the workingman to London, and to flood the metropolis with competitive labor, the hope of obtaining permanent and well-remunerated employment, which shall enable him to marry and commence housekeeping, with the prospect of decently providing for the comfort of a family, is undoubtedly the most powerful. It need not be asserted that such a result is one of the great prizes in the lottery of a working-man's life—a prize which every man hopes and intends to win, but which few eventually realize, and which even those who attain to it do so at the cost of health and the sacrifice of years of life. It was in pursuit of this prize that, urged by motives which have ever proved the most powerful stimulants to the energies of man, I again entered London in March, 1833, to place myself in the ranks of industry, determined never to flag or falter in the contest, and never to recognize even the possibility of such a thing as voluntary idleness or a breach of economy.

It was a fortunate thing for me that I found the trade pretty brisk on my arrival. Having secured a cheap but tidy lodging in Westminster, I proceeded on the second day of my sojourn in town to look out for employment. It was quite a matter of accident that my first application was made at a small printing-office in the rear of the south side of Ludgate-hill, and almost under the shadow of St Paul's. I was taken on at once, and a frame was allotted me in a room with four others; three apprentices and a superannuated journeyman almost totally past work. The books in hand were mostly religious publications, and I fell to work at once upon a Dissenting magazine, published monthly. Before the week had elapsed two additional hands joined; and as the month grew older, and publishing day drew on, a third made his appearance, whose periodical duty it was to put the magazine together (or, technically, to make it up) and send it to press. This man, whom I shall call Smart, was a rather eccentric genius, and altogether an anomaly among working-men. He had been apprenticed to a printer, and learned his trade; but having become impressed with the notion that he was born to astonish the world, had abandoned his employ and entered a Dissenting College. Here he had acquired the accomplishment of talking *ad infinitum,* but had ingeniously omitted to furnish himself with anything worth talking about. His tongue vibrated incessantly, one might have almost thought involuntarily, from morning to night; and though he knew, as he must have known, that for half the time he had no listeners, he talked on notwithstanding. From College he had been translated to a country pulpit, in a midland country, where, he told us, he had 40*l*. a-year "and the run of his congregation;" so that he could manage to live without spending more than half his salary, small as it was. He had to preach three times on Sundays and twice in the week, and to " do" the school and the prayer-meetings. Besides his regular salary, he sometimes made a " half-sov." by " supplying" vacant pulpits. He declared that he never studied his sermons —couldn't do it at the price ; that it was trouble enough to pick out a text. He boasted that he never found himself at a loss, which I could readily believe, and assured us that the best way to get *out* of a " fix, when a fellow finds that he is going to stick in the mud in the middle of his preachment," is to get *into* a passion, when a little gasping and incoherency will pass for a good deal of feeling and enthusiasm. He initiated us into the art and mystery of bleeding the congregation, or, as he termed it, " milking the fold."

" It does not do," said he, " in these small places, to fix beforehand the day for a collection ; if you did the chawbacons wouldn't find their way to chapel: that's a green move, and never pays in the provinces. No, no ! Look out for a fine day and full pews, when you've got the fat farmers and their wives and daughters, and perhaps the squire and his lady— that's the nick—pitch it into them comfortable, all about Isaac and Jacob, and Laban and Esau, and the oxen and asses, and the herds and the flocks, and the pastures and the corn-fields Then, when the old chaps begin to wag their rosy gills, and to wake up in their own element, that's your time—stick it into them—the ' day appointed,' that's your weapon 'My dear friends, this is the *day appointed* for the quarterly collection.' It is a dead nail, that, never knew it to fail. I've ' dished' a matter of 2*l*. 10*s*. by that move in my own little place."

In such a style this ex-ecclesiastic would run on for the hour together, to the amusement or indignation of his hearers. He knew the private histories and secret peccadilloes of all the "great guns and holy bolies,' as he called them, of the Dissenting denominations, and retailed them liberally, with the flippant volubility of a man in whom the organ of veneration was altogether wanting. Concerning his own private history he did not think it necessary to be quite so communicative; but I learned from other sources that through his characteristic levity and superficiality he had lost ground among the denomination to which he belonged, and that he had been *persuaded* to resign his ministerial pretensions and had returned to the exercise of his profession, in which he was assisted by the patronage and recommendation of the religious body of which he had been an organ and was still a member. He was a smart man, in the American sense of the term, and contrived to make more by his eight or ten days' work on the magazine than some who labored on it for a whole month.

At that time I knew nothing of London work, and its somewhat peculiar regulations. Mr Smart took the benefit of my ignorance by depriving me in his own behalf of my just share of what printers term "fat," a word the professional signification of which cannot be accurately imparted to the general reader, but which describes a species of advantage occurring more or less in all sorts of work, and which ought justly to be equally divided among all the hands engaged, in proportions corresponding with the labors of each. But Smart was not the only peculator I had to contend with. Of course, I could not long remain ignorant of the usages of the business; and I now discovered that the overseer, Mr. Y——, who was supposed to be a secret small partner, and who had a reputation among the body for "exalted piety," and with the ostensible proprietor of the office for admirable management, made no sort of scruple of cheating when he could. For instance, I wrought until twelve o'clock at his request for four successive nights, and till after one for the two following; but not being aware that I was entitled to anything extra for the night-work, I charged nothing in my bill for it, and when, a month afterwards, having discovered my mistake, I made a claim for the amount, he refused to pay it on the ground that I had forfeited it by not charging it at the time.

Although doing much more work in this office than I was ever paid for, owing to the "admirable management" of the overseer, I yet earned a great deal more than it is generally possible to do in the larger houses where the scale is rigidly adhered to. The reason was, that I wrought longer hours, and was allowed to work as many hours as I chose during the day. I was in my frame every morning at six, and seldom left before ten, often not till midnight; but my health and constitution were then first-rate, my habits frugal and temperate; and fatigue, if it came at all in the week, came late on the Saturday, and was dissipated by the repose of the Sunday. My bills were rarely less than forty shillings, and often above fifty weekly; but they were seldom paid without a hint that I was earning too much money, and it was plain to me, though I could never comprehend for what reason, that I should have been more welcome had I written less. During the first two weeks of each month, the old man, who seldom earned above a dozen shillings, and myself were the only journeymen compositors employed. There were twelve apprentices in all, nine of whom wrought in a room by themselves upon the best work the house afforded. Upon the whole, the establishment ought to have been immensely profitable, as the amount of wages paid weekly could hardly have been a third of the value of the work done. Much of the press-work was monopolized by a machine in the cellar, driven by an Irish engine of flesh and blood—and potatoes—who turned the handle for half-a-crown a day, finding his own steam; and the whole of the reading was ground off for a pound a-week by a young parson waiting for a "call."

Before I had been here two months there came a Greek volume to be printed, with Latin notes and scholia. This, which was fortunately considered too hard a bone for the apprentices, turned out an extremely good job for the compositor. The old man and I were taken from the magazine and set about it—but after a few trials the old man gave it up as a bad job, knowing nothing of either language, and being half blind with age. After the first few days, when I had thoroughly mastered the Greek case, I found it an easy thing to earn, at the hours I was working, twelve shillings a day upon it; and I labored diligently to make hay while the sun shone. But yet I could not get it out so fast as it was required, and therefore a Greek compositor was advertised for, and engaged to assist. When I heard that a Grecian was coming, I expected, as a matter of course, to see a first-class man, one of the gentlemen of the trade, and was not a little astonished to behold a wretched grimy specimen of humanity, nearly forty years of age, fluttering in rags, and literally scaled with filth, with scarcely a shirt and but an apology for shoes, inducted into the next frame to mine as my coadjutor. He was a positive scarecrow, but his appearance was no index of his ability. He rained a perfect storm of Greek type into his empty case as he began distribution, and picked it up again when he commenced composing with proportionate rapidity; and I expected that he would reap a tremendous harvest and make short work of the whole volume. But I found that his industry was of a very fitful kind and required a vigorous stimulus. He had hardly been two hours at work, and earned as many shillings, when he assailed the overseer, who just then entered the room, for an advance of wages, on the ground of utter destitution through recent illness and want of employment. The overseer looked at what he had done, and handed him half-a-crown, with which he shot down stairs at once, and returned in a few minutes with a pint of gin, a penny loaf and a lump of cheese. The whole of the gin disappeared in the course of the next hour; the bread and cheese furnished his meals for the remainder of the day. He left at seven in the evening, borrowing a few shillings "to pay his lodging." He "showed" again next day at a quarter to ten—again borrowed his gin-money, and wasted an hour in emptying the bottle in small sips "to steady his nerves" before he began work.

He was not long of discovering that I was a stranger to the customs of the trade, and took upon himself to lay down the law for the conduct of the work we were upon. He first proposed that we should work in pocket—he taking the Greek and I the Latin—a proposition which would have been advantageous to both had he possessed average industry. Finding I would not have a partnership, he informed me bluntly that I had no business to work the hours I did, and that I was robbing him by taking more than my share of a profitable job. An appeal was made to the overseer, and knowing his dislike to heavy bills, I was fearful of the result; but the work was wanted in a hurry, and he decided in my favor, recommending the Grecian to use equal diligence and earn as much as he could. For some days after he made a show of extraordinary industry, and certainly did a great deal of work. New type was now supplied to us as fast as it was wanted, as no proofs were to be returned for press until the whole was in the hands of the editor. I felt now pretty sure of getting three-fourths of the whole to my own share, and labored on sedulously for three months, receiving between three and four pounds every Saturday night.

At the end of this period a very unsavory fact came to light. The overseer, whose "admirable management" was no match for the tactics of the ragged Grecian, suddenly discovered, upon examining the accounts, that more money had been paid to us than the composition of the whole work should have cost, while a pile of "copy" yet remained untouched. We were called down and "blown up." A stormy explosion was followed by a rigid scrutiny, our several pages were examined and proved—when it came to light that my gin-drinking comrade had been "writing horse," as it is termed, or charging for more than he had done, to the tune of 14*l*. 10*s*. The rascal confessed with a leer that he had been regulating his bills by mine, but said he was willing to do the work for which he had been paid. Thus he managed to get an equal share after all; for there was no other remedy than to let him work out his debt, which he did at his leisure, much to the mortification of the printer, who disobliged his employers by the delay, and still more to time, who saw myself swindled by the tricksy manœuvre of a lazy scamp out of some weeks' profitable employment.

Meanwhile other hands had been engaged upon the magazine, and I found myself in the very unenviable position of a hanger-on, with not above one-third of my time employed, and that so unprofitably that my receipts were reduced to the level of those of an apprentice-boy. I was obliged to draw upon my previous savings to pay current expenses. It was now the beginning of August, and knowing by this time that a flood of hands would be discharged upon the trade very speedily, from the approaching cessation of business in the Government houses, I was anxious to get into some remunerating employ before that awkward crisis came. I consulted the old man, with whom I was a favorite, as to what was best to be done. He had a grandson, he said, apprenticed to a compositor who had "farmed" a newspaper, and was doing it cheap for the proprietors with their own materials. He thought they were about increasing the size of the paper, and might want a hand or two. At my request, he gave me a note to Mr. B——, upon presenting which at the office in a street running out of the Strand, I was, to my utter amazement, introduced by a sooty little urchin to the identical "sheep's-head delinquent" who seven years before had decamped with my sovereign from the dingy crib in Clare-market, and who now, perched upon a high stool in a little closet lined with lamp-black and curtained with cobwebs, and holding my opened note in his hand, was lord in the ascendant of the typographical department of the —— newspaper. He was clad in a new suit, extra genteelly cut, wore a gaudy gold ring on his little finger, and a brilliant bob in the breast of his shirt;

but the habit of dirty fingers, too strong for his gentility, had spotted his clean linen with dabs of dust; and the habit of beer ' in moderation" had stained his light waistcoat with the trickling signature of John Barleycorn. I knew him instantly, and could scarcely refrain from laughing when I contrasted the present mixture of dirt and finery which his figure presented with the wretched habiliments of 1826. I saw, too, that the recognition was mutual, and was far from enjoying the distressing state of confusion and incoherency into which my apparition had thrown him. His first impulse was to leap from the stool and seize me by the hand; but before he had half done it, a second thought impelled him back to his seat, upon which he fidgeted about, and read and re-read the note I had brought, looking over it at me as I stood before him with as unconcerned a countenance as I could assume. He changed from red to pale ten times in as many minutes, and was evidently at a complete nonplus, and unable to deliver himself from the dilemma into which my arrival had thrown him. At length he ventured upon a question:—

"How long have you worked in London?"

"Only since last March."

"Was you ever in London before?"

"I was here in 1826, but could not find work."

"Well—and where did you find it?"

(I thought I would give him a little relief.) "I was fortunate enough to meet with a *kind friend* who advised me to go to France, while I had the means I went over, and stayed there till the Revolution. I have always felt grateful for that advice, and always shall feel so."

My examiner buried his face in an old proof as I spoke, and the stool on which he sat rang with a tremulous motion against the ground. When he had made a show of reading to the end of the paragraph, he said in a voice of forced indifference, "Well, I'm busy now; call in the morning, and I'll give you a frame."

I was as glad to get away as he was to get rid of me, and left the house with the intention, for sheer humanity's sake, of troubling him no more. Upon turning the matter, however, over in my mind, I became aware of two very good reasons why I should keep the appointment he had made. In the first place, if I did not go near him he would probably imagine that I should divulge his former failing to the members of the trade, and in subjecting him to the terror of that I should be inflicting upon him the very trouble which I was really anxious to spare him, and, in the next place, there was no reason upon earth why any previous misconduct of his should operate to my present disadvantage, or even prevent him from making me reparation, if he chose to do so, in any way that might offer. One thing I decided upon, and that was, utterly to ignore the adventure of the sheep's-head supper unless he should himself choose to revive it. So I called the next morning at the time appointed. I had done right. He was plainly relieved to see me; and, leading me up-stairs to the composing-room, gave me a frame next to that of his son Jem—the little Jem that had pawned the flat-irons—now a really good-looking stripling of fifteen, and as sharp-witted, fast-handed a compositor as any of his age.

I never had reason to regret the policy I had pursued in this instance. Though B—— never made any allusion to our first meeting, he made me manifold reparation for the trifling loss it had occasioned. Besides the work which he threw into my hands on two days and a night of every week, he procured me the translation of certain French documents, for which I was paid at a much higher rate, and he allowed me many indulgences which I should never have received or expected at the hands of a perfect stranger.

B—— was making money fast, and bade fair to become a man of wealth and consideration in time. He "made up" the paper with his own hands, and went through the business with a systematic rapidity and dexterity not to be surpassed. With the exception of a " turnover" from the country, and myself, he had no journeymen to pay. He had eight apprentice-boys besides his own son, and all these he housed and fed, and having them continually under his own eye, had trained them to discipline and punctuality, and made their co-operation nearly as efficient as that of regular journeymen. He would infallibly have made his fortune, and done more than he did towards the ruin of the working-printers' interests, had he possessed sufficient foresight to have bought shares in the newspaper he was printing, and thus secured its continuance. This, if he thought of it at all, he deferred and neglected until it was too late. The proprietorship underwent a complete change about two months after my engagement commenced. A printer of some standing became a shareholder to a large amount, and owner of the "plant" of materials; and B—— received one fine morning notice of the approaching termination of his contract, and was left at the end of a month with his son and eight apprentices as his entire stock-in-trade. He was not an atom daunted by this untoward catastrophe. Too well inured to fluctuations of fortune to suffer his philosophy to be disturbed, he buttoned up his pocket, by this time tolerably well lined, turned over his boys, some of them "for a consideration," to parties who were but too willing to have them, and giving me a letter of recommendation to the new printer, snapped his fingers at the world, and, conscious of the improved value of his services from his late experience, threw himself upon the market.

Between the magazine and the newspaper, working three days a-week upon what I could get by the one, and two days and a night upon the other, I had managed to do tolerably well. I applied without loss of time to the new printer; but he, having already a good staff of hands, declined my services altogether. It was now November; the trade was dull as the weather, the dirty Grecian, who, notwithstanding his large earnings, had not spent one penny on his wardrobe, still clung tenaciously to the few author's proofs, and was not got rid of without some difficulty, and more pecuniary loss, when, towards the end of the month, the last sheet was sent to press. My circumstances were not much improved by his departure. I could not expect to displace the man who had succeeded me upon the magazine, and who, to the great mortification of Parson Smart, had vindicated his rights, and secured to himself a full share of the advantages which the other had been used to monopolize. I hung about the office day after day, doing little or nothing, and, to get rid of the miserable torment of idleness, employed myself at the fireside in poring over an old German grammar which I found lying in the dust on an old shelf. While thus engaged one morning, and superintending the general "dangle" of chops, steaks, rashers, and red-herrings, which were to be discussed at the dinner-hour, H———, the old man, brought me the morning's *Times*, and pointed to an advertisement for a printer well versed in every department, to take the management of a small office. I was heart-sick of the horrible aspect of November in London, with next to nothing to do, and I wrote off to the advertiser by that day's post, and offered, if he would pay expenses down, to traverse the seventy miles between us and talk the matter over. I received an answer by return of post, acceding to my proposal, and the next morning, having nothing to delay me, mounted the coach, and descended at the advertiser's door about five in the afternoon.

I found my principal in the person of a cutler, a little, active, grizzle-pated man of fifty, occupied behind his counter in riveting a pair of scissors. He invited me into a little dark parlor, and producing my letter, began upon the business at once "I am going to start a newspaper," said he. "in this town. There is not one here, and I have made up my mind that it will pay. I am no printer—have hardly seen the whole of the business of printing in operation ; and, to be plain with you, unless you are master of the whole art and mystery, you will not do for me. But I know the thing is easy enough ; and I have two lads whom I intend to teach the business—when I know it myself. You may have them at your disposal as soon as you like, if we come to terms; but you must act candidly, and make no mystery of anything."

I represented to him that one man could not compose an entire newspaper, and that it would be necessary to have several hands besides, as well as an editor and reporter.

"I shall be editor and reporter myself," said he, "and I think one good hand may do very well when the boys begin to be useful. In the meantime, there will be a month to prepare and get out the first number. I have no office yet. The types and press will be in town to-morrow, and we are clearing out a place over the way to put them in. I can borrow assistance from my friend the printer in the market-place, with whom I shall not interfere, and whom I have been urging for this last year to start this thing himself, but he has not the pluck. This place is as dull as a prison for five days in the week, but we have a capital market on Wednesday, the day we shall publish the paper. I shall cut what I want out of the London papers, and add the local news and the state of the markets all round the county, which I have been in the habit for some time of supplying to the *County Gazette*. The paper will be small, four pages, the size of the *Dispatch*, and the type big enough for the old farmers to read without spectacles."

I told him that I had no notion that the thing would succeed, even if we were able to do it. He said he did not care a rivet about my notions; he had not sent for me to give him my notions, but to do his work, if I chose to do it at a fair price. Was I willing to make the attempt, and leave him to play the fool if he liked? That was the question; and, further, if I were disposed to sell him my labor, what was the price of it? Conceiving that I had an original to deal with, I withheld all further objections, and let him have his own way. As to price, I demanded the standard "stab." wages, thirty-six shillings a-week. This, he said, was exorbitant, and more than he would pay; and we were on the point of parting on the subject of wages, when he asked what I would take if he boarded and lodged me. I said I would allow fifteen shillings for that; and, after trying in vain to knock off the odd shilling, he finally agreed to give me a guinea a-week, and to find me a home, for six months certain.

Our agreement concluded, my employer rung the bell, and ordered a strapping wench, who answered the summons, to show me to the spare room, to carry my trunk thither, and then to prepare tea, and be quick about it. Having taken formal possession of my quarters, which looked pleasantly upon a third of an acre of garden-ground at the back of the house, and removed the stains of travel from my face and person, I descended to the tea-table, where I found the whole family assembled, consisting of my principal, his wife, with an infant in arms, a grown-up daughter of twenty, and two lads of fourteen and sixteen. There were two younger boys absent at school, who made their first appearance at home at the Christmas holidays. During the whole of my domiciliation among them, I was received and treated in all respects as one of the family, and never had cause to regret the engagement I had formed. The next day the materials, which had been bought a bargain from the assignees of a bankrupt printer in a neighboring town, were unloaded from a wagon into a long room prepared for their reception, over a cart-shed opposite our dwelling When I had opened the various packages, and made myself master of their contents, I was not a little chagrined at the sight of the trumpery outfit they presented to view. When all were at length displayed and arranged in some sort of order, I told my employer that it would never do to make a beginning with such a plant, the full value of which was not forty pounds altogether.

"I should wonder if it was," said he, "since I gave but twenty pounds for the lot. But if they have served to print a newspaper already, I don't see why they should not do so again." With that he drew from his pocket a number of the defunct *County Advertiser*, printed and published by the former owner of the rubblish before me, and put it into my hands.

It was a curious and unique specimen of the newspaper-press; four small pages of wretched, last-dying-speech-looking print, intersected with gaping blanks of white paper, with hardly one entire column plainly legible, through having been worked at a ricketty press; the type was of all sizes, from that of the largest Church-bible print to that of the smallest used in a newspaper. All sorts of miserable shifts and contrivances had been resorted to to accomplish the fourth page; f's had been turned upside down to do duty as j's; h's had consented to stand upon their heads out of a similar friendship for the y's; c and e had made common cause together; and, which was worst of all, two, three, and even four different sizes and sorts of type had been pressed into the service of one paragraph. My employer stared at me as, with looks of mortification and contempt, I conned this precious document.

"Well," said he, "what do you think of that? Can't we do the same?"

"Heaven forbid!" said I. "This is all I have to say: that if you expect me to become a party to such an execrable abortion as this, you have mistaken your man. I must have proper materials, or I don't go to work. As for that lot of rotten timbers, which was once a press, I shall not take the trouble to put it together, since it can do no better than this. I would rather forfeit my expenses, and return to London."

"Stop!" said he, "not so fast, if you please. I have intended to procure another press, but thought we might make a beginning with this until we feel our way."

"No," I replied, "such a beginning would ruin the attempt. You may buy a press for thirty pounds, and you must spend as much more for type ere we can begin."

This was a species of opposition he had not expected, and he hesitated a good deal before he made up his mind. He left the place suddenly, without saying a word, and returned in a few minutes, with his friend the printer of the town. This gentleman settled the business in a few words; the press was condemned to the flames, and a second-hand iron one ordered from Distaff-lane; and a fount of long-primer, for which the town-printer had no use, was exchanged for a quantity of placard and hand-bill type of no service to us. With this alteration in the stock I declared myself content, and then, with some degree of satisfaction, set about the purgation of the cases, all in a state of villanous disorder, and making preparation for the first number. The indefatigable proprietor was in the office early and late, and made himself master of all the details of the business, and actually picked up the column which formed his first "leader" with his own fingers. The type, which had been more abused and neglected than fairly worn, gave a good impression from the platten of an excellent "Stanhope," and the addition we had made to it prevented the necessity of recurring to any of the horrible contrivances above mentioned.

The town destined to be enlightened by the new publication, though not the capital of the county, yet contains a population of near seven thousand, and boasts one of the largest and best-frequented markets in the country. It is surrounded with extensive and well-stocked downs and sheep-pastures, where hundreds of thousands of those animals, under the care of shepherds, who for months together never see the face of man, wander, with their guardian dogs, in blissful unconsciousness of the farmer's shears or the butcher's knife. More than a dozen villages, situated beneath the abrupt declivities of the high grazing-grounds or on the banks of clear streams, are the abodes of the graziers and sheep-farmers, who form, with their drovers and attendants, the dense and motley population which crowds into the town on the early dawn of the Wednesday's market. The number of "traps," or light spring-carts, which at noon, on market-day, line the back thoroughfares and approaches to the town, for miles in length, afford substantial evidence, by their neat and trim condition, of the comfort and prosperity of their owners. The market-place, though large, overflows into all the surrounding approaches with a plethora of horses, oxen, pigs, sheep, and poultry, and provender for cattle; while every trader erects his "standing" for the day of business which is to recompense him for the idleness of the week. Cheap Jack appears upon the scene with his heavy-laden cart, and roaring like a cataract through his battered tin trumpet, intones his litany of lies in a voice of thunder, and most effectually shears the yokels who shear the sheep. By two or three o'clock in the afternoon, the business transactions of the market are generally over, and then commences the ceremony of wetting the bargains made, without which they would not be thought to stand good. Every birth of commerce is baptized in "gin-tickle," and libations in strict proportion to the amount of traffic flow freely down the throats of the thirsty votaries. As the evening draws on the "traps," gigs, and dog-carts draw off; the burly graziers and farmers, swaying from side to side and staggering like tottering nine-pins, are hoisted by the publican, ever careful of his customers, into their separate vehicles, and by eight or nine o'clock the market is clear, the streets deserted, silence resumes her reign, and the dull town, asleep in the starlight, shows not a symptom of life or breath save a few glimmering lights, and not a sound is heard but the slow-pacing regular foot-fall of the guardian of the night

When I first beheld the multitudinous market I was no longer surprised at the speculation of my employer, and only wondered that it had been so long delayed. He knew well what he was about. He had long before deposited his securities and got his paper from the Stamp-office; and having well placarded the town for three weeks, and puffed the adjacent villages, till not a soul remained ignorant of his intentions, he published the first number on the appointed day, and got rid of the whole impression before noon. A second edition was exhausted by sunset, and altogether six hundred copies went off on the first day. He would not print more, though there were demands for the paper up to Friday morning—judging it as well, he said, to have the thing inquired after. This speculation succeeded, and paid a good profit, as the projector had anticipated, from the very first. The expense of production, beyond the cost of stamped paper and my wages, was next to nothing. The elder lad collected advertisements and local news, the younger composed slowly but correctly within a month. The cutler made himself a pair of editorial scissors, and used them with so much good judgment that his second and third pages, small as they were, contained all the news of the week. He wrote his own leading articles which he suited admirably to the taste of his customers; and he chronicled the state of the markets of the county with such fidelity and carefulness as to become an authority on that particular branch of news among surrounding editors. In short, he did the work, as he had intended to do it, well and thoroughly, and reaped his reward in the patronage and approbation of the public.

I had quite enough to do, and often worked late at night during the first two months, notwithstanding I had assistance from the office of my employer's friend, the established printer of the town. But as the paper made its way, and the number of standing advertisements increased, and as the lad under my care became more rapid and skilful in his work, my labors lessened in proportion, and I enjoyed the opportunities of leisure which now became frequent. In compensation for working all Tuesday night, and till late in the day on Wednesday, I had the whole of Thursday to myself, when I wandered on the Downs, and, as the spring advanced, fished for trout in the brooks—and in wet weather pursued my studies in my own room, or by the fire-side at home. Long before the termination of my six months' engagement I saw clearly enough that it was not the intention of my employer to renew it. I had fulfilled the mission for which he had hired me, and had taught him and his boys all that they needed to know of a business which, for all useful purposes, may be as easily acquired in six months as seven years. I was not therefore surprised when, at the end of April, he asked me what I intended to do at the termination of our contract. I told him at once that I should return to London, and informed him at the same time that he would have to pay my expenses back, as my services were not to endure for twelve months. He said he was perfectly willing to do so; and engaging in my stead the town printer's apprentice, now out of his time, who had given us his assistance all along on the nights previous to publication, he gave me my discharge, together with a moderate gratuity as a token of regard, and paid my fare to London in the latter end of May, 1834.

I returned to town five-and-twenty pounds richer than I had left it six months before, and with health and spirits renewed by my country sojourn, as well as somewhat wiser from the experience I had acquired. Not relishing the idea of again hanging-on upon the magazine, which, as I understood from Parson Smart, whom I met in the street, was still in the same hands as when I left London, I applied for work and obtained it in a house occasionally employed by Government in the manufacture of blue-books, and sometimes by the India House in the production of volumes of an analogous nature. I arrived just in time to witness a very profitable dodge, by which John Bull, whose pockets lie invitingly open to the experiments of the ingenious, was made to contribute a tolerably round sum to the hoards of the printer. It happened at this particular juncture that the India Board had ordered a good thick volume upon the affairs of Hindostan, to be printed in demy quarto: the bountiful Providence that watches over the interests of the master printer had so ordered it that Government should give directions for printing the same volume in foolscap folio, the standard size of the blue-book boluses which the public are supposed to swallow for the correction of their internal disorders. The printer employed on that occasion by the Government immediately transferred his job to him of the India House, who being of an economical disposition, printed both from the same type, first working, as the several sheets were ready for press, the quarto edition for the India House, and then, swelling out the pages to the folio size by the insertion of blank spaces between the lines and headings, working the folio copy for the Government. By this ingenious manœuvre the whole expense of composition and reading was saved on the Government edition, and the public had a thousand or so of quarto pages for which they paid a folio price, nearly three-fourths of which price was a clear gain to the colluding typographists.

The work in which I was directed to take a share, was a volume of corporation matters, containing a large number of municipal charters, the whole of which were written in lawyer's hand in Latin, if Latin one may call such canine stuff as the monks and clerks of the feudal ages, in their learned ignorance, perpetrated so plentifully. It was now that, for the first time in my life, I became acquainted with the anomalous mode of conducting business which prevails among the working printers in the larger offices in London. I have mentioned in a former section of these reminiscences that my knowledge of Latin, such as it is, never put a pound into my pocket: it might and would have done so on the present occasion had I been allowed to reap the advantage of it, but that would have been decidedly against the regulations of the trade; and I was virtually reduced to utter ignorance of the language by being placed upon the same level as those who had never learned it. This was accomplished in the following manner; and in describing the method pursued, I do no more than describe the system which is in operation at the present hour in all large houses—which is recognized by the Printers' Trades Union, and which the masters find themselves compelled to countenance. Not only were the hours of labor limited, by agreement among the working themselves, to a certain number for every day, before or after which it was forbidden to touch a type—a plan which, in the present instance, prevented my working before eight in the morning or after eight at night, or making any use of the time allotted for meals—but the amount of work we were severally permitted to execute was also limited to the capacity of the meanest workman in the companionship. Sixty hours, or ten hours a-day, was decreed as the working time of the week; and in order, it would appear, to keep all the hands upon the same dead level, no man could be paid for more than sixty hours' work, whatever amount he might perform. The work being almost entirely Latin, the quantity to be done in an hour had been calculated upon the presumed ignorance of all the workmen engaged upon it, and was but little more than two-thirds of the usual number of lines. Entirely ignorant of the extraordinary principle upon which we were doing business, I wrought for the first week with all the energy of which I was capable, and at the end of it had eighty-two hours to charge, and which, of course, I expected to be paid for. The general bill paid eightpence an hour, owing to an unusual number of blank and short pages, for which compositors charge the same as for those full of matter; and I looked, as a matter of course, for 2*l*. 14*s*. 8*d*. But shortly before the hour of payment, the clicker came round with some small scraps of paper in his hand, containing the bills for the week of the several compositors, and presented me in my turn with mine, which ran thus:

Sixty hours £2 0 0
On the shelf, 22 hours

"On the shelf," thought I, as I blushed up to the ears with the combined consciousness of mortification and ignorance. "What blessed mystery is this?" There was nothing for it but to confess my inexperience to a comrade, and demand an explanation.

"Oh," said the beery genius to whom I applied, "it's all right. Strike me sensible! I'll show you the fake as clear as mud! You see, my fine fellow, you're a precious sight too hungry—you've put the steam on too fast—you want to come the fire-eater over us. You'll find it's of no use doing more than your hours in the long run, leastways except it's for your own convenience. If you've got a score of hours on the shelf this week, you needn't do but forty next, you'll have the whole sixty all the same. You thought yourself in luck, I suppose, because you had nothing to do in your proofs? That last proof of mine took me three hours to correct."

"In luck!" said I. "I have taken the trouble to learn the language."

"Have you?" retorted he. "Then I can tell you we are not going to pay you for it. You'll find it don't do to be greedy; you must take what comes, and *mike* (be idle) a bit now and then, if you are such a fast man."

I was astonished at this disgraceful explanation of the mystery, but soon found that, absurd and mischievous as is the principle involved, my companion had stated nothing but the truth. My superfluous earnings went to swell those of my coadjutors, and I had gained the privilege of being as lazy as I chose on the following week, three days of which would enable me to get up to the average.

The second week, so soon as I had made up at my leisure the required number of hours, which happened about noon on the Thursday I sat down quietly under my frame to the study of the German grammar, considering that a better use of my time than working for the benefit of my companions. In the course of the afternoon, the overseer came round, and seeing me sitting still, demanded the reason. I told him I had done my week's work; that if I did more I should not be paid for it, and had therefore declined taking more copy. Though he must have been perfectly aware of the system pursued, he would not appear to recognize it, but flew into a passion, and swore he would not keep his frames idle, adding, that if I did not choose to proceed with my work, he should put another man in my place, and I might quit the house at once. Thus I was compelled to work the rest of the week, or at least to make a show of working, and again had ten additional hours on the shelf on the Saturday night. This continued so long as the Latin copy lasted. At the end of six weeks I had shelved seventy hours, which, for all I know, are on the shelf to this day, since I never got anything for them, probably through my ignorance of the proper mode, if there be any, of turning them to account. The reader will see that the operation of this execrable system of management is to reduce the character and efficiency of the best workman to that of the worst, or at least to the average standard, and to clap an extinguisher on industry and emulation: it is, in fact, the compositors' scheme of protection, and has the inherent vice of all schemes of protection, inasmuch as it is fit for nothing but to secure to the idle and inefficient workman a greater share than he has a right to of the rewards of the more industrious and effective, at the expense of the latter.

When the charters were completed we grew more busy and wrought longer hours; and I was now amazed at the latent powers of some whom I had looked upon as drones while working on a foreign tongue, and who now did seventy-two hours weekly without attending longer than when but sixty were required of them. Some additional hands were now put on the work, and among them, to my mortification, I recognized one of my quondam companions in the Rue du Pont de Lodi. This fellow, who was a Cockney of the worst school, whose conversation was made up of obscenity and slang, and with whom, from a natural antipathy to the species, I had never associated in Paris, soon began to make himself offensive to me, and to render my position anything but pleasant. At his instigation I was immediately dubbed "Professor," in allusion to my attempts at tuition in France. Sham disputes and altercations were got up on various topics, and finally laid before me for decision. My opinion was demanded with ironical gravity on the simplest points of grammar and punctuation, and if I refused to give it, a general groan of the most dolorous and wailing character was growled from every throat. If, for the sake of quietness, I gave my honest opinion, it was received with universal thanks and the most profound expression of obligation, equally disagreeable and tantalizing. I resolved to hold my peace, and let things take their course; but my temper, which was never one of the meekest, drew me into a difficulty. My tormentor, feeling secure of his game, from the general sympathy of his companions, thought fit one afternoon to make some offensive personal remarks, which so exasperated me, that I foolishly walked into his frame, hauled him out, and with a blow between the eyes felled him to the ground. For this I was "chapelled" on the spot—that is, I was tried by a general jury of the whole room for a breach of the peace, and fined five shillings by sentence of the "father" of the chapel for striking a comrade. There was much amusement at my expense; the "professor" was pronounced "pugilistic," and that epithet was henceforth added to the sobriquet with which I was honored. The money was transformed into gin and beer, and drunk on the spot, and three hours were wasted in hiccuping jobations upon the enormity of my offence. Ironical references to me on difficult questions were now more numerous than ever; and each man, as he came up to my frame on his pretended consultation, armed himself with a huge letter-board as a shield against my fist, and peeped over it with mimic fear and terror as he made his request. All this occasioned me considerable loss of time, as well as infinite annoyance.

The *Times* newspaper was taken in daily, and it was the office of each compositor in turn to read the debates and leaders aloud for the benefit of the rest. When it came to my turn, they could never understand my "professional" mode of reading, and made me many humble requests for explanation. Seeing that nothing would please them, and finding myself baited beyond endurance, I resolved to put an end to it one way or other.

While cogitating some plan for the purpose, my eye fell one morning upon an advertisement in the first page of the *Times*, which I hastily copied out in my bill-book, and which was to the following effect: "The services of a gentleman are required who will take charge of the boys of the —— School, out of school-hours, and render occasional assistance in the classes. Address, stating qualifications and terms, to X. Y. Z.," &c. &c. Thinking it at least worth trying for, and hoping it might emancipate me from my present uncomfortable position, I forwarded a note to X. Y. Z, giving myself the best character my conscience would allow, and referring to Dr. D——, at F——d, who I knew would give me a testimonial. By return of post, I received a direction to apply personally to the Head Master, the Rev. Mr. E——, in the town of——, on whom rested the onus of selecting from the various applicants. I procured leave of absence from the overseer, and next day set off by coach to ——, to try my fortune with the reverend pedagogue.

CHAPTER IX.

I am engaged at the Grammar School—Farewell for a time to the Printing Office—Enter upon my new duties—My Companions and Coadjutors —Up in the morning early—The Mortal Body—"Plugger"—The life of an Usher in a School—Value of Time—Arrival of "Tater," and establishment of the drill—A mutinous Militia—The Whisker Synod— A domestic Revolution and a Barring-out—Precautions against Starvation—Physical force triumphant—The Christmas Holidays—Parson Smart and my Sheep's-head Patron again—I go to work temporarily on a Weekly Paper—A Popular Author and Burglary Historian— The Mysteries of Romance Writing—The Mushroom Literature which springs up in a night—Desperate resources of Genius—I surrender my post.

I DESCENDED from the coach at the gate of the grammar-school about twelve o'clock in the day, and was ushered into the presence of the comely and portly pedagogue, the Rev. Mr. E———, who sat reading, in his morning-gown and easy chair, in a well-curtained study surrounded with the gilded tomes of authors in all languages, living and dead. Though on the verge of threescore years, the head-master was yet a handsome man, majestic in figure, affable in manners, and the very incarnation of condescension and considerate politeness. He received me graciously, and having listened to my application, proceeded to test my qualifications for the office I proposed to undertake. He spoke French with a sort of home-made accent, but with perfect grammatical correctness, and even idiomatic propriety; and condescended to receive, or pretend to receive, information from me on the subject of the syntax of the participles. He examined me in Latin, and bade me first construe and then scan a passage in the Heautontimorumenos of Terence. With the translation he professed himself more than content, but candidly told me, what was true enough, that I appeared to have paid but little attention to quantity, and advised me by all means to study it sedulously. I promised to do so—a promise, by the way, which I have very indifferently kept, having never yet been impressed with the importance of knowing the pronunciation of a tongue which nobody speaks. I then produced a small portfolio of drawings, with which he was pleased; and he said that that accomplishment would make me popular with the boys, who, most of them, took lessons from a drawing-master twice in the week. He read the testimonials which I produced, declared himself perfectly satisfied with regard to them, and then entered upon the question of salary. This, after some fencing on both sides, was finally settled to my perfect content, at a sum which would allow me to save quite as much as though I were earning full wages as a compositor, while I expected to be leading a life of comparative leisure, an expectation which the result was far from realizing. I returned to London in the afternoon, pledged to enter on my scholastic duties on that day fortnight, by which time the boys were expected to re-assemble for the half-year.

The next morning, which was Saturday, I gave the overseer a fortnight's notice, in conformity with the regulations of the trade; and on his expressing surprise and persuading me to stay, I made him acquainted with the step I had taken, and with my reasons for taking it. He instantly sent for my tormentor, and after rating him soundly, by way of retributive justice, told him, that, since he had forced me to leave, he also must take his departure, and gave him formal notice to quit in no very flattering terms. The rest of my short time at the office passed quietly enough. There was a marked difference in the conduct of my companions, who, so far from molesting me as before, seemed now willing to make amends for past annoyances. They expected, in fact, that I would remain after the other had left, and were not a little surprised to see me pack up on the second Friday morning, and take myself off.

It was nearly nine o'clock in the evening, when, accompanied by all my worldly goods, I arrived at the grammar-school in the town of ——, where I was destined to take up my residence for twelve months. Having inquired for the reverend principal, he came forth from his study, and leading the way into a large room looking upon the lawn which abutted upon the turnpike-road, introduced me to four gentlemen who, seated round the window in the twilight, had watched my arrival, and, engaged in conversation, were waiting the appearance of an early supper. Two of them, like myself, were strangers, and had not been an hour in the building when I first joined them. One was the new writing-master, a man of extraordinary skill in his own proper department, who, with an entire devotion to his art, nourished a profound contempt for every other species of accomplishment, save only the arts of cricket and fives-playing. The other was a young man of about five-and-twenty, with a remarkable talent for silence, and, as we were not long of finding out, with no other talent of any kind. The two old hands, who, by way of distinction, called themselves the "stickers," were the youngest of the party. Y——, the mathematical teacher, was but seventeen years of age, but he was on the way to become a sound mathematician and algebraist, though he was hardly fitted for a school, owing to his fiery and uncontrollable temper. T——, the classical teacher, was one year older, and was a model of gentlemanly deportment, as well as of personal beauty—astonishingly well read, for his years, in the Greek and Latin classics, and the best German writers to boot—and endowed with a patience which stupidity could not ruffle or obstinacy abate.

We who were the new-comers, were of course anxious to obtain what information we could respecting the nature of the occupations upon which we had entered. Neither of the "stickers" was a whit loth to gratify our curiosity to the fullest extent, and the whole economy of the school, which was but of comparatively recent establishment, the characters of the various masters, and the whimsical legislation of the Council in London, who had the absolute government of the whole affair, were passed under review with a degree of candor which would have astonished the parties concerned. The head-master, who received 400*l*. a year for his Greek and superintendence, was known among the boys by the endearing appellation of "the Pelican," from the singular and sole mode of punishment which he was ever known to inflict himself, and which consisted in his taking the delinquent to his own study, and there cramming him with Greek adapted to his capacity in *vivâ voce* lessons, thus feeding him, as the boys said, with his own life-blood. Whenever coporeal punishment was resorted to it was executed by the wardens, who acted as a kind of police in the play-ground, to keep the boys from wandering out of bounds. Next to the head-master were two second masters, one classical and one mathematical, at salaries of 200*l*. a-year each. These had separate studies of their own, and kept themselves totally aloof from the teachers, never exchanging a word with them, save in controlling their functions during school-hours. Of the boys, many were the sons of poor parents, and received their education for nothing; others were the sons of gentlemen, and paid for instruction; but all were treated rigidly alike, there being but one table and one kind of dormitory for the whole.

By the time we had discussed these particulars pretty freely it was eleven o'clock; and as we had to rise at half-past five, F——, the writing-master, took his candle and went up stairs towards bed. In two minutes he burst into the room again in a towering passion, and called us to follow him. It appeared that some young blackguard had grossly insulted him on his first entry into the long dormitory through which he had to pass to his own chamber. He had marked the delinquent, and was determined on redress. The mathematician ran down stairs to the steward's room, and brought up a small whip, which he thrust into F——'s hand, and we all mounted the stairs to witness the vindication of our authority. The large room was as still as death; not a breath was audible from above a hundred pretended sleepers. F—— marched to the simulating culprit and, uncovering him, dealt him such a punishment with the whip as set him bellowing with anguish. The noise of his roaring brought up the head-master, who found himself compelled unexpectedly to take the part of his subordinate, who, being a perfect stranger, had been gratuitously insulted, and who, by this prompt and vigorous assertion of a claim to respect, procured for himself a greater share of it than either one of his colleagues ever enjoyed during the twelve months of my stay in the school.

I was quartered in a double-bedded room with the silent youth who had come down to take charge of the junior classes, and to prepare them for the instruction of the teachers of the next degree. He relaxed his taciturnity a little when we were closeted together; and, after sundry "Hems!" and clearings of the throat, asked me, in a voice of deep solemnity, if I knew "whether they allowed grog after supper; had heard they did, but had not seen any to night."

I told him I did not concern myself about such trifles.

"A trifle do you call it? I am surprised at such a term. Sir, I wish you good night." And in five minutes he was asleep.

We were all roused from our slumbers at five in the morning by the clanging of a bell that would have almost waked a watchman. One part of my duty, in which the silent man was bound to co-operate, consisted in rousing 200 boys from bed, and getting them down to the lavatory, where they were taken charge of, the elder ones by the wardens and the younger ones by the servant-maids, and washed and combed, or compelled to make their own toilets, by the time the bell rang for prayers, at a quarter before seven. My coadjutor declined to rise at the instigation of the bell, and I had to rout up the whole school myself. He made his first appearance at the breakfast table at eight, and, pleading a bilious head-ache in excuse for his tardiness, devoured four or five rounds of hot toast and butter, and drank a quart of cocoa by way of specific. After breakfast, the new-comers were formally introduced to the boys, and the latter were made acquainted with the nature of our duties and the species of authority of which we were the delegates. I found the office I had undertaken not in very good odor. I had been appointed to the exercise of a function suggested by the Council in London, and which the scholars regarded as an infringement of their liberties; and I soon saw that if I was to be of any service, it must be by the exercise of forbearance and kindness, and not by the assertion of any species of authority; and I endeavored to regulate my conduct in accordance with this conviction.

I was subjected to a much more severe examination from the boys than I had undergone from the head-master. Being open to consultation on every subject, I was continually questioned upon all; and before twenty-four hours had elapsed, there was not a boy in the school who was ignorant either of what I did or did not know. This point settled, they bestowed upon me the sobriquet of "Omnium," in allusion to my various smatterings of knowledge, and left me pretty much to myself, all but the studious few who really meant to profit by such assistance as I could give. Their examination of my silent coadjutor was less satisfactory. They could get very little indeed out of him, but all that was in him they got; and they dubbed him, "Mortal Body," in allusion to his drowsy temperament and dogged silence. This genius stayed with us but a single month, proving a hindrance rather than a help. His whole idea of tuition consisted in the hearing of lessons gabbled over by rote, a system which was of no use at all in —— School, where the boys were taught instead of being órdered to learn, and where lessons were never committed to memory in any set form of words. We managed to get his history out of him before he went. *In vino veritas*, and in brandy-and-water, too;

so we got him grog after supper by pleading his delicate stomach with the matron, who sent him a "bottom of brandy" from the infirmary stores every night, which unlocked his tongue and made us acquainted with his past life. He was the son of a tradesman in Islington, and, having taken a violent fancy against business, had made the astounding blunder of supposing the life of an usher one of indolence and ease. Young as he was, his name was on the books of every school-agent in London. He had been despatched by these worthies successively to half the private boarding-schools in the kingdom, from all and each of which he had been bandied home again, generally with a quarter's salary, as the only mode of getting rid of him. He assured us that he had paid ninety pounds to J——n alone, whose best customer he was, and " who always treated him like a gentleman." He had not a single accomplishment beyond a tolerable share of penmanship, yet he never scrupled to apply for any situation that was vacant on the scholastic list, and he passed a good portion of his life in travelling about the country, at other people's expense, to and from the various appointments obtained by his unblushing pretensions. He had visited nearly all the celebrated schools in England, and could give a good account of the dietary of most of them, though he recollected nothing besides. He would eat, no matter what the viands, for a full hour after the rest of us had done supper, and would fall fast asleep on a bench in the school-room at eleven o'clock in the forenoon, having lain till eight when he ought to have risen at five. He disappeared one morning without beat of drum, being quietly dismissed by the good natured governor, whose patience he had thoroughly exhausted

With the departure of the Mortal Body my duties underwent some modification. The junior French classes came under my charge, an arrangement which brought me unpleasantly into collision with an ignorant fellow who had somehow secured the appointment of French teacher at a liberal salary, through his influence with the Council, but who, bred on board ship, was neither Frenchman nor grammarian in any sense of the term. He had contrived to pick up a small stock of phrases, and pretended to teach the language by conversation. The boys had nicknamed him "Plugger," in consequence of a habit he had of stopping both nostrils with his thumbs, in order to give effect to the French nasals—a help to pronunciation, however, in which he did not allow his pupils to indulge. He had been for three years indoctrinating the whole school upon his peculiar system, and of the whole two hundred pupils there were not yet to be found three who could read a verse of the French Testament at sight. I commenced operations on a different plan, combining Hamilton's method with oral instructions in grammar In the course of a month my classes read the Testament fluently—not from any merit of mine, but simply because they could not help doing so with daily practice in such a method. The "Plugger" took occasion to resent my interference; and though I had commenced with these classes solely to please the head-master, not being compelled to it by the terms of my engagement, the old gentleman found himself obliged, for the sake of peace, to put an end to my endeavors, in this department. In all other respects the studies of the school prospered satisfactorily. The mathematical master was a man of sterling qualities, in no way ignorant of his attainments and capabilities; and he was, fortunately for the school, a thorough proficient in the art, most difficult of acquirement of imparting instruction. He studied hard, and never lost a minute, withdrawing to his own room the moment he was released from school. I may mention that he subsequently carred off the highest degree at Cambridge, gained a fellowship of 500*l.* a-year, and is at this hour occupying a post the possession of which is a guarantee both of reputation and fortune. The classical master was of a different stamp. He was married, and thus had no chance of a fellowship. During the year he was absent for months together, keeping his terms at Trinity College, Dublin, from which he managed to squeeze out a degree by dint of a little ingenious hocus-pocus His subordinate, T——, was an infinitely better scholar than himself, and invariably took the upper class of pupils, even in his presence. The classical master is at the present moment a curate in a country town, upon eighty pounds a-year, " with a wife fat, dusty and deliquescent," and six young scions of the Church.

I have stated that at the sudden disappearance of the Mortal Body my duties underwent some modification; I shall describe them as they had settled into a habit within two months after my arrival, for the benefit of all hungry aspirants to a like post. At about a quarter after five in the morning, after the merciless bell had effectually banished the drowsy god, I turned out of my bed, and in five minutes was marching through the dormitories and arousing the sluggards. This ceremony had to be repeated several times—the older lads never rising without a dose of " cold pig." By about half-past six the bed-rooms would be empty and the lavatories full, the boys washing and being washed by the maids. Those who were first down enjoyed a game of play in the grounds, where I was always supposed to be present, to prevent boxing-matches and the breaking of bounds. At a quarter to seven the bell rang again for muster and prayers in the great school-room. Prayers were read by one of the masters, and being concluded in ten minutes, the old gentleman drew off his classes of Grecians to the Greek room, and left the rest to the care of his subordinates. I now took my stand at the head of an English grammar class; and while going through the lesson for the day, cut up a hundred turkey-quills into pens, or mended those made the day before. Two or three hundred serviceable pens were the consumption of the day, which F—— and I were expected to supply. At eight o'clock the whole school marched in to breakfast, under the superintendence of the head-master. This was despatched in about twenty minutes, when, grace being said, the boys burst into the play-ground, which I was obliged to patrol till they were recalled to school, at a quarter past nine.

I had now a couple of hours to make my own toilet and occupy as I chose. I devoted them to the study of German, under the guidance of T——. At a quarter past eleven my arithmetic-class was ready for me. At twelve the boys, again dismissed, required the superintendence of two of us until dinner, and after dinner till two o'clock. The afternoon was fully occupied with a class in the Delectus and the writing-classes, to whom I was general pen-mender. Each boy wrote but for a quarter of an hour each day, and in any copy-book that came to hand—leaving their ranks in turn to fill the vacancies at the writing-desk as fast as they occurred. At half-past four the school was dismissed to tea, and was again under my charge till seven, when all were once more assembled for an hour and a half. This period was devoted to mathematics and general history, but in fine weather was frequently passed in a ramble through the fields or in a game at cricket. At half-past eight the bell rang for supper, which was immediately followed by prayers, and at nine each of us marched off to get our several companies to bed. This was no easy business. Bolstering was very much in vogue, and when, in the dark, a hundred or two of sturdy young rebels were battling it in their night-shirts, it was next to impossible to restore order or to recognize the ringleaders. Fifty times have I sat by the hour together at a bed's foot, fiddling or fluting them to sleep; and often when, deceived by their audible snoring, I have left them in fancied repose, I have been compelled to return with lights, and all the assistance I could procure, to quell some horrible tumult which shook the house to its foundation. Sometimes it was a pitched battle, fought by the light of a smuggled candle, between two rival chiefs, whom we would surprise covered with blood and gasping with passion. Sometimes it was a descent of the Grecian phalanx, who would take it into their heads to go down with their bolsters, and "slaughter the Helots" for the fun of it; and whatever was the occasion of the riot, it was seldom quelled without our mingling in the contest armed with weapons of a more substantial description.

In spite of all we could do, and we usurped a deal more of authority than, under proper management, we should have been allowed or had occasion for, the discipline of the school, out of school-hours, was of the worst description, while we were worried and harassed almost beyond endurance. It was rarely before ten o'clock that we enjoyed a quiet hour, and though we generally pursued our studies till twelve, it was at the cost of much weariness and physical exertion. I had never before been so thoroughly impressed with the importance of time. With the exception of F———, the writing-master, every man in the establishment hoarded his minutes like guineas, turning every one to account in some way or other. T——— wrote every sermon he heard at church into Latin as it fell from the lips of the preacher; while Y——— pored over his prayer-book, pencil in hand, and covered the margin of every leaf with algebraic figures and formulas, or mathematical diagrams. The masters rose at the first peal of the morning bell, and worked hard privately until called into school. Each had an object before him, and strained every nerve to accomplish it. I was too much an imitator not to do the same; and giving my French for T———'s German, contrived to make some progress in the language, in spite of the scantiness of my opportunities

In the meanwhile, the effect I had been engaged to produce remained as great a desideratum as ever. The boys once familiarized with my position, soon learned to treat my unsupported authority with indifference; and the Council in London, resolved upon securing better discipline by some means or other, sent down a young Irish gentleman well salaried, and invested with authoritative control over the boys during the intervals between school-hours. "Squire Tater," as the rogues christened him, as soon as they heard the Hibernian accent, was an accomplished man of about thirty, who to a competent knowledge of chemistry, languages and practical science, united some harmless military experience, picked up on parade. He brought with him a small chemical laboratory, and gave lectures in the school room of an evening, illustrating them with amusing experiments. He became a prodigious favorite in the course of a few weeks. His gentlemanly manners won the respect of all whose respect was worth having, but his popularity unfortunately declined as rapidly as it had arisen. He had received orders from the Council to drill the boys, and to initiate them into the mysteries of right-about face, marching, wheeling, and forming squares, &c. &c. The urchins looked upon this as very good fun as long as it was a novelty, and flocked to the drill with all the eagerness that could be desired. But the novelty soon wore off, and the old love of trap, taw and fives, returned with renewed force. Now came the struggle. Tater, with the assistance of the ushers and wardens, forced them to the drill in separate squads, but he could not force them to obey orders; he began to apply his rattan, and the boys broke into open mutiny. Day after day the play-ground was the scene of riot and misrule. Some semblance of obedience was enforced by our combined exertions; but the mutineers held a secret council in the bed-room, the object of which was to get rid of Tater from the establishment. They entered into a conspiracy to effect their purpose, and they were successful; though by what means they carried out their plans so fully and secretly has always been an impenetrable mystery to me, and remains so to this hour.

The council, hearing of the dissatisfaction of the boys on the subject of the drill, came down to the school in a body, to witness the operations of their new officer and to inquire into the cause of the grievance. They consisted of a body of elderly gentlemen, wealthy cits, for the most part, who had the management of the funds by virtue of the will of the patron and founder of the school, who, at his death, had largely endowed it. They reviewed the boys as they were drawn up in rank and file—and their chairman addressed them on the importance of discipline and the value of a habit of obedience to orders. We were astonished that not a voice was heard in complaint; the reason was, that the rebels had determined to take the law into their own hands, and had not intention to compromise the matter. But though the Council saw nothing to object to in the conduct of Tater, some of their number found cause of offence in the amplitude of his whiskers. Like other geniuses, Tater was in advance of his age, and in reference to those facial ornaments which it is now the fashion to cultivate to an unlimited extent, was full fifteen years before his time. As he walked majestically in front of his disaffected bands, you might have imagined that his head was wafted along by a pair of raven wings, so broad and black were the bushy appendages of his face. The Council actually sat two hours in deliberation on the subject of these voluminous phenomena—and ended their discussion by sending for the unconscious possessor, and proposing in plain terms that he should reduce them to an amount somewhat approximating to average pilosity. A rather singular and somewhat stormy scene ensued. One of the Council, a junior member, who had sat chuckling secretly over the ludicrous perplexity of the elders, declared loudly for the integrity of the whiskers, on the principle of the sacredness of private property; and Tater, encouraged by the countenance of an ally, read them an indignant lecture on the subject of their proper business, winding up his oration with an oath, binding himself to prefer the preservation of every single hair to the salvation of all the bald pates in Christendom.

The whole school, from the head-master to the sleepless "boots" who, ensconced behind two hundred and fifty specimens of chaussure, passed his days and nights in the consummation of Day and Martin's blacking, enjoyed the whisker agitation, and one and all sided with the grower in defence of the crop. If Tater would have moderated his drill, and have been content with a limited authority, he might now, perhaps, have recovered his popularity and influence; but, presuming on the approbation which the Council had expressed of his plans, and presuming, too, on the sympathy of the boys, instead of relaxing he began to play the martinet, and to enforce with military rigour obedience to his commands. The more he hectored and stormed, the less compliant and submissive, and the more noisy and insolent, became the unwilling recruits. At length it was apparent to all of us that a crisis was approaching, and that an end must be put, either by the strong arm to the mutiny of the boys, or by the veto of the Council to the ceremonies of the drill. The boys did not think fit to wait for either alternative.

One night, as we were all sitting round the supper-table in the council-room, while Tater was amusing us with a fluent and rapid lecture on the subject of carbonic acid gas, we were suddenly startled by a voice on the stairs over head, which shouted in thundering tones " B, A, R." In an instant there was a rush from all the smaller dormitories to the principal bed-room, which was followed the moment after by the sound of heavy blows struck by ponderous hammers, succeeded by three tremendous cheers, the last prolonged by yells, hootings, and imitative cock-crowings for several minutes. We started up, electrified, from our seats. Tater turned as pale as death. Some of us ran to the study of the head-master, whom we found already aroused by the tumult, and, with his two coadjutors, about to proceed to the scene of action. Accompanied by the steward, wardens, and trembling maid-servants, we made our way in a body to the large room. This room, which contained about seventy beds, had the door taken off for the sake of ventilation. The entrance was, however, effectually blocked up, and we saw that all attempts to gain admission would be ineffectual for that night at least. The rogues had taken the whole of the bedsteads, which were of iron, to pieces, and by the aid of strong staples forced into the solid joists on either side, had erected a wall of iron bars not two inches apart. Against these they had piled mattresses one upon another, over which they had bent other rods fastened by similar means. To all the appeals and interrogations of the masters they replied only by a cheer, and refused to hold any parley until the next day, when, and not before, they declared themselves willing to treat on the subject of their grievances. As nothing else was to be done without creating a disturbance in the town, it was judged best to leave them unmolested for the night, the masters probably thinking that the demands of appetite might reduce them to submission in the morning. We could see from the play-ground that the mutineers had provided themselves with lights, which were not extinguished till long after midnight; and hours were passed in uproarious frolic before they retired to rest.

The next morning we commenced operations, after the usual clanging of the bell, with six pupils, instead of over two hundred. These were examined as to the cause and the originators of the barring out. They informed us of what we knew already—that the cause of all was the interference of Tater with the out-door sports; but of the contrivers and ring-leaders they professed to know nothing, and neither threats nor the promise of reward could extract from one of them a syllable in betrayal of their comrades. They were evidently mortified at being shut out of the conspiracy and the glory it involved, a circumstance which had resulted from their own tardiness in answering the signal. After we had breakfasted, we followed at the heels of the head-master to hear the terms of the capitulation, but our summons was answered by the declaration, made by the lips of the youngest child amongst them, a little pet of seven years of age, that the republic would not rise till eleven o'clock, when they would make known their ultimatum. The Pelican, anxious to prevent the odium of exposure, retired, and when a couple of hours had elapsed again summoned them to parley. He was answered by an elder spokesman, who, disguising his voice by speaking through a roll of paper and the teeth of a comb, now declared that they had resorted to insurrection to free themselves from tyranny, that they were resolved upon the dismissal of Tater from the school, and that until they had obtained a promise from the master that he should be dismissed they would never surrender, but would one and all starve first. This declaration was instantaneously corroborated by an overwhelming cheer from the whole body of insurgents. The terms proposed were considered such as could not be entertained; and, after some attempts at expostulation, the head-master informed them that if they did not pull down their fortification by one o'clock, he should feel himself compelled to send for workmen and effect an entrance by force. They answered this threat by "three cheers for the Pelican" and "three groans for Tater," and with the determined asseveration, often repeated, that if a breach were effected they would defend it with their lives,—ending with a tremendous roar of "Liberty or death!"

There were no symptoms of concession in the course of the afternoon; and about four o'clock the head-master, perplexed with the state of affairs, sent for a couple of carpenters, with a view to effect a forcible entrance. This was no easy matter. The elastic iron bars, backed by the wool mattresses, would not yield to the blows of his mallet. Tater came to his assistance with a crowbar, with which he succeeded in bending aside two or three of the rods; but he got an ugly cut in the wrist from the point of a carving-knife, in the hands of one of the defenders, and retired wounded from the field. Further attempts at force were now abandoned: the insurrectionists repaired the breach and strengthened the barricade with additional mattresses, buttressed within with the solid bedstead and furniture of the writing-master's chamber. Night came on, and they celebrated their triumphs with renewed shouts and uproar.

Next morning we were astonished, on descending to the school-room, by the unexpected apparition of nearly sixty boys, instead of six, whom only we expected to find. They were all young children under eleven years of age, who had been ingeniously got rid of as so many useless and bread-devouring mouths by the self-imprisoned garrison. From them we learned, that though the fortress was well victualled—abounding at present in hams, polonies, salt beef, bread and biscuit, and bottled beer, yet, as a long siege was expected, and a determined resistance resolved upon, a council had been called, and the resolution formed of getting rid of those who, from their tender age, could be looked upon only in the light of non-combatants. This had been accomplished by cramming each little appetite into a pillow case, and letting him down, at the first dawn of day, by means of ropes, into the play-ground, a height of at least twenty-five feet. These involuntary deserters did not add, what was the fact, that they had been busy for a full hour in collecting every vessel they could lay hands on, and returning water to the thirsty mutineers by the same conveyance. Young as these children were, they were as intractable as their elders on the score of impeaching, and would afford us no clue for discovering who were the contrivers of the conspiracy.

The affair now began to assume a more formidable aspect, and it became necessary to resort to decisive measures of some kind to bring it to a termination. With any other man than the Rev. Mr. E——, the authority with which he was invested would have been inducement enough to have brought about submission by force; but our head-master had all along constituted himself the bulwark of the boys against the very authority which he himself delegated to his subordinates; and he could not endure the thought of jeopardizing his popularity. He held a long conference with his two coadjutors in his study. To this conference Tater was at length summoned, and induced by the united representations of the trio, much against his own judgment, to send in his resignation. He drew up and signed the document with due formality, and the head-master then proceeded alone to apprise the insurgents that their demands were complied with. On his promise that no one should enter but himself, they pulled down their barricade and gave him admission, crowding around him, as he afterwards told us, with every demonstration of affection How he graced his surrender

I had never the means of ascertaining; but it must have been admirably done; because the boys returned immediately to their duty, and, doubtless in performance of some pledge which he had, during an hour's interview, solemnly exacted, conducted themselves throughout the remainder of the "half" in a manner, so far as discipline was concerned, almost irreproachable.

I am aware of nothing worth recording that took place during the rest of that term. As autumn came on, and waned into winter, my duties grew still less agreeable. To rise in total darkness, and to turn out to promenade by star-light in the play-ground covered with snow or slippery with ice; to sit for hours in the wintry draught twenty yards from the fire, blowing my chilblained fingers in the vain attempt to thaw them sufficiently to mend a pen; to urge the shivering children to activity, to save the suffering and plague of frost bitten toes —these were some of the pleasures incidental to the winter season. I was but too glad when the Christmas holidays drew near, with the prospect of release, and the six weeks' recess which I should be allowed to spend as I chose. By about the middle of December half the boys had departed homewards. On the 17th the duties of the school were discontinued, and, within three days after the din of departure had subsided, and with the exception of a small band of twelve or fourteen, self-dubbed the *miserrimi*, the school was empty. The unfortunate boys left behind, who had assumed, partly in jest and partly in sad earnest, the above sorrowful appellation, were the sons of parents who were either too poor or too indifferent to the longings of childhood to pay their expenses to a distant home. Three, indeed, were orphans, and these, from the experience of former years, had become reconciled to their lot, knowing that they were well-cared for at school.

I had looked forward to the termination of the "half" with the fixed resolution of making good use of the leisure of the recess in prosecuting my studies. But, from some inexplicable cause, no sooner was the whole day my own than the old mechanical instinct to be doing something tormented me so effectually that I found it impossible to fix my attention sedulously, even for an hour, on the tasks I had cut out I found that I could not study with earnestness unless in hours redeemed from days of constant employment. If this fact appear strange to the reader. it must be because he is not a working-man, or has never experienced the necessity of making time for himself, to all who have, it will appear no mystery The place was deserted. My coadjutors had all joined their Christmas circles, and yet I, in possession of perfect seclusion, and surrounded with books, was too restless to make use of either.

Wearied out with uncomfortable excitement, in the afternoon of the second day I packed a few changes of linen into a small knapsack, and set forth on the frost-bound road to walk to London I traversed Blackfriars-bridge as the bell of St. Paul's was striking seven, and popped in upon Parson Smart, at the office of the magazine, in the middle of a long preachment on the subject of justification by faith, the doctrine of which he was learnedly endeavoring to beat into the brains of a hard-headed Cockney. I heard the rattle of his eternal mill at the foot of the stairs, and waited a moment or two at the door to listen to the well-known sound. My appearance, for a wonder, put an end to his homily, and he darted out of his frame to seize my hand. While we were talking up the last six months, who should enter the room but my sheep's head friend and patron B——, with his son Jem ? They were out on the hunt, the trade being very brisk just then, for a couple of hands to assist on the —— newspaper, and had "dropped up promiscuously" as my old companion observed, for the chance of finding one there. I immediately volunteered my services, though I had not come to town in search of work, and was gladly accepted , and upon informing B—— that I had no lodging to go to, he invited me to his own home, where he said he could, if I liked, "*conodger* it very well, and stow me and my traps comfortable." I accompanied him to his house, near Hatton Garden, and met a hearty welcome from his wife, and a steaming pot of "egg-flip," a composition of beer, spirits, and eggs, to which, as I had travelled far, and the night was bitterly cold, I was not coy of paying my devoirs. After breakfast next morning, I went with him and his son to the office, not a hundred miles from St. Martin's Church, and commenced work on the paper, filling the frame of a regular hand who was absent through sickness. I wrought here a whole month of my holiday, and saved half my earnings, which were not very great. For three days of the week we had little to do, but had to make up for our inaction by unflinching labor as the day of publication drew near.

One of the main attractions of the paper which we had to produce weekly, consisted, or was supposed to consist, of a romance of the burglary, cut-throat and gallows class of literature, a chapter of which was advertised to appear in every number. This production, which was doubtless a source of gratification to a certain class of readers, was one of infinite annoyance to the compositors and all parties subordinately employed upon the paper. The author was a gay and fashionably-dressed gallant, something over thirty, and apparently one of that class of geniuses who can never do anything till they are goaded to exertion at the last moment. Instead of sending his manuscript to the printer in decent time, he never sent any manuscript at all; but came himself some few hours before the newspaper went to press, and mounting a seat in a closet next the composing-room, set about the perpetration of his weekly quantum in the very jaws of the press gaping to be fed. A sort of easy, sloping-backed stool was prepared for his accommodation, in which, with the full consciousness of genius upon him, he lounged languidly, and threw off the coinage of his brain. His method of composition must, I imagine, have been perfectly unique, and was certainly as troublesome a process for all persons concerned as can well be conceived. I shall describe it for the benefit of aspiring geniuses, and for the sake of showing the public the workings of the inspiration of romance under the spur of necessity—and so many guineas a column.

On the first arrival of the "popular author," whom, by raising myself by stepping on the bed of my frame, I could, and sometimes did, overlook, he would seat himself in front of a broad white quire of vellum, would seize a pen, and, dashing it into the ink, would suffer his right hand to droop at his side, and, distilling the black drops on the floor, employ himself for twenty or thirty minutes in stroking his whiskers, which had naturally a propensity to hang down in the bandit fashion, upwards toward the middle of his face, occasionally wetting his finger and thumb and twisting them into a curl. Suddenly, the right hand would be cautiously raised, and a few words dropped stealthily upon the paper. Then came another long and deliberate sweep at the whiskers, varied with a pull at the chin and a convulsive grasp at the scowling forehead; then a few more unwilling syllables, and then a bout at the whiskers, and so on, and on, till an hour or more had elapsed, when he would ring the bell violently. The ever-watchful "devil" would dart into the closet, and re-appear in an instant with the first edition of the "copy." Here it is; and this, be it remembered, is all the progress that the action of the romance is destined to make for the present week:—

Bluster knocked at the door, and asked if Slackjaw had come.

The woman said no; and the captain brushing past her, entered the room on the left. Slowgo and Bluebag were there before him.

"Where's that hell-hound, Slackjaw?" cried Bluster.

"Vy," said Slowgo, "that ere's a rum kvestion. How the —— can ve tell?"

Suddenly the sound of footsteps was heard without, and Slackjaw immediately after entered the room.

Bluster suppressed his wrath; and the party sat down together to confer and arrange their plans.

"Whereabouts is the crib?" asked Bluster.

"About a mile the tother side o' Bow," responded Bluebag.

"Is the barkers all right?"

"Righter nor a trivet."

"And Jad meets us at the Whitechapel gate?"

"That's the fake."

"At one o'clock if I'm fly?"

"One's the number. 'Tis now 'leven. I wotes for a drop o' heavy afore we starts."

"D——," roared Bluster, "if I'll have any gettin' drunk afore business."

"Just pots round," insinuated Slowgo; "that won't hurt us; and the night's infernal wet and windy."

The captain conceded "pots round;" which being duly discussed within an hour, the party arose and repaired to the appointed spot. They found Jad in the shadow of the turnpike, and, guided by him, pursued their route. It was near two in the morning when they came in sight of the house which it was their "business" to plunder.

No sooner did this precious morsel of "copy" appear than it was cut up into eight or ten small pieces, and in a very few minutes a proof of the whole was in the hands of the author, whose occupation for the remainder of the night it was, by a process well understood and exceedingly profitable to the geniuses of romance of the present day, to spin it out to the required length of from two hundred and fifty to three hundred lines of minion type. Directly a proof was obtained, the types were distributed, as we knew from experience they would not be worth correcting, and we lay upon our oars awaiting the second edition. This generally employed the author for another hour, and by dint of numerous insertions and interlineations, with some few substitutions, was made to assume an appearance somewhat like the following —

It wanted a little more than an hour of midnight when Bluster knocked stealthily three times with his knuckles at the door of the house indicated in the last chapter.

The door was opened by a foul-faced and filthy figure in the garb of a woman, who carried a farthing candle, which she shaded with her left hand, and threw the light full in the face of the captain.

Bluster asked in a hoarse whisper if Slackjaw had yet arrived.

The hag doggedly replied that he had not, and grumbled something about "too much of Slackjaw in that house already."

Bidding her hold her tongue, and flavoring the injunction with a curse, the captain, brushing past her, entered the dingy little parlor on the left, where Slowgo and Bluebag, who had arrived before him, enveloped in a cloud of tobacco-smoke, puffed their short-pipes by the light of a glimmering fire in a rusty grate.

"Kiddies all," said the captain, as he stepped into the reeking chamber.

"Nothing but," growled Slowgo in response

"Where's that —— hell-hound, Slackjaw?" asked Bluster, evidently irritated.

"Vell now," says Slowgo, "that ere's vat I calls a rum sort of a kveer kvestion; how the —— should ve know vere he is?"

"Less of your jaw," retorted the captain, who wanted but little to render him furious "I want none of that"

Suddenly the sound of hasty but cautious footsteps was heard without; they stopped at the door, and the three gentle taps announced the arrival of a confederate. The grim hostess was heard leisurely ascending the stairs, and a minute after the door was noiselessly opened, and the dilatory Slackjaw entered the room.

The arrival of the cracksman seemed to appease in some degree the irritable captain; he suppressed his rising wrath, and after a few guttural salutations had been exchanged, the party sat down together to confer and arrange their plans.

"Whereabouts is the crib we're a goin' to crack?" asked Bluster

"About a mile the tother side o' Bow," responded Bluebag. "I knows the track fast enough."

"How about the barkers, Slackjaw?"

"Right as a trivet," said that worthy, showing the butts of a brace of pistols stuck into the breast-pocket of his coat.

"And Jadder meets us at the Whitechapel gate?"

"That's the fake."

"At one o'clock, or else it's no go."

"One's the chime. 'Tis now past 'leven. I wotes for a drop o' heavy afore we starts."

"No, that be d—d. B—t me if I'll have any getting drunk afore business. Crack the crib, and bag the swag, and then get drunk as h—. That's my maxim."

"Just pots round, captain," insinuated Slowgo. "That won't hurt us. The night's infernal wet and windy. Hang it, let's have a little drop inside as well as out."

The captain conceded "pots round." A gallon of beer was brought in by the angry amazon, who coolly helped herself to a long draught before she left the room. Bluster drank a double share, by way of keeping his men sober; and having discussed the contents of the can within the hour, the party arose and repaired to the appointed spot

They had a good hour's walk before them. Doggedly and silently they proceeded on their way, and came within

10*

sight of the turnpike-gate just as the heavy bell of St. Paul's rung out ONE! They found the ever-punctual Jadder lurking in the shadow of the toll-house, and, guided by him, pursued their route. When they had passed through the straggling village of Bow, Bluster inquired of Jadder whether the cart was already in waiting on the spot.

"All right," said the other. "Solomons is there with his blind blood-mare, and Levy's trap. Ten mile an hour, and room for all of us."

It was near two in the morning when our reckless adventurers came in sight of the house which, standing invitingly alone, and at least a furlong from any other dwelling, had aroused the cupidity and daring of the burglar's jackall, Jadder

This second edition of "copy" was cut up and divided like the former, and a quarter of an hour supplied the author with his second proofs. The types were again distributed, and again we waited for a third edition of copy. This came forth in due time, presenting an appearance as different from the second as the first had been from that. Descriptions of Slowgo and Slackjaw were interpolated; oaths and slang ejaculations were knowingly sprinkled about among the conversations, as so much spice in the savory mess A speech is introduced from the hostess, who is bullied into silence by Bluebag. Slackjaw supplies a paragraph on the merit of his "pops," and establishes his claim to the gallows by the gratuitous confession of half a score murders. Bluster blusters after the model of Ancient Pistol struck silly; and some spicy descriptions of the exploits of Solomon's blood-mare are added in a style that would edify the votaries of the turf. These voluminous additions swell the chapter to more than half its required length; and the author is now asked whether he will have the matter of the third proof distributed. If he consents that it should remain, it is a sign that no more merely verbal interpolations are coming, or at least very few, but that the additions to be made will be of separate paragraphs only. Another hour passes away, and the fourth edition of " copy " comes into our hands—the author sometimes handing it to us himself—the overworked devil being found proof against "kicking up," fast asleep on the floor. We now begin to see the end of our labors. The author has left his characters, and called upon the elements to contribute their quota of matter to his hungry columns. The rain now begins to rush down in torrents, the wind can do no less than howl a perfect hurricane; the thunder roars, and the mad lightnings leap from their hiding-places. All of a sudden the raging tempest abates; the stars twinkle brightly beyond the scudding clouds; the moon rises over the distant range of hills; she is horned like the crescent, and suggests an allusion to the turbaned Moslem; or she is a week old; or she shines in full splendor; or she is in her last quarter, and glares ominously on the scene—or perhaps she don't rise at all, but hidden in her "secret interlunar cave," refuses her placid countenance to a deed of violence—perhaps of blood! But wind, rain, hail, snow and tempest, and moon or no moon, all contribute their several portions to the two feet two inches of small type which are indispensable to enable the popular author to turn over his long column decently, and pocket his five or ten guineas, as it may be, creditably to himself. The fourth edition, however, seldom finishes the chapter. A fifth and often a sixth is required before the necessary quantum is made up. Single lines of a parenthetical character were frequently the last resource of our exhausted genius; and I have known a hiatus of more than a dozen lines filled up in extremity by " Ha!" " Ugh!" " Indeed!" " You don't say so!" " The devil?" &c. &c., ejaculations which were kept standing on a galley in separate lines, to be had recourse to in a case of last emergency. When at length the deed was done, and the imprimatur had issued from his lips, our son of genius would light a refreshing cigar, and with both hands occupied in the propulsion of his obstinate whiskers upwards and forwards, would stalk grandly down-stairs, deposit his gentility in a cab, and rattle home to bed.

During the third week of January the man whose frame I had been temporarily filling, recovered sufficiently to resume his labors, and I was not sorry to surrender my post. Dr. D—— from F——d, his wife, and Ellen arrived in London on a visit to the doctor's son, a few days before I resumed my duties at school. I shall not attempt to describe my pleasure at the meeting with her who was the object of all my hopes and exertions. Four happy days we spent together rambling among the lions of town, without once making the discovery of a fact which annoyed the good doctor beyond measure, namely, that the fog, frost, and slush of London were altogether intolerable and not to be borne.

CHAPTER X.

I return to the Grammar-School—New Regulations—I resolve to leave—Am paid off and return to London—Search for Employment—A model Master Printer, not for imitation—I find work on the Surrey side—Enormous gains of workmen—Cold Comfort—Pleasant Anticipations—A sudden check to them—Poor Parson Smart—" Wanted a Schoolmaster"—A Crowd of Competitors—A confident Character—A Parish Beadle—A midnight Examination—Claims of Candidates—The Schoolmaster elect—Decree of Mr. Bundle—Dissatisfaction and Tumult—Farce of advertising in some cases—A Roadside Professor—Geography made easy—" Strike flat the thick rotundity o' the Globe"—First Literary Attempts—A dishonest Patron—I am employed in a Government House—Economy of a "fast" Printing Office—A permanent Post—A home visit and dispositions for matrimony—I am married.

I PACKED Ellen and the Doctor and his lady, together with a hundred of his volumes of divinity, which he had taken the opportunity of his visit to town to get substantially bound, into the Old Company's coach one cold starlight morning; and as the heavy vehicle rolled off westward, I returned to my lodgings and made up my knapsack before it was yet light, and sat down in a melancholy mood to wait for the starting of the short stage which was to carry me back to the school. I took leave of B—— and his family at the early breakfast; my host, as he shook me heartily by the hand, assuring me that he should come down to the school some day, and find me out when I least expected it.

It was now near the end of the month, and I found most of the boys re-assembled at my return. By the first of February the numbers were complete, some new boys having filled up the ranks of those who had finally left. Several of these were almost grown men, whose education had been deferred for want of means or opportunity; and their influence had a bad effect, especially upon the elder boys, who began to ape the airs and pretensions of the new comers, and to repudiate the obligations of obedience and established rule. It soon became evident that the whole school considered the compact, whatever it was, which they had made with the head-master at the barring-out as virtually at an end. They were more unruly and troublesome than ever; and the good-natured governor soon found it necessary to direct the constant attendance of the whole force of ushers and under-masters in the play-ground when the classes were dismissed. In addition to these grievances, I was docked of one of my two hours in the forenoon, in order to assist in shoving a small class of the new comers over the asses' bridge, to qualify them for joining their more advanced comrades.

I had now literally not a moment of time at my command from five in the morning to nearly ten at night, unless I abstracted it furtively from hours of duty, or saved it from the single hour in the forenoon, after washing, dressing, and shaving. My colleagues as well as myself rebelled against the new measures, which all our representations to the principal failed to modify. We should have broken out into open mutiny had we been the subjects of rigorous supervision, but as that was very lax, we could evade much that was preposterously required of us, and relieve each other in some small degree by acting together in concert. Still we were all discontented, and weary with a never-ending routine of duty which brought no satisfaction in the performance, but increasing complaints instead. Quarrelling, fighting, riots, and pitched battles were more frequent than ever. These last were conducted so secretly that we did not even know when the affairs came off—the first intimation of which would be the sudden apparition of black-eyes and bloody shirts in the ranks at prayer time or in class.

As spring drew on, and the days grew longer, matters grew worse and subordination was a thing unknown. The slovens could not be induced to wash of a morning, or the fighters to go to bed of a night. Bolstering became a perfect mania; and the only chance we had of getting the turbulent crew to sleep was by walking them completely off their feet by long and late rambles round the country, and bringing them home thoroughly fagged and weary at the hour of bed-time. I began to get sick of my post, and often I asked myself why, with the means of doing otherwise, I submitted to lead a life of perpetual discomfort and drudgery. As this feeling became stronger, my assiduity grew less; and having no prospect of fulfilling my duties satisfactorily, I candidly confess I grew careless of fulfilling them at all, and sailed with the stream which it was vain to attempt to oppose. When the warm weather came, sickness and fever broke out, from the want of proper ventilation in the rooms. Many of the boys were moved off to the infirmary, and some died. The head-master now became anxious, and interfered personally to restore order, enforce the morning ablutions, and prevent riots and fighting. He gave me a long jobation, to arouse me to the performance of an impossible task. I told him I should prefer resigning it unless it were reduced to practicable limits—that I had too much to do, and could from that cause do nothing effectually. Ever courteous and kind, he promised to revise my functions, and drew up a schedule of them for my guidance, which left me three hours a-day unemployed. Of course I acted on these instructions; but that produced an explosion of wrath among my coadjutors, and sent each of them breathless with indignation to the study of the old gentleman for a corresponding schedule. I was recalled, and we were directed to submit a plan of our own. This was never done, and things went on as before.

One evening in May I punished with a moderate caning a young varlet for letting loose a swarm of cockchafers, which he had collected for the purpose, to buzz round the old gentleman's head as he read prayers under the gas-lamp. The fellow thought fit to roar immoderately because the head-master was within hearing, though on other occasions he never condescended to "give tongue" as he called it. The old gentleman came at the cry and beckoned me away. He lectured me, rather harshly for him, on the assumption of authority I was nettled at his patronage of an unmitigated young blackguard, and retorted on the total absence of anything like authority anywhere on the premises. We came to an open, though, on his part at least, a perfectly polite rupture. I proffered to leave at the conclusion of the "half," without waiting for a quarter's notice—and the proffer was accepted. I went to my bed that night with a feeling of satisfaction which I had not experienced before for twelve months. The prospect of release from this harassing life gave me new spirits, and I now longed for the holidays as eagerly as did the greatest dunce in the school.

The next day, as I was sitting at tea with my colleagues in the council-room, there came a thundering peal at the outer door, and an important-looking personage was shown in who advanced and seized me by the hand almost before I was aware that it was my old friend B——. He had brought down a column cut from a French newspaper, and would wait while it was done into English He had made a holiday of the occasion, and tremendously overdressed himself; and really, what with rings on his horny fingers, emerald studs in his breast, frizzled hair, and a waistcoat of kaleidoscope pattern, cut quite a grand and gaudy appearance. The lads were all going out to cricket, and F—— volunteering to take the custody of my division, I remained at home and discharged the commission my friend had brought. It was done in the course of a couple of hours, and then I accompanied B—— a mile or two on the road to town, and consulted with him as to the next step I should take. He told me I might "cut grass" on the paper if I chose, and he would take care I should not starve, and that I should have full employment on the first vacancy; but he said I might perhaps do better by applying at Stamford-street, where he knew they were busy, and some of them writing "howdacious bills, the like of which was never known afore." B—— paid me handsomely for my translation, and promised to keep on the look-out, and to let me know if anything worth having turned up.

Just before the Midsummer vacation the annual examination of the pupils took place. It happened unfortunately that the wretched discipline was too apparent to escape the notice of the visitors. The progress of the pupils was considered creditable in all respects but one. There were good Grecians, Romans and mathematicians among the boys; but they were wild as colts, and there was no deference to authority, which, indeed, they had never been taught to respect. The French classes did not come under review, so that the eccentric system of Plugger escaped remark; but the management of the school became the subject of a searching investigation by the Council, at the instigation of the patrons who attended the examination, and the result was that the indulgent Pelican saw himself compelled to tender his resignation, which was accepted, and he resigned on the following Christmas after my departure. He was testimonialized by the boys, who presented him with a handsome silver salver, graced with a laudatory Latin inscription, in gratitude for the identical course of management which had rendered his dismissal imperative.

I had no sooner pocketed the cheque for my quarter's salary than I turned my face towards Westminster, where, engaging a lodging in the shadow of the Abbey, I took up my abode, and set forth, the day after my return, in search of employment. I had mastered German enough to read most of the poets, and any narrative prose work; and I thought, before applying for English work, I would see whether my French, Latin, Italian and German might not be worth a few shillings a week in the market, and so be made substantially useful. With this notion in my head, I called at an office in the immediate neighborhood of the Strand, where works in all tongues, especially Bibles, were constantly in course of execution. I requested to speak with the principal, and, after some time, he came forth from a very dirty closet, and demanded my business. When he understood that I was a compositor seeking employment, he scowled upon me, with a pair of leaden eyes like a couple of bullets stuck into a dab of yellow mud, and fiercely inquired why the devil I troubled him? Why did I not ask for the overseer? I answered that I had some small skill in languages, and that I was desirous of turning it to account, and that I conceived that he would be the better judge of my qualifications.

"Oh! that's it, is it? Well, what devil are your qualifications? Come, out with them, don't keep me waiting here all day! —— you! what do you know?"

I mentioned French.

"French!" said this wholesale printer of Bibles, "d—— French! You don't call that anything?" adding, in language which cannot be printed in his own broad English, "*Nos crepitamus Gallicam linguam,* every devil of us. French is no recommendation here, I assure you."

I told him I read Latin.

"Latin, eh? We do no Latin here, and we should be very little better for you, I fancy, if we did. What's the Latin for *frisket?*"

I told him I did not know.

"I thought not! A devilish fine Latin scholar you are! —— me if I think you know what a frisket is! What else do you pretend to?"

I answered that I read Italian and German.

"Italian and German, eh? I am bound you do!—and Spanish to boot, of course!"

"No, I did not say Spanish."

"More fool you! 'Tis as easy to say Spanish as not. I'll warrant that all the German there is in you came out of a German sausage. What else?"

"I replied, "Nothing else."

"Then," said he, "you are of no use here. If you were well up in the Arabic, Persian, Sanscrit, or even in the Tamul or Bengali, confound you! you might be of some service, and I wouldn't mind giving you three-and-thirty a-week as a reader. There! cut your —— stick, and don't come here boring me again with your —— French flummery and Spanish liquorice!"

With that, this externally and intrinsically dirty beast turned on his heel and vanished into his congenial den. I was in no humor to waste any of my small stock of politeness upon such a specimen of the brute, and I walked silently down the dark staircase with something like a feeling of gratification, arising from the consciousness that it was not in the power of Fate, to transform me into anything so disgustingly contemptible as the wretch who had given me such a reception.

This adventure, to use a common but not very elegant phrase, completely took the conceit out of me, and taught me how small is the real value of philological studies to a practical printer. I made up my mind, once for all, to pique myself no more on anything of the sort, and resolved to keep my private studies in the back-ground, and to pursue them quietly for the sake of the enjoyment they afforded. Recollecting B——'s advice, I turned my steps towards Duke-street, Stamford-street, and made application to one of the overseers for a frame. After what I had just gone through, I thought the civil questioning of Mr. V—— the perfection of politeness. I was engaged immediately, and informed that I was to commence operations at once. In half an hour I had fetched my implements of labor from my lodgings, and, following the overseer into an enormously long and narrow room which bore the name, and in no small degree resembled the locality, of " the quarter-deck," one end being raised like the poop of a vessel of war, I was set to work directly upon the columns of the " Encyclopædia Metropolitana." This was a species of labor which required a good deal of fagging perseverance to yield the average "stab" wages; but in the course of a month I was transferred to another companionship employed on Government work sent from the Stationary-Office, upon which I did much better.

This printing-office was the greatest in extent, and, considering its size, the best managed that I had seen in England. A little army of workmen were continually employed, and yet anything approaching to confusion was rarely seen. An immense amount of work was got through weekly. In a large building in the centre of the court-yard above a score of machines were grinding away from morning to night, and frequently all night long. At any hour of the day, the portly figure of the stalwart proprietor might be seen moving hither and thither, wherever a master's eye was most required, while two sons, each in control of a large department, superintended, conjointly with the overseers, the movements of the vast machine. The type was cast on the premises, and the nuisance of standing still for want of material was a thing unknown. Here I wrought for several months, early and late, and, during a good portion of the summer, on Sundays as well as other days. Papers on the subject of the Post-Office kept us going night and day. The total eclipse of the sun, which came off one Sunday afternoon, was not allowed to interrupt us for more than ten minutes; and it was voted an astronomical "take in" because it did not necessitate the lighting of candles.

I was very well satisfied with my position, and indeed had not much time for grumbling; but there was an envious spirit at work among a large section of the men. A favored companionship, located in a room rather appropriately called "The Treasury," were making enormous gains, earning continuously, it was said, ten pounds a-week per man, through the profitable nature of the work and the generosity of the proprietor, who refrained from appropriating an advantage he might rightly have claimed, and allowed his workmen to reap the benefit of a species of labor unprecedentedly lucrative. The good-natured principal was assailed with anonymous letters from parties who fancied themselves aggrieved because they had not a share of the coveted gains, though it was a fact which could not be denied that the best workmen were those who were reaping the extraordinary harvest. Ultimately, though not until some time after the period of which I write, this captious spirit led to the reform of the grievance which had given rise to it; but it was reformed in a mode which, whatever satisfaction it may have afforded to the grumblers, yielded them no profit. The mode of payment by piece-work was abolished in the Treasury companionship, and the men, paid for their time at so much a-week, retained the same description of work, the abnormal profits of which went to the proprietors.

I remained pretty constantly employed during the whole of the winter of 1835—6, and my health suffered some rude shocks from the alternations of heat and cold consequent upon the absence of fires at a season when the neighboring Thames was almost blocked with ice—contrasted with the sudden and overwhelming rush of steam into the pipes which warmed the rooms whenever it was convenient for the surly old stoker, who made his bed on the top of the boiler, to turn it on. As the spring came on the work slackened materially, and a good many of the hands withdrew; but just as I was expecting to be discharged, I was transferred to another room, and placed in a better position than I had yet occupied.

I had made up my mind to get married in the course of this year, and looking upon the unexpected improvement in my prospects as an evidence of the permanency of my present post, I began the usual preliminary process of "persons about to marry." I hired part of a small, neat, new house in the neighborhood of the office, and set about furnishing it by degrees as substantially as the state of my funds would allow. By the middle of May I had spent about fourscore pounds in lining my nest, in which I passed all my leisure-hours, strumming upon a tolerable piano, for which I had exchanged a ten-pound note, and anticipating the wished-for arrival of her who was to transform my first-floor and kitchen into a paradise.

One morning, however, my harmonious practice and celestial anticipations were suddenly put to a violent death by a command from the overseer to abandon my present post in favor of a youth thrust headlong into the house by a celebrated man of science who had a volume to be printed, upon the back of which he had mounted his protégé, a needy relation, as a rider. The patronage which ensconced a poor relative in an office for which he was but indifferently qualified, deprived me of remunerative employment at a moment when all my happiness depended upon its continuance. I was transferred suddenly and without ceremony to a companionship half employed upon the Tract Society's works, the pious paragraphs of which appeared to me the perfection of literary rubbish, for no other reason that I am aware of than because it was impossible to earn a fair day's wages by composing them. Mr. V—— kindly informed me, that if I could meet with anything better I might accept it at a moment's notice; and accordingly I began to look out in all directions, and to bestir myself in the inquiry with an activity proof against rebuff.

I made a call upon Parson Smart, whom I found suffering from serious and alarming symptoms and spitting of blood, and altogether changed in manner and character from his former self. He still wrought languidly at his frame, but had received notice, which was not to be mistaken, he said, to "put his house in order." His rattling volubility was changed for an ominous and brooding silence, broken only by heavy and involuntary sighs. He promised to make inquiries on my behalf, and hoped that he should have the satisfaction of serving me. He put a worn copy of Beza's Testament into my hand at parting, and bade me read it sometimes, and think of him as kindly as I could when he was gone. My spirits, already depressed, were not improved by the change which had come over the poor parson, who, it was but too plain, would soon cease from his labors. The same afternoon I obtained temporary employment at the printing-office of the *Literary Gazette*, where, however, I remained but a few days, returning again to Duke-street when the job I had been engaged upon was finished.

On returning home one evening, I found a note from poor Smart, inclosing an advertisement cut from that day's *Times*, and expressing a wish that the situation it offered might meet my wants; and advising me to lose no time in my endeavors to secure it. The advertisement was headed "WANTED, A SCHOOLMASTER," and had been inserted in all the London morning papers of the day. By the contents of the whole paragraph the reader was informed that the mastership of a parish school in one of the suburban districts of the capital was vacant; that the annual salary would average about 120*l.* at the lowest; that a good and commodious residence was attached to the school-house, with a garden for the master's use. It was further stated, that a knowledge of the Lancasterian system of instruction was indispensable; that all the candidates were to attend in person on a given day and hour, and were to come provided with testimonials of ability and good moral character; and it was expressly stated, that if competent persons attended, the election would take place there and then.

The reader will readily conceive that in my then position I read this announcement over with no small interest. Circumstances had made me fully competent to undertake the duties required to be performed. I was thoroughly familiar with the system of instruction indicated, and my imagination speedily installed me in the office, with my laughing Ellen at my side; and I saw myself surrounded by fifty or a hundred docile boys eager for knowledge, and emulous in the noble conflict by which it was to be acquired. The income of 120*l.* a-year was amply sufficient for all my wants; and I already enjoyed it in perspective, as well as the house and garden and the golden leisure which the occupation of a schoolmaster so circumstanced affords. I wrote that night to the address of the advertiser, informing him of my intention to become a candidate, and sent letters by the same post to Dr. D——, and to my old colleagues and superiors at the grammar-school, for testimonials of character and ability. I resolved to do all in my power to get possession of the appointment; and pending the arrival of my testimonials, I proceeded to make inquiries in the near neighborhood of the school, in reference as well to the circumstances which occasioned the vacancy as to the comfort and desirableness of the post. These were all answered to my perfect satisfaction; the late master had died out, after having held the office for twenty-five years, during which period it was supposed, as he had carried on an evening-school on his own account, that he had not realized much less than 250*l.* a-year. Some of the neighbors, indeed, from the fact of his having portioned off several daughters very liberally, estimated his income at much more, taking into account certain annual bonuses which some of the parents, well-to-do in the world, made a practice of presenting at Christmas-time.

Well furnished with testimonials and good wishes on the part of the givers, in a series of documents which swelled my pocket-book almost to bursting, I mounted an omnibus on the afternoon of the appointed day, a full hour before the specified time, and in forty minutes was set down within a few hundred yards of the domicile which I most devoutly hoped was to become my future residence. It was a neat and newly-built house, having a third of an acre of garden-ground behind it, well stocked with flowers, vegetables and fruit. A gothic portico at the top of a flight of steps overshadowed the doorway, and a verdant lawn, as large as Temple-gardens, lay green in the sunshine in front of the building. While ascending the stone steps which led into the school-room, the door of which stood wide open, I was made aware by the sound of voices that mine was not the first arrival. As I stood in the entrance, rather astonished at the sight of twenty or thirty individuals of various ages, one of them laughingly invited me to walk in and secure a seat while there was yet room; an admonition for which there appeared no reason, as there was abundant sitting-room for at least a hundred persons. I took my seat with the rest, and was drawn into conversation with an intelligent man upon the subject of our gathering. The time specified for our meeting was six o'clock, to which it still wanted a quarter of an hour, and yet more than two dozen competitors were present. As the critical moment approached, numbers more came in, and long after the hour had struck new-comers seemed to rise spontaneously out of the ground, and crowded into the long-room, until all available space was disagreeably crammed, and seats were no longer to be found.

The group of candidates thus tumultuously assembled presented a rather motley and very varied picture. Some wore an aspect of maturity, and were plainly far beyond the age which the public announcement had declared eligible, while others were extremely juvenile in appearance. Some had evidently held hand-to-hand contests with misfortune, and been long used to grapple with adversity; and others again, judging from their genteel garb and adornments of rings and jewellery, seemed already above the position to which they aspired. Not a few, it was clear from the palpable traces of intemperance in their looks, were of a scampish and dissipated class, to whom anything like the observance of punctuality and order would have been intolerable; and one could hardly help wondering what possible inducement could have led them thither. Here and there a melancholy individual, with integuments worn threadbare and in the last stage of presentable decency, sought to shelter himself from the general gaze by crouching on his seat and drooping his head upon his folded arms. Several, probably abashed by the presence of numbers, produced books from their pockets, and either were or affected to be so absorbed in their contents as to be insensible to the increasing noise and tumult around them. One, a youthful Irishman, with no demonstration of a shirt, and a hat which, though half the rim was wanting, he wore jauntily over his sandy locks, read in a loud whisper from a few tattered leaves of a Minellius's Horace, any part of which, I felt assured, he was prepared to construe categorically if put upon his mettle. All, strangers to each other, wore at first an air of restraint and embarrassment, which some of them, however, shook off with surprising facility, and by degrees the hum of conversation grew louder and louder.

Having thrown open all the windows for the sake of air, we awaited with tolerable patience the arrival of the party who were to make the election. It was a fine summer's evening, and the declining sun shone pleasantly upon our faces. A few favorite and venerable jokes were bandied about the room, and not a little slang emanated from time to time from a group of rather seedy specimens who had congregated near the staircase which led up to the board-room where our fate was to be determined. Among these was one particularly talkative and elate, who gratuitously enlightened all around him on the subject of the election, and their probable chances, which he unceremoniously declared to be *nil*. His vaticinations were voted an annoyance by some of the more mature, and he was civilly requested "to keep himself to himself." "I shall keep more to myself than you expect, old fellow," he replied. ' In the mean time, as this is but a dry job, I'm blessed if I don't send for a pot of heavy, if you like to go halves, or I'll toss you for the Joey." With that, hailing a boy from the window, he despatched him to the ———'s Head for a pot of stout, which the landlord was to score up to his old customer, whom for the nonce I shall denominate Mr. Benjamin Boggle.

Meanwhile time passed on—seven o'clock struck, and then eight, and not a soul present save the candidates. Weary with waiting, and perhaps hopeless of success from the number of competitors, many now took their leave, and before the electors came, which was not until half-past eight o'clock, and the last rays of the sun had disappeared, not above half of the original number remained. The adjudicators, who at length, preceded by the parish beadle, arrived upon the spot, consisted of seven or eight middle-aged burgess-looking individuals, and a young man in ecclesiastical garb, the curate of the parish. They were headed by an elderly personage of forbidding and stolid aspect, who had plainly left his good temper, if he had any, at home, as being of no use on the present occasion. Grumbling audibly, as if offended at our numbers, he led the way up-stairs, bestowing just a nod of recognition upon Mr. Boggle as he passed him at the stair-foot. The committee, as they called themselves, made a factotum of the beadle, who for that night at least had no sinecure. As it was discovered that the room up-stairs was not large enough to contain us all, we were requested to send up our testimonials for examination: the beadle came round and collected them in a large basket, and we remained below during their perusal. By this time we were in complete darkness, and much clamor was raised for a light, which was accorded after half-an-hour's outcry—a single tallow candle being mounted against the wall.

A long and weary interval was now passed in extreme discomfort and dissatisfaction, from which many were fain to escape by flight, leaving their testimonials behind them. I and my acquaintance of the hour, having nothing better to do, were, however, resolved upon seeing the matter out, last as long as it might. At length, at near half-past ten at night, the beadle proclaimed from the stair-head that "Hall the trusty-menials was so satisfactry the boord couldn't make no chice, and tharfore them gemmen as was present an' had no 'bjection to go under a zamination was invited to come forrad at once in the boord-room." There was immediately a general rush to the staircase, and as we were by this time reduced to about a third of our original number, we all managed to squeeze into the chamber. But here a new difficulty arose; there was not at the table room for more than half of us. The leader, whom we now knew to be the churchwarden, suggested that we should be examined in two parties, and the division was made as we stood, all on the right hand of the speaker taking their seats at the table, where abundant writing-materials were provided, and the rest waiting for a separate turn.

From the conversation of the party at the head of the table, who were all parish functionaries of one sort or other, it was plain that a more incompetent set of judges upon such a matter as that in hand could hardly be found; but the curate was a host in himself, and really applied to the business with earnestness. The questions which we had to answer all bore upon moral or theological subjects, and had been prepared with perhaps too severe a judgment I had accidentally seated myself next to Mr. Boggle, whose proficiency in slang, in which he was a marvellous adept, made me curious to ascertain what might be his theological notions. If I was intent on watching him he fully returned the compliment for I found him copying in a bouncing hand every word I wrote in answer to the first question—an attempt at fraud which I baffled by writing rapidly, and suddenly turning over the leaf The second question was ' What is faith?" I took care, by writing my reply under the shield of my first leaf, to leave the observant Boggle to his own resources, and had the amusing satisfaction of seeing him write in answer 'Faith is belief— and the Belief is 'I believe in God the Father,' &c &. to the end of the creed as it stands in the Church of England Catechism." A subsequent question demanded an explanation of the phrase "All dangers ghostly and bodily" Mr. Boggle was a devout believer in ghosts and goblins, and he piously expressed a prayer against all bogies, phantoms and apparitions as the deadly enemies of his salvation.

It was a curious and not uninteresting sight, that midnight assemblage. The curate sat smiling encouragingly by the side of the burly churchwarden, while his compeers, the parish functionaries, were fast dropping off to sleep, and giving sonorous tokens of their happy oblivion of all that was going on. Some hard-headed competitors, rubbing their skulls and knitting their brows, now and then jotted down a word or two, and then turned their eyes to the ceiling for inspiration. Others, scribbling away as if for dear life, seemed resolved that quantity at least should not be wanting to their argument. At the back of each one stood another anxious expectant in solemn silence, anticipating with exultation or dread, as it might be, the same difficult ordeal.

When we had written replies to about half-a-dozen questions, a ceremony that occupied very nearly an hour, we were requested to sign and forward to the head of the table all our manuscripts, and vacate our seats for the remaining candidates. It was strange, however, that the same questions were not propounded to the second batch; and complaints were preferred on this account from some of the first party, because, as they alleged, it would be impossible to arrive at an equitable judgment unless all were subjected to the same test. These complaints were overruled on the ground that as the candidates last examined had heard the questions already put, and had, perhaps, seen some of our replies, they would be much more likely to improve upon them than to give superior replies impromptu to new questions. New questions were therefore submitted to the new examinees, who got through their business in about the same time, or rather less than an hour. During this lagging hour I had the honor of Mr. Boggle's conversation, and he assured me that *he*, and none other, would be the person chosen, as I should see if I were fool enough to stand it out.

When the second party sat down the curate warned them not to be so long about their replies as their predecessors had been, and assured them that what was sought was merely evidence that they could return intelligent answers to the questions propounded, and that brevity would carry it in preference to diffuseness. His representations were to no purpose;

the few who had anything to reply were resolved to answer at the fullest length, while others, as in the former instance, wrote little or nothing. Before they had finished, the curate, looking at his watch, regretted that he could stay no longer, and took his departure. The churchwarden put the few remaining questions from the list, and recommended despatch, "as there had been a great deal too much bother about the business already."

When the whole of the manuscripts were completed and delivered to the churchwarden, who by this time had joined his companions in a refreshing nap, the synod were waked up by the beadle, and we were all desired to withdraw again to the school-room, and there await the result of their deliberations. Before complying with this desire, one of the candidates requested to be heard for a few moments in support of what he considered an especial claim to be preferred before others. As his request was not denied, he proceeded to state that he had filled a similar and more responsible position for many years; that he had been in the habit for a long time of lecturing on scientific topics, and had a course of lectures then in progress, and that, in addition to his regular duties, he would, should they appoint him, pledge himself to give periodical elementary lectures in the school-room for the benefit of the pupils, their relatives and friends. This speaker was followed by another who had lived long on the Continent, spoke the German and French languages well, and offered to add to the usual curriculum instruction in those tongues, at the option of the children's parents. He, again, was succeeded by a third, of musical pretensions, who proposed, if they would elect him, to put up a capital church-organ in the school-room, and impart to such of the pupils as had ears and voices regular instruction in psalmody and chorus-singing; and he talked learnedly and at some length on the humanizing effects of music on the popular character. The lofty pretensions of these three were angrily resented by a fourth orator, who, mounting upon a stool, piously thanked heaven that he neither lectured, jabbered French, nor fiddled, which he begged the committee to believe was perfectly true "upon his honor," but that he knew what it was most desirable that the children should learn, *and how to teach it them*, as his testimonials would certify. This sarcasm put an end to further tempting displays of the sort, which might else have detained the meeting much longer; and we all adjourned, not without some wrangling and ill-humor, to the school-room below.

Our numbers were now reduced by repeated desertions (for several had slipped away during the examination) to about thirty, and a more hungry, thirsty, angry and discontented crew it was never my misfortune to witness; always excepting Mr. Boggle, who, solacing himself with a hunch of cold beef and bread, washed down with a second pot of stout, seemed in excellent spirits and temper. He could not, indeed, contain his satisfaction, and broadly told us all that what he had before hinted we should find true; namely, that *he* was the lucky individual—"the identical flute" destined to "leather the lads of the parish" in that identical room. "And good reason, too," said he, "old Bundle, the churchwarden is my father-in-law, and I've got four kids and another on the stocks, and devil a bob I've earned this four months." He added, for our further delectation, "I'm the only fellow in the parish what has put up for it, and I've canvassed every rate-payer, and got more than half the votes promised me already." " What have votes to do with it?" asked one, "the advertisement stated that the election would be made here to-night; I don't understand you." " Then I'll put you up to snuff: the election *will* be made to-night, but it will be the election of six or seven as will be allowed to canvas the parish, and I don't care which of you it is; I've got my circ'lars all ready, printed, sealed, and directed, and shall lug in most of the votes, I reckon, before to-morrow night." These extraordinary tidings were received with not a little indignation, the expression of which mightily amused Mr.

Boggle, who drank to the luck of the disappointed candidates, and expressed a hope that they would all "go in and win" another time; he had no objection, so long as they did not stand in his way

Several more now took their departure, some with loud expressions of contempt and anger, and by the time the beadle made his appearance at the top of the stairs, with the list of persons who, as Boggle had predicted, were to be allowed to compete for the situation, we numbered hardly a score. The beadle having bawled out, "Them gemmen whose names I'm a goin' for to call over is invited upstairs, and them as don't hear their names mentioned is declined," proceeded to read the list. It consisted but of eight persons, among whom were numbered myself and my acquaintance of the night, and of course the confident Boggle. We all obeyed the summons, and, perfectly well prepared for what was to follow, ascended the stairs. Mr. Bundle, with great pomposity, informed us that we had been selected by the committee for the excellence of the replies we had furnished to the questions proposed, and added that we might all proceed at our earliest convenience to canvas the parishioners; that a list of the rate-payers would be hung up in the school-room on the morrow; and that the choice would, of course, fall upon him who should obtain the greatest number of votes. This address was not received with half the complacency with which it was delivered. A number of voices began to protest at once against the measure, and to insist upon the terms of the advertisement being literally fulfilled. One, bolder than the rest, denounced the whole conduct of the affair as an infamous deception, and demanded that the replies of Mr. Boggle to the questions propounded should be read aloud for the satisfaction of those whom he was declared to have excelled. This was a contingency to which that sagacious personage had never given a thought, and it staggered him not a little; but his natural impudence befriended him, and he demanded in turn that the whole of his rivals' performances should be read as well. The old churchwarden, however, knew the game he played, and said he should permit nothing of the kind—"did they want him to go through the whole precious business over again? he had had enough of it for one bout. If any gentlemen was discontented he was at liberty to withdraw." This was adding fuel to the fire; the noise and confusion increased until at one moment I positively thought it was coming to a fight; but such a climax was luckily spared us, disgust predominating over anger in the bosoms of most of us. Threats of inquiry and public denunciation on the part of some of the defrauded and disappointed competitors were met by a scornful laugh from the committee, in which he who might now be considered the successful candidate heartily joined. At the command of old Bundle, the beadle now began putting out the lights; the committee took unceremonious leave by a private door, and in thorough disgust at the unprincipled transactions of the night we found our way into the streets at about two o'clock in the morning.

Having more than five miles to walk, for there was no conveyance to be found at that hour, I was glad of the companionship of my intelligent acquaintance, who certainly had the best title among all the competitors to the vacant post. I found he was much less surprised at the events of the night than I was, and bore the disappointment with more philosophy than I could pretend to. "I place little reliance upon such advertisements," said he; "it often happens that every thing is settled, as was the case here, before the announcement appears in the newspapers. Indeed its insertion is frequently but a matter of ceremony, in conformity with established precedent, or perhaps with the terms of the original endowment of the charity." I asked him if he thought Ben Boggle's name would have appeared in the list of eligible competitors had the curate remained in the room until that was drawn up. "Perhaps not," said he; "I saw the curate throw down his manuscript with a gesture of dislike But that is nothing, he would have canvassed the parish, for all that, under the auspices of his father-in-law, who has too much influence in the place to be easily withstood, and, being first in the field, he would have carried the day." "It appears to me," I remarked, "that the business of the night was purposely delayed, and protracted, perhaps, for more reasons than one. It might be desirable to get rid of half the applicants, as well as to weary out the curate, who could hardly be supposed favorable to the election of Mr. Boggle." This my companion thought very probable, but questioned whether, had the curate stayed, he could have prevented the ultimatum which had been arrived at, and which, it was plain enough, it was the determination of the sapient synod, the partizans of the churchwarden, to bring about.

It was broad daylight when I got to bed that morning, and being much fatigued with the harassing business I had gone through, the long fasting and the two hours' walk homewards, I did not rise until after ten in the forenoon. While hastily despatching my late breakfast, and ruminating on the events of the last night, a stranger was shown into my room who had been inquiring for me long before I had risen. He was a stalwart countryman, little short of seventy years of age, clad in a cloak of primitive quaker cut, corduroy breeches and top-boots, with a spotted Belcher neck-tye and a white hat, at least six inches in the brim. I thought at first that he had made a mistake, and introduced himself to the wrong person. Upon questioning him however, it appeared that he had been recommended to me by some persons at the office of the magazine, where I was well known, and where he had applied to have a small book printed, without having, in his supreme ignorance of literary matters, conceived it at all necessary to prepare a manuscript. He supposed, in fact, that the printer would know what he wanted, and furnish him with it as readily as a tailor would with a suit, or a saddler with a harness, and was very much taken aback to find that he must write the book, or get it written, before the printer could have anything to do with it. Still he was not to be deterred from his purpose, and, at the recommendation of some of my old companions, he had sought me out to enlist me in his service. I soon gathered from his garrulous narrative that he was by profession a toll-keeper, that he farmed a turnpike-gate, where he had sat for the last five-and-forty years at the receipt of custom; and that he had filled up his leisure for nearly the whole period by the study of geography, which he had made his hobby, and in the knowledge of which important science he considered himself second to no man living or dead. His object in coming to town was to make known to the world a discovery of his own, which he had been twenty years in bringing to perfection, and which he plainly considered would confer upon him an undying reputation. Having acquainted me with thus much, he untied a large greasy portfolio, and displayed to my expectant gaze what he termed a portable substitute for a terrestrial globe in the shape of a large pasteboard card of two feet square, upon which the land and water of the earth were rather curiously mapped out in one circle. Starting from the centre, as the North Pole, the meridians of longitude were drawn straight in all directions to the uttermost circumference of the circle, which was supposed to represent the South Pole. Of course the parallels of latitude were drawn at equal distances in circles round the centre, and the equator was marked by a darker line at the distance of half the diameter. The continents of Europe, Asia, and North America, were cramped and huddled together in the narrow meridians at the centre, and all together scarcely filled so much space as the island of New Holland, or Australia, which was necessarily made to crawl like a huge sea-serpent round nearly a third of the outer circumference. But, as the good man justly observed, these unfamiliar shapes, among which South America figured as a parallelogram, were no hindrance to the efficiency of his instrument, in order to the perfection of which he was compelled to give both hemispheres at one view. By means of a number of movable indices turning upon a pivot in the centre, and a graduated margin at the circumference, also furnished with movable points, together with a few other devices which it is not necessary to describe, he had rendered his machine available for all the purposes of a terrestrial globe, the use of which he felt confident that it would ultimately supersede, to his world-wide renown and personal emolument. He showed me how any problem which could be worked upon a globe could be also worked, and with greater ease and rapidity, by the help of his invention, which could be manufactured at less than one-third of the cost of a globe of a relative size.

Under the guidance of this strange and confident genius, and encouraged by a retaining-fee with which he qualified the commission, I set about the authorship of a small elementary treatise on geography, written for the purpose of introducing his "Planisphere," as he called it, to the notice of the public. The book, which barely amounted to 100 small pages, including the usual number of problems, and an explanation of the mode of solving them by means of the new machine, occupied me about a fortnight: and as the old gentleman paid me handsomely for the labor, I had no cause to be dissatisfied with my first feat in authorship. What was the result of my patron's speculation is more than I can say. The instrument, in a much more simple form than that in which I first saw it, and explained its use, is now to be purchased at most of the map-sellers in the Metropolis, and is in the hands of thousands of pupils in families and private schools; but the name of the Old Essex turn-pike man, who was indisputably the first inventor, and who expected to be immortalized by it, has given place to that of the all-engrossing publisher, and already ceased to be remembered.

This first literary attempt was followed by another of less fortunate issue. The old geographer recommended me to a pretentious fellow who had undertaken the sale of a part of his impression, and who had been a lottery-office printer in the neighborhood of Cheapside. This worthy engaged me to get up a couple of pocket-books for the ensuing year, it wanting yet some weeks to midsummer. At least a third of their contents was to be original or translated matter, and each was to contain a score or so of charades and enigmas, and a set of quadrilles. I contracted to supply matter for both, with the exception of the almanack, for ten pounds, and set about the business with my usual industry. I translated tales and sketches from the German and French, procured original papers from my old coadjutor T——, who was still a "sticker" at the grammar-school, tortured my dull brains in the construction of conundrums, transformed ten popular airs into a couple of sets of queer quadrilles for the pianoforte, and in little more than three weeks presented my manuscripts to my employer, with a demand for payment. He said he had made no stipulation for ready money, and declined paying anything, at least until the books had passed through the press. Before that consummation came about, he contrived to pass himself through the Bankruptcy Court, having first established his son in the business; and I, some eighteen months after, received from the assignees three-and-sixpence in the pound as the reward of my labors. This clever genius afterwards attained to civic honors, and, for aught I know to the contrary, enjoys them yet.

Having despatched this commission without receiving the sum agreed on, and having, moreover, a strong presentiment that it was never intended to be paid, I began to renew my search for regular employment. It was nearly the middle of July when I received information from B—— that hands were wanted at a house well known in the profession as a wholesale manufactory of blue-books. I applied without loss of time, and fortunately obtained an engagement which held out the prospect of permanency, and promised to yield an income above the average earnings of the trade. The house in which I found myself located bore the stamp of antiquity and dirt, both to a degree perhaps unrivalled in London. Originally a small office, it had, through the active and spirited management of a progenitor of the present owners, enlarged its bulk by elbowing out its neighbors in various directions, and appropriating their dwellings to its own use. Thus, though now an extensive establishment, it was little better than a ruin, and had to be periodically surveyed and shored up with beams and timbers to support the monstrous weight of metal with which every floor was oppressed. Nearly two hundred men, besides the necessary supplement of boys, were busily employed throughout the whole of the session of Parliament. Many of these were far advanced in years, and had passed the whole of their working lives upon the premises, and had brought up their sons to follow the same career. Considerable sums had been spent in repair of the frail tenement within the recollection of the youngest lad; but the oldest inmate, even he who had never left the office for a week together for nearly half a century, could not certify to the outlay of a single sixpence for purposes of cleanliness or sanitary precaution.* The ceil-

---

* A word here upon the treatment of working-men by employers. The compact between master and man, by which the former purchases the labor of the latter, appears to be the only thing kept in view by either of the parties. But the employer is morally bound to regard the health of the workman, if for no other reason than because the workman is in no condition to take care of himself. This obligation is, in London at least, almost universally repudiated. Men are crammed together in dark, damp and beggarly holes, where not a tithe of the air necessary to a healthy existence can penetrate, and where, in an atmosphere above a tropical heat, and saturated with reeking, villanous odors, they are frequently compelled to work sixteen hours out of the twenty-four the whole seven days of the week, it may be for months together; or they are buried in cellars or sheds pervious to every blast of the wintry winds, and are debarred from the sight of a fire the live-long day. Any place, in short, the vilest den or the most fetid hovel, is accounted good enough for the operations of the workman; and here he is subjected to a severity and continuance of labor which no man would be ass enough to impose upon a beast that was his own property, and for which if he did, the Society for the Prevention of Cruelty to Animals would haul him before a magistrate. In a word, the employer contracts for the labor of the workman and takes his life into the bargain, and he will continue to do so as long as

ings are black as printers' ink with the candle-smoke of two or three generations, and the walls, save where they were polished to a greasy brown by the friction of the shoulder, were of the same color. The wind and the rain were patched out from the clattering casements and the rotting window-frames by inch-thick layers of brown paper and paste. Type of all descriptions, old as the building itself, or shining new from the foundry, was abundant as gravel in a gravel-pit, and seemed about as much cared for. Pots, pans, dishes, and cooking-utensils ground the face of it as it lay upon the men's bulks, and the heels of the busy crowd, as they tracked their sinuous path through the piles of forms stacked together in every available space, razed the corners of the pages nearest the ground. Everything like comfort, order, economy, and even decent workmanship, was sacrificed to the paramount object of despatch—the turning out the greatest possible quantity of work in the shortest time. So great was the disorder consequent upon such a system, that, notwithstanding the plethoric abundance of materials of every sort, those wanted were rarely to be found at the instant they were required; and the most villanous shifts, in the use of which the men displayed an ingenuity which nothing but long practice could have matured, were resorted to, to meet the demands of the moment. The result of all this was shown in the appearance of the work produced, which, being done for the Legislature, nobody thought of criticising, and which came damp from the press with the aspect of printing a century old, impressed by some supernatural agency upon the modern composition of gypsum,

the latter is fool enough to submit to it. In the case of printers, the Legislature, which embodied its mercy towards the factory hands in the Ten Hours Bill, virtually enacts that printers shall work for fifty hours at a stretch, or even more upon occasions, and that they shall see neither waking wife nor child, nor church-pew nor pulpit, for six weeks together, when that friend of the people Joseph Hume, or my Lord Who-ever-it-is, at the helm of affairs, deems it expedient that the public stomach shall undergo a course of blue-books rags, and rubbish, which, under the name of paper, is palmed upon the Government, and becomes the transitory vehicle of the public and national records.

I was set to work upon papers relative to the Poor-Laws, which were then undergoing the reform so much needed, and though my habitually methodical disposition revolted at our headlong mode of despatching business, I soon grew reconciled to the slovenly haste which reaped the same remuneration at the week's end as would have been awarded to the most careful attention. The work was abundant, and we wrought late every night—and all night long two or three times in the week—though the men gained little or nothing by the extra night-work, in consequence of the idleness which necessarily followed the next day.

Before the session closed at the end of August, I had been given to understand that I might consider my occupation permanent; and, having concerted the previous necessary measures, I availed myself of the opportunity, in the second week in September, when the whole office took their annual holiday and devoured their customary "weigh-goose," to take my first trip by railway as far as Maidenhead, and starting thence by coach to Bristol, presented myself in the evening at my father's house.

I had been absent more than three years; and though, from continual correspondence with home, I had been made acquainted with all the events of the family circle, I was not prepared for the total change which greeted my view. I found the old couple alone in the snug cottage. Tom had married and settled five miles off two years before; Polly was governessing it in the heart of Wales, and my fair little Patty had been carried off by a young parson, to grace the lot of a poor curate's wife in a rural village a hundred miles away. My parents were not at all disposed to join in the melancholy impression the sight of their solitude produced upon me; and when I regretted that the family should be so broken up, said that I ought to regard the matter in a different light, as instead of growing less by loss from death, they had almost doubled in number since I parted from them. On inquiring for Ned, I found that he had managed the whole of my matrimonial preparations—had put up the banns at St. James's—had arranged the wedding to come off on the morrow—and was then off to F——, in order to return with the bride before breakfast in the morning, having first made his dispositions for a merry party.

And a merry party there was, and no mistake about it. I rose early in the morning, and, setting forth on the Bath Road, impatient for a sight of Ellen, had walked a couple of miles beyond Keynsham, when I met the phæton coming up Salford Hill, and containing, as I had hardly dared to expect, the Doctor as well as his protégé whom he had resolved upon "giving away." I was soon mounted by the side of my future wife; and at nine o'clock we descended at the cottage-door amidst a crowd of laughing faces assembled to do honor to our union.

I passed the next two hours in a kind of dreamy babble of which no distinct impression remains upon my memory. Then the rays of the sun were streaming on the monumental tablets in the old church, and the weird words were said which bound two loving hearts in one fate; and then I walked slowly through the antique porch with a *wife* hanging upon my arm.

CHAPTER XI.

Marriage and Manhood—I keep my own counsel—Memoir of Charley Crawfish, a "woman's husband" and a compositor of the old school—Doings of the "Cock Sparrow"—Charley's Portrait—Sixteen shillings' worth of Love—A Printer's Wedding—Grand musical procession—The Bride in hysterics—A "Jerry"—Congratulatory address—Spiritual union—Pleasures of Housekeeping—Home Joys—Paternal Counsels—A public Execution—The Rush to the Gibbet—Conduct of the mob—The victim of the Law—Death in the air—The Gallows good for Trade—Reflections on British killing by Law—Executions in France—The Influence of the Hangman upon the crime committing class—Effects of "Gallows Literature"

I SPENT the first quarter of my honeymoon in a ramble among the pleasant places on the banks of the Wye, in a visit to the old and dilapidated Abbey of Tintern, an ascent to the summit of the Wynd Cliff, and an excursion to Newport, Cardiff, and Swansea, and a return-voyage up the Channel. To Ellen all was new and beautiful; and there was a novelty and a beauty equally agreeable to my own perceptions, owing, perhaps, to the new feelings of half-delightful, half-serious, responsibility with which I now began to regard everything in the world. For months before the indissoluble knot was tied I had not been able to get over the impression which haunted me, as well sleeping as waking, that the event in which I was so much interested would never in reality take place; indeed, that in the course of circumstances, it never could take place; and that some portentous interference of fate or Providence would in some way or other assuredly prevent it. Now that, notwithstanding all my apprehensions, everything had come to pass precisely as I could have wished it, I am afraid that my pride kept at least equal pace with my gratitude, as I certainly began to entertain a much more exalted opinion both of myself and my merits than I had previously done. A wet day's journey on the outside of the Bristol coach, lasting from six in the morning till nine at night, during which we were both soaked to the skin, was the first gentle and admonitory introduction to the inevitable troubles of life which we were henceforth to share in common. We laughed them off then, and have never made very serious grievances of them to this hour. There are ten thousand little *désagrémens* which may spring up any day of one's life, which if you choose to receive with open arms will stick by you as permanent guests, but which will disappear without beat of drum if they be not honored with notice. I imagine the practical philosophy which leaves such trifles to take their own course was instinctive with both of us, and therefore the uninterrupted peace of our little household hitherto must perhaps be attributed as much to constitutional causes as to any individual merits to which we might lay a just claim.

I think it is Emanuel Swedenborg who makes the assertion that marriage renders the husband more a man *homo* and more a man *vir*; and supposing that that renowned visionary intended marriage with a proper object, at a proper season, the assertion is perhaps at least as true as anything in his Celestial Arcana. In the case of working-men, it is especially a fact that those who are well married are the most efficient, the most respectable, and the most intellectual and humanized (I cannot think of a better word) of their class. It is unfortunate, however, that in too many instances the advantage is all on the side of the male; and it has many a time been a marvel to me that men in this rank of life, often in superior circumstances considering their status, are content to see the mothers of their children leading a life of perpetual drudgery and discomfort. That share which a father is morally bound to take in the nurture and training of his offspring is not unfrequently repudiated altogether by the working-man of

London, who conceives, perhaps not without some show of reason, that if he undertakes and performs the duty of providing food, shelter and raiment for his family, no more ought to be required of him. It is true he has but little time for more, especially if he be a printer, the late hours at which men in this profession now labor, and the uncertainty of a release from labor at any specified hour, preclude the possibility of any regular intercourse between the father and his children: and it is no wonder that a duty which cannot be regularly fulfilled should be neglected altogether, or devolve upon the mother to fulfil as she best can. But, letting that pass for the present, if a well-assorted and well-timed marriage makes the husband more a man in all respects than the belated bachelor can ever be, there is a species of marriage infamously prevalent among the lazy classes of the industrial order, the existence and disgrace of which are but very partially known or appreciated, and which has a very contrary effect. I allude to the transformation which is brought about when an idle, boozing, and shammocking scamp weds an industrious girl profitably employed in some humble profession, for the sake of living, in whole or in part, upon the fruit of her labors, and who invariably becomes more idle, more drunken, more worthless—less a man *homo*, and less a man *vir*—a " woman's husband," in short, and nothing else in the world; unless, indeed, as is pretty sure to be the case, her tyrant and tormentor. I could, if I chose, make some curious revelations on the subject of such matches as these, which are by no means rare, and which, indeed, would be far more abundant than they are were it not for the fact that females in profitable professions— for that is a *sine quâ non* with your lazy suitor—are but seldom to be met with, or have too much good sense to contract engagements with men of doubtful character

I had said nothing to any of my companions on the subject of my intended marriage, for several reasons, and for one in particular, which would have effectually debarred any confidence of the kind had I been ever so much disposed to make it. This was the knowledge of the, to me, unsavory fact, that in all printing-offices *of any pretensions* the wedding of a comrade is signalized in a way far more ostentatiously ceremonious than flattering to the adventurous Benedict. I had not been back a week at my post before I had ample reason to congratulate myself upon the reserve I had maintained. I was then one among a numerous band of witnesses of the official celebration of the wedding of one of my comrades, which, as it reveals some of the characteristic mysteries of the inner world of the workshop, I shall chronicle precisely as it occurred, for the benefit of the world outside. The person to whom this unenviable honor was paid on the present occasion was " Old Crawfish," who had been nearly fifty years in the house, and a brief sketch of whose biography may well precede the account of the ceremony.

Charley Crawfish was brought into the world amidst the peculiar odors of printing-ink, seething pelts, and damp paper, being born in the narrow court or close in which stood the office where he wrought during the whole working period of his long life. His parents were of the most necessitous class, and, engaged in a continuous struggle for the means of subsistence, had not the power, even had they the inclination, to provide him with anything more than such an education as could be had for nothing. At a charity-school in the neighborhood he learned to read fluently and to write a little; and, thus qualified, he was thrust into the office at the age of twelve, at a salary of three shillings a-week, as warehouse, errand, or reading boy. It was now that his education really began. The social atmosphere of a printing-office at the close of the last century was infinitely worse even than it is at present. Intemperance, now the exceptional, was then the general stigma of the trade. Compositors, comparatively few in number, from the dearth of knowledge among the lower orders, or perhaps from the prevailing idea that a good education was indispensable for a printer, were proportionably independent, and were virtually the masters; while the pressmen, who had already earned for themselves the *sobriquet* of "pigs," were the drunken despots and tyrants of the profession. Among such surroundings Charley picked up his knowledge of the world, from which of course, his principles were to be deduced. At the age of fourteen he was apprenticed and turned into a frame to acquire the art of a compositor under the tuition of a journeyman, who, for a per-centage of his first six months' wages, taught him his easy business. He served his seven years, and, that term accomplished, found himself suddenly, at the age twenty-one, in the receipt of earnings amounting to double the average of the wages of a compositor of the present day, and varying from three to five pounds a-week during the greater portion of the year, and averaging half those amounts during the remainder. The sudden influx of riches developed his character in its full bearing. It was a very simple one indeed, consisting but of one trait—the sole, single, and undivided devotion of body and soul to himself What other men regard as a weakness or a blot, self-seeking or self-gratification, was Charley's pride and boast He was himself his own household god, and continued for nearly half a century at once the devout priest and gratified idol of the self-erected shrine. Soon after he was out of his time, he took simultaneously to matrimony and brandy-and-water. He married an industrious lass who drove a thriving trade in caps and clear-starching at one end of the court, and he immediately after joined a "free-and-easy" at the "Cock Sparrow," round the corner at the other end. It was observed that for the first few weeks of his matrimonial bliss he would hesitate on leaving the office of an evening, undecided which way to turn, attracted by the seductions of Hymen on the one side and of Cognac on the other. His affections, however, eventually surrendered to the brandy-and-water, the attractions of which grew stronger and stronger with each revolving year, while those of his busy wife and her quiet fireside waned and dwindled to the vanishing-point. The evening club which he frequented was the resort of prosperous tradesmen who had made their way in the world, devotees of gravity and grog, who met nightly, not to roar in drunken cadence the strains of patriotism or the joys of Bacchus, but to discuss the affairs of the nation over a philosophic pipe moistened with diluted spirits. Charley Crawfish sat them all out. One by one the Cock Sparrow, "with his bow and arrow," killed them all off; in thirty years not one of the original throttles of the Cock Sparrow club remained above-ground, save and except Crawfish alone, who, by this time swollen to double his natural size, had inherited the president's chair and controlled the orgies of the nightly assembly. Six glasses of brandy-and-water were his stated complement for the evening, save on extraordinary occasions, in honor of which he would enthusiastically " turn the figure," as he termed it, to the tune of " thrice again to make up nine." Of course it is almost needless to remark that his family—for he had a family—were dependent upon the industry of their mother both for support and training ; and she managed—how, Heaven knows—to bring up the children and launch them into the world, it was averred by those who knew him well, without any assistance or co-operation on his part. When I first saw him he was a rotound and portly figure of threescore, with the remains of a once handsome countenance bloated and animalized by sensual indulgence. A pair of sparkling black eyes surmounted by shaggy brows overlooked a Roman nose, which was rivalled in protuberance by a lower lip borne outwards to the horizontal position by forty years' goblet-pressure. He stooped a little and staggered much beneath the weight of some nineteen stone upon a pair of sturdy-looking legs, bandaged and " full of holes," which he anathematized vigorously, and swore that they were walking him into his coffin. He had just buried his wife and worn crape for three months when, feeling the want of somebody to look after his " shaky pins," as he called them, he was in search of a second helpmate, whom of course he was ready "to love, honor and cherish" as he had done the first. The blandishments of threescore, and the tenure of his ulcerated limbs, to say nothing of his brandy-and-water habits and his irascible alcoholic temper, were not very successful among his fair acquaintances. After a vain attempt at a courtship according to the old-established formula, by which he gained nothing more than a rather fierce feminine philippic in reference to his conduct towards his dead wife, he was driven to resort to other tactics. He made overtures to a sturdy charwoman whose services he had occasionally engaged after the death of his partner and drudge, and qualified his matrimonial proposal with another strictly mercantile, offering to allow her so much a week for housekeeping if she would only consent to make him happy. The coy bride, that was to be, objected to the smallness of the amount offered—she was willing to take him for better for worse, but not for less than sixteen shillings a week; she could not love, honor and obey, and bandage his bad legs night and morning, for less money; and further, knowing what she knew, namely, that the late Mrs Crawfish had not seen the color of her husband's money for the last five-and-twenty years, she was resolved, before the knot was tied, to have a contract drawn up and properly witnessed and signed previous to going to church To these not very amatory conditions the limping swain was compelled to subscribe before she would take him in hand; and accordingly the necessary document was prepared and executed in the presence of a select few of the bridegroom's comrades. The marriage had taken place at St. Andrew's Church, Holborn, on the morning of the Sunday previous to my return to the office; and the first day of comparative leisure in the following week was chosen for the official celebration of the affair according to the rites and ceremonies of the established "chapel"

On the morning of the celebration, long before the arrival of the decrepit swain, his frame was converted into a shady bower of verdant foliage by means of fresh-gathered boughs of evergreens, tastefully arched over the top, and ornamented with ribbons, true-lovers' knots and transfixed hearts, with here and there a plump-haunched Cupid nestling among the leaves. All the approaches through which he must pass to arrive at the bower were less liberally decorated with the same significant symbols, which were also seen fluttering on the shoulders or breasts of the various members of the companionship. So soon as the aged Benedict made his appearance, he was bowed and congéed with the most ceremonious respect by all hands to the decorated bower, where a high stool being placed for his reception, he sat in smiling state to enjoy the honors of the *fête*—a proxy having been appointed, in deference to his age and "shaky pins," to bear the part of the bridegroom in the procession. Congratulations now poured in upon him thick and fast, couched in language which it would be inadmissible to repeat, all received with perfect good humor and evident relish, and retorted with equal spirit and excelling want of decency by the object of them, amid roars of laughter on all sides. At length, at a given signal, a tremendous explosion of discord is heard in the room above, whither the masqueraders had retired to dress, and the procession is heard lumbering down the stairs amidst the clang of a species of overwhelming dissonance for which a printing-office alone could furnish the instruments. They consist chiefly of empty chases (square iron frames) of various sizes suspended by cords to act as triangles, and struck by a cross-bar or poker, emitting a portentous wailing jangle, in the pauses of which the blast of a tin horn, the crash of a watchman's rattle, the scraping of a fiddle, the thin wheeze of a dozen penny trumpets, and the flumping of a paper gong are distinguishable at intervals. The procession now forms in line at the foot of the stairs, and advances at a slow, pompous and marching step to the sound of its peculiar music. It is headed by the master of the ceremonies in a cocked hat, white waistcoat, peak-tailed coat of fashionable but antique cut, tights, black stockings and pumps, who clears the way with a long old-fashioned cane. He is followed by a simulated blind fiddler, ludicrously ragged and patched about the head, like Munchausen at his worst, and furiously rasping away at the tune of "Sir Roger de Coverley," or "Kiss my Lady." Then come a long file of followers, whose appearance it is impossible to describe with anything like accuracy, seeing that it varies on every occasion, according to the whims and comic humor of the individuals composing it. The most horrible disguises are generally those which elicit most mirth, and are therefore most in request. On the present occasion they were in number about thirty, mostly masked with hideous visages, goggle eyes, vampyre mouths, and tongues long enough to tuck under the arm, and nearly all bearing upon their heads cylindrical caps of paper stiffened with paste and pointed at the top, of the height of several feet, and ornamented with colored emblems. In front, and next to the blind fiddler, marched the proxy bridegroom genteelly dressed in his best suit with a white favor in his button-hole, and leering affectionately at the personated bride who hung upon his arm. This impersonation of the bride is looked upon as the cream of the joke. The person selected to play the part was the tallest, stoutest and strongest fellow in the house, and he was dressed precisely in imitation of the black doll that hangs suspended over a rag-shop, save that he carried before him two stuffed mountains of bosoms, perfect phenomena in their way, and glittering with jet polish, surmounted with a hideously grotesque black mask. In every room that he passed through, and that was every room in the house, it was his business to faint and go into hysterics, in the execution of which duty he performed most astonishing feats of strength, flooring his attentive partner by the convulsive extension of his arms or legs, and upsetting his supporters on all sides till half of them were sprawling on the floor, and invariably refusing to " come to" without the indulgence of a long and strong pull at a black bottle borne by the master of the ceremonies for the sole sustentation of *the lady*, and ostentatiously labelled "Old Tom."

As might be supposed, it frequently happens that the real bridegroom, particularly if a man of unobtrusive habits and character, holds this ceremony in utter abomination, and does all he can to escape from it. To escape, however, he is not allowed; and once in the grasp of his black and brawny bride of the hour, he is dragged around the whole circuit of the house, an unwilling sacrifice to the mirth of his companions. Any attempt at expostulation on his part is met by a general chorus of low and dismal groans which effectually drown his remonstrances, while his sable Dulcinea, fanning his face with an enormous gilded fan of the last century's manufacture, encourages him to the display of a manly fortitude by endearing appellatives and the proffer of restoratives from the black bottle with the label. In the instance I am recording, however, the bridegroom of the hour being a proxy, entered fully into the spirit of the farce, and played his part with such energetic demonstrations of affection so ludicrously conveyed as to convulse the spectators with laughter; leaving the bride at liberty to devote himself to the display of such soft feminine airs as would have astonished a professor of gymnastics.

Upon its entrance to every room, the procession was received by that indescribable salutation known in printing-offices under the appellation of a "jerry," a slang term for a unique species of alarm which can at any time be instantaneously produced, and which, when well executed, would give a stranger the impression that every joist, beam, timber, and plank in the building was undergoing simultaneous fracture, and the whole edifice coming down with a crash; it is, however, effected by the simplest means, merely by the employment of some fifty pair of hands in raking rapidly the numerous small boxes which contain the capital letters with some hard material, and as many feet in stamping heavily upon the ground. When the "jerry" and the succeeding cheer had subsided, the master of the ceremonies introduced the fictitious bride and bridegroom to that particular companionship and invited them to attend at the bower of love and beauty (pointing to the ebony bride), to drink the health of the new-married pair. The invitation was, of course, accepted with due acclamation, in the midst of which the procession moved on, with a grand instrumental crash, to complete the round of the premises. When the whole house had been thus perambulated from the topmast to the ground-floor, the *cortége* returned to the large room, where the bridegroom, enthroned on the stool in front of his bower, was receiving the congratulations of a hundred men, who, in acceptance of the general invitation, had repaired to the scene of action. At the information of the approaching music, a lane was formed amidst the dense crowd, through which the whole procession in Indian file moved forward to present their individual obeisance to the bridegroom. These consisted of a strange variety of speechless antics and grimaces, accompanied with low bowings and semi-prostrations, and sundry clever but delusive attempts to pierce the fat paunch of the grinning Benedict by butting at him with their pointed paper caps.

When all the masqueraders had rendered due homage to their fat idol, the father of the chapel, giving three blows with a mallet upon the imposing-stone, made an imperative demand for silence, while the master of the ceremonies should deliver an address to the bridegroom, to which the attention of all present was politely requested. Then followed the address, delivered with a loud, deliberate, and distinct utterance, that not a syllable might be lost; the orator pausing at every period to allow time for the subsidence of the roars of laughter with which every sentence was greeted. Of this address it is impossible to present the reader with a single line, out of regard to mere considerations of decency. Enough to say that it was perfectly unique in its character—that every conceivable joke upon the subject of matrimony, intensified in obscenity by the powerful alembic of a depraved imagination, was brought into

LIQUID CONSUMMATION OF THE CONTRACT.

requisition, and a hundred technical expressions peculiar to the trade, endowed for the nonce with an indecent signification, added a welcome savor to the much-relished display. These addresses are perfect marvels of the sort, exhibiting, as they generally do, the connexion of language studiously decorous and well-chosen, with ideas grossly filthy and disgusting. They form, I believe, a portion of the literary treasures of the printing-office, and bear in their composition the evidence of careful compilation and selection from a stock of probably hoarded witticisms and humorous allusions, applicable to the subject of matrimony in connexion with the technicalities of the business. When the address was finished, amidst a crowning cheer of applause, a space was cleared for a dance. The blind fiddler was lifted upon the " stone," and " Sir Roger de Coverley " was danced *con amore*, accompanied with the falling of the towering caps, the rejection of the masks, beards and ugly visages, and the gradual but complete denudation of the masquerading attire—even the blind fiddler himself shaking off his rags and patches and revealing the well-known features of Sam P——, famous for the fury of his fiddling and his frenzy for frolic.

Thus ended the ceremony; the contracting parties were now considered to be officially united in wedlock, and it only remained to cement their union and the good fellowship of the house with the customary libations of gin and beer. The merits of these two liquids were sententiously discussed, with mock gravity, by two separate parties each maintaining the superiority of their favorite beverage. Old Crawfish, who always professed a horror of neat spirits, voted in favor of beer; the bouncing bride defending her feminine weakness in favor of the more stimulating draught. The master of the ceremonies settled the question, in virtue of his office, by deciding that both were better than either; and, with a delicate allusion to the alliance they had already celebrated, proposed their instantaneous combination in one matrimonial gallon can. This was accordingly done; and the precious mixture being renewed as often as necessary, the healths of the virtuous couple were drunk with due honors by all assembled, and, it now being one o'clock and the liquor out, the meeting was dissolved. Most of the men returned to their work in the afternoon, as though no interruption had occurred, but, as always happens on such occasions, a certain class, foes to half measures and eager to "wet the other eye," drew off in a body to the neighboring public-house and wound up the mummery of the morning with a night of drunken uproar and debauch

I esteemed myself fortunate to have escaped such an ovation, rather than have undergone which I would have abandoned any advantages that a printing-office could afford. I kept my own counsel, and passed with my comrades for a bachelor for the best part of a year after my marriage. I had now considerable leisure upon my hands, seldom working by candle-light during the whole of the recess of Parliament We spent the long evenings of autumn and early winter, when the weather was fine, in contemplating the mighty world of London, with its ever-moving tide of population, under the mysterious aspect of night It was a novel and wild pleasure to Ellen to stand aside awhile, in one or other of the crowded arteries of the great Babel, and watch the unending flow of the living stream of human forms emerging from the gloom and vanishing again in a moment into the mist and darkness; and we uttered on such occasions many profound and sagacious moralizings, with which it is not my intention to regale the reader. Arm-in-arm we threaded without weariness the interminable thoroughfares of commerce, and, gazing with unsated eyes upon the gorgeous spectacle of wealth, industry, and art arranged in the dazzling shop-windows, enjoyed the gratuitous exhibition with a thousand times more pleasure than we could possibly have done had we been the undisputed possessors of the whole. Then, at times, we concocted plans of economy; and, armed with the neatest of baskets and a capacious great-coat pocket, went to market together in order to put them in execution. The country girl from the hill-side was completely bewildered by the noise and tumult of the New-Cut market on a Saturday night where the throng was so dense and every door and counter so besieged by clamorous buyers that her quiet voice could not be heard, and I was obliged to come forward and lend my lungs for the occasion. Then, having supplied our own wants, we would linger on the skirts of the throng and observe with curious eyes how others managed their weekly expenditure. Young wives and elderly matrons, intent upon provisioning for the Sunday's dinner, haggled and chaffered and cheapened the coveted morsel, and palavered and cajoled the saucy butcher or the unctuous butterman till they got what they wanted, either the object of debate or a curt and surly rebuke that sent them in search of it elsewhere. Then sometimes we would both snatch a hasty peep into the gin-shop at the corner, where squalid poverty rioted drunkenly in rags, and purchased the hunger of the morrow with the unreason of to-day; and where brutality in fustian jacket bullied and beat the partner of his self-wrought wretchedness and robbed his offspring of their daily bread; and then, without a doubt, we moralized once more. Ah! those were happy days, when we were beginning to play the game of life, and, like children at school unwilling to peril the loss of a new toy, played it " in fun " and not in earnest.

With the colder and less favorable weather came longer evenings and a cosy fireside—in the little kitchen when we were alone, in the first floor when a friend—of whom, Heaven be praised! we had very few—favored us with a visit. Upstairs we played duets on the piano, and rehearsed again and again the songs and ballads which formed our little stock of music, occasionally supplemented by the purchase of a new piece, or the painful copying of a borrowed one; and downstairs we rubbed water-colors on the plates and dishes, and splashed landscapes on the snowy sheet, which we often found prodigiously yellow, and anything but snowy in the morning, through my wife's liberality in the article of gamboge. She rubbed out the colors while I drew an outline, and then read aloud while I washed them in; and so we made pictures, and devoured books, and created a world of our own in which we lived like absolute monarchs, with none but ourselves to govern.

My father, who had nothing else to contribute towards establishing his children in the world, forwarded us his blessing and good wishes in a letter, which, from experience of the value of the advice it contains, I shall publish *verbatim*, for the benefit of young couples all and sundry. Thus he wrote.—

Oct 21, 1836.

"MY DEAR SON AND DAUGHTER,—I cannot refrain from following you with the expression of my wishes for your welfare, and some counsels which my anxiety on your account will not suffer me to suppress. They shall be few and short, as the more likely to be remembered. You are neither of you aware, so much as you will be some years hence, that each of you is more dependent on the other than upon all the rest of the world put together for daily and hourly comforts and the peace of the heart habitually at ease: these are mainly promoted by the little nameless amenities without which the ripplings of life will become waves of trouble It is therefore desirable that each should bear it always in mind that your temporal destinies are indissolubly linked together, and a *little* unkindness is a *great* wrong in either of you.

"After a few months, I trust both your minds will settle down into that incomprehensible consciousness of *oneness* which, while it is the most mysterious is also the sweetest, purest and loveliest of all human affections But the exquisite delights of such a relation can only be preserved by each maintaining a course insuring the utmost confidence and respect of the other. A cross look, an unseemly word, negligent inattention to known wishes—will scatter the complacent comfortableness as a harsh handling destroys the bloom of a fine piece of fruit. I wish both of you may be able to avoid everything of the kind; it is better to be a little painstaking to suppress the first rising of such sort of things than to destroy in one moment the complacency which no after-care can ever restore.

"I am glad to learn that my son is joined to a companion whose departure from home is matter of regret to all who knew her, and most so to those who knew her best. If I mistake not, her capabilities and aptitude to create domestic comfort are far beyond a sackfull of gold; and I trust his good sense as well as his affection will afford them fair play. On the other hand I beg to remind my new daughter that the husband has a thousand elements of disturbance in his daily avocations to which the wife is an utter stranger; and it will be her privilege and her title to the respect of all whose respect is worth having, to make his own fireside the most attractive place in the universe for the calm repose of a wearied body or excited mind. The minor comforts, which are the most valuable because the most constantly in requisition, will depend more upon her looks, her manner, and the evidences of her forethought, than upon all the other occurrences of life.

"A long and diversified experience of the ways of men compels me to the ungracious counsel: Put no unnecessary confidence in any man, and be particularly cautious in dealing with a company of men, be their individual worth whatever it may. Reduce to black and white whatever is of the slightest importance to "good understanding" and expect nothing that is not so explicitly detailed and insured.

"My best wishes and trembling prayers go with you.
Your AFFECTIONATE FATHER."

One Saturday morning towards the close of November or beginning of December, I have forgotten the precise date, a letter was put into my hand at the office. It was from my quondam friend and employer the cutler editor, as whose agent

I occasionally acted, and who charged me with a commission to procure him certain "sorts" from the foundry and transmit them by coach, in time for his next impression. Not choosing to disappoint my wife and lose my dinner, I deferred the visit to the foundry until after work in the evening; when, upon arriving at Chiswell-street, I found the men in the act of leaving, but was informed I could have the materials I wanted as early as I chose on Monday. On Monday morning, accordingly, having risen rather earlier than usual and breakfasted by candle-light, I set forth to execute my commission before proceeding to work. Crossing Blackfriars-bridge, and barely noticing that there was an unusual concourse of foot-passengers of the laboring and lower sorts, I turned up Ludgate-hill, where I found the crowd still greater, less equivocally disrespectable, and all hurrying forward at a rapid walking-pace. Intent upon the object I had in view, I pushed forward as rapidly as the rest, and turning sharp round into the Old Bailey, came suddenly upon a spectacle which, of all others, was the farthest from my thoughts It was the morning of an execution. A thick damp haze filled the air, not amounting to an actual fog, but sufficiently dense to confine the limits of vision to a few hundred yards. The beams of the level sun threw an almost supernatural light of a dim but fiery hue into the mist which they yet had not force enough to penetrate; and there, darkly looming with grim and shadow-like outline against a background of lurid vapor, rose the gallows upon which a wretched fellow-creature was about to be death-strangled and dangled in expiation of the crime of murder. In a moment the commission I had in hand vanished from my thoughts, and, impelled by a fearful and morbid curiosity, I suffered myself to be borne by the pressure behind, every moment aggravated by the arrival of trampling multitudes to the spot, towards the object of the general gaze. One minute afterwards, I saw that the attempt to retrace my steps would be not only vain but dangerous; and, compelled to make the best of what I could not now avoid, I was pressed onward as far as the outlet of Fleet-lane, when, contriving by main force to get my back against the end of a stout trestle upon which seven or eight fellows were mounted, I managed to maintain my position until the horrible ceremony was concluded.

It wanted yet full twenty minutes to eight o'clock, when I stood fast wedged within a few fathoms' length of the scaffold. As far as the eye could pierce through the misty glare, was one unbroken sea of human heads and faces; the outer masses reeling, staggering and driving in fitful currents against the firm, compact and solid centre, fixed and immovable as though charmed to stone by the horrible fascination of the gibbet. Far beyond and above all, the tower of St. Sepulchre's, magnified by the morning haze, showed like a tall, transparent cloud, from which was soon to burst the thunder-peal of doom upon the miserable man who had shed his brother's blood. The subdued murmur of the immense mob rose and swelled like the hollow roar of a distant but angry sea. Here and there a tall and burly ruffian, pre-eminent above the crowd, signalled his fellow in the distance, or bellowed a ghastly witticism upon the coming horror across the heads of the throng. Women— if women they are to be called, who, like vultures to the carcase, flock to the spectacle of dying agonies—of all ages but of one indescribably vicious and repulsive class, had pushed, and struggled, and fought their way to an eligible point of view, where they awaited with masculine impatience the close of the fearful drama of which they formed so revolting a part. Children of tender age, who must have taken up their position ere the day had dawned, and before the arrival of the masses, made an unsightly addition to the scene. A boy of nine, borne aloft on the shoulders of a man of sixty, who stood by my side, expressed his uncontrollable delight at the tragedy he was about to witness. At every window in the houses opposite the debtors' door, and indeed wherever a view of the gallows could be obtained, parties of pleasure were assembled for the recreation of the morning. The roofs, the parapets, the protruding eaves of the shops, all were populous with life ; the very lamp posts and projecting sign-boards were clung and clustered over with eager beings impatient to assist in the funeral obsequies of the victim of the law

And now a violent surging and commotion in the centre of the living mass gives token of a fierce quarrel which has ripened to a fight Shrieks, yells and cheers of encouragement issue from a hundred throats, while a crew of tall and powerful blackguards elbow and trample their way to the scene of action, and the glazed hats of the police are seen converging unerringly to the disturbed spot Then there is the flourishing of gilded staves, the sound of sturdy blows followed by a roar of execration, and a gory-visaged culprit is dragged forth, defrauded of his expected banquet, and consigned to a cell in the nearest station

The tumult has hardly subsided when another claims attention. A brace of pickpockets, taking advantage of the fight, are caught in the too confident exercise of their profession; and these, much easier captives than the fighting Irishman, are led off in their turn to the same vile durance.

By this time, weary and actually sore with the repeated violent collisions I had undergone in sustaining my post. I was glad to make a bargain with the man perched above me, who, for a bribe of a few pence, allowed me to effect a footing in his front. I had scarcely accomplished this when the church-clock in the distance rung out the quarters. . The crowd, listening for this, had been comparatively silent for the last few minutes, and the note of the bell was acknowledged by a kind of shuddering deprecation for silence, by the instant uncovering of innumerable heads, and the involuntary direction of every eye towards the debtors' door. As the fatal hour at length pealed forth the door was slowly opened, and there came out upon the scaffold, not the mournful death-procession which all were awaiting with such intense interest, but its grim herald and precursor, the crime-honored aristarch of kill-craft, the great stage-manager of the law's last scene, whose performances are so much relished by the mob—the hangman, bearing the odious strand of new rope coiled upon his arm. He was received with a low but universal hum of recognition from the vast multitude now breathless with the exciting anticipation of what was so soon to follow. With an apparent perfect unconsciousness of the presence of a single spectator, he proceeded to mount to the cross-piece of the gibbet, to which, with an air of professional dexterity, he deliberately attached the loathsome cord, occasionally pausing and measuring with his eye the distance to the level of the platform. During this operation he was favored with a running fire of comments and counsels, garnished with infernal jokes and sallies of insane humor, from the mob who stood nearest. Having made the necessary preparations, he withdrew for a few minutes, amidst the mock cheers and congratulations of some kindred spirits below.

The awful pause which ensued was but of brief duration. Too soon a group of dark figures slowly emerged from the open doorway, among which I could discern the chaplain reading the burial-service, and then the quivering criminal, his hands clasped in prayer, yet bound together in front of his breast: he was supported by two assistants, and was already, to all appearance, more than half dead with mortal terror. These demonstrations of insupportable anguish on the part of the principal performer were received with evident and audible dissatisfaction by a large portion of the spectators of the drama. Derisive sneers on the want of "pluck" manifested by the poor, horror-stricken wretch were expressed in language which cannot be repeated; and in many a female but unfeminine face hardened by embruting vice and callous to every feeling of humanity, I read a contemptuous scorn of the timorous sufferer and a proud and fiend-like consciousness that they themselves would have dared the dark ordeal with less shrinking. The very boy mounted on the old man's shoulders at my side called his grand-dad" to witness that "the cove as was to be hanged wasn't game,' a declaration which was received with a hoarse chuckle and a corroborative verdict by the standers-by, while the repulsive ceremony went on with fearful rapidity. In less than a minute the light of day was shut for ever from his eyes, his ears were dumb to the last prayerful accents from human lips, and the body of the malefactor, sinking with a sudden fall until half concealed by the level platform, struggled in the final throes of agony for a few moments—mercifully abbreviated, as some well-experienced amateurs at my side plainly pointed out, by the coadjutors of the hangman pulling heavily at the feet in the inclosure below—and then swung senseless, veering slowly round upon the now-deserted stage.

The very instant the "drop" fell, and while the short gasping cry from a thousand lips which hailed the close of the tragedy yet rung in the air, the scene assumed a new character the elements of business were borne into the arena of pleasure. Three or four nondescript specimens of the street-orator, who were standing just beneath me, drew suddenly forth from the depths of their long-tailed greasy coats of serge each a bundle of damp paper, which they flourished into flags in a twinkling, and while the death-struggle was acting before their eyes, eager to turn it to account and to realize an honest penny, filled the air with their roaring intonations of "the last dying speech, confession and behavior" of the murderer of the season. Their example was imitated by fifty others on different parts of the ground, and the chorus of their united voices formed but a beggarly requiem to the departing spirit. The tragedy ended, the farce, as a matter of course, came next The body had to remain suspended for an hour, and during that hour amusement must be provided, at least for that portion of the spectators who can never have enough unless they have the whole of an entertainment To swing a live cat from a side avenue into the middle of the crowd; to whirl a heavy truncheon from one broken head on a mission to another; to kick

HANGING, A RIDICULOUS CEREMONY. 279

maul and worry some unfortunate stray cur that has unhappily wandered from his master; to get up a quarrel or a fight, if between women so much the better—such are some of the time-honored diversions chosen to recreate the hour which a sagacious legislature presumes to be spent in moral reflections upon the enormity of crime and the certainty of its bitter punishment, in the presence of the law-strangled dead.

I had never before seen a public execution in England, but I knew perfectly well—as who does not know?—the feeling with which such exhibitions are regarded by the lower orders, and I had often revolved in my mind the probable cause of that feeling. In now witnessing thus accidentally the whole ceremony, I thought I perceived one source of it, and that not a trifling one, in the ceremony itself. It struck me, and I have no doubt but others have received the same impression, that with all the actual horrors of the dismal process, in addition to a great deal that is disgusting, there is a great deal more that is essentially though horribly ridiculous in our national legal method of public killing. The idea of tying a man's hands, of drawing over his face a white night-cap, through which his features yet remain dimly legible, and then hanging him up in the air is manifestly a ridiculous idea—and connect it with what dreadful realities we may, the sense of the comic or absurd will predominate in the minds of the populace, ever alive to the appreciation of the preposterous or the discrepant, and never willingly disposed to serious reflection. The vagabond kennel-raker, the nomadic coster, the houseless thief, the man of the lowest order of intellect or of morals, sees the majesty of the law descending to the punch-and-judy level, and getting rid of its criminals by the same process as the hunch-backed worthy adopts to get rid of his tormentor—and being accustomed from his infancy to laugh heartily at the latter exhibition, he is not likely to retain for any length of time a grave demeanor in presence of the former one. A flogging in the army is allowed by all unfortunate enough to have witnessed it to be a far more impressive spectacle than a hanging at the Old Bailey. Strong men are known to faint at the sight of the one, while boys and women find amusement in the other. If the object of either exhibition be to deter the spectators from offending against the laws, why is the discrepancy between the effects of the two all on the wrong side? unless it be that the one exhibits the semblance at least of Justice vindicating her violated authority with a deserved though terrible measure of severity, while the other comes into view as a mere hasty and bungling business of killing, the vulgar and beggarly details of which it is impossible to connect in imagination with her divine attributes.

Some years before, I had witnessed in Paris the execution of two men for assassination. The crowd on that occasion, in the Place de Grève, was as great as now in the Old Bailey; but their decorum, I am bound to state, was infinitely greater. I can only account for this difference in favor of a population among whom human life is at a far greater discount than it is with us, from the fact that among the French a public execution is a much more impressive spectacle than it can be made to be in England. The guillotine bears a higher character, perhaps because it wears a more serious and terrible aspect than the gallows; and the functionary who controls its avenging blade does not, as with us, bear a name the synonym of all that is loathsome and repulsive. It is the same class of men and the same order of minds that flock together to gaze at public executions wherever they take place; but I question whether, in any other country than England—except, perhaps, among our offshoots, the Americans—a class of traders could be found corresponding with our hawkers and bawlers of last dying speeches, who congregate with their lying wares around the foot of the gallows, watchfully waiting for the commencement of the death-struggle, to them the signal of commerce, and then, at the precise moment of horror, unanimously exploding from their hoarse throats "a full, true and particular account, for the small charge of one halfpenny." The meanest mud-lark in all Gaul, the infamous and malodorous *chiffonier* of Paris, would recoil with disgust from such a species of traffic, the prevalence and prosperity of which at such a time among the lowest orders of London, testify perhaps more than any other single fact to the degraded state of the popular feeling in reference to death-punishment by the hands of the hangman.

Second to the influence of the hangman, and the scene in which he figures in the production of a degrading and disgraceful estimate of the terrible solemnities of justice, is that of the press. What the Old Bailey or the Horsemonger-lane exhibition is to the uneducated spectator, the broad-sheet is to the uneducated reader; and it requires no great discrimination to recognize in the publication of every minute particular of deeds of violence and bloodshed, looking to the avidity with which such details are seized upon by the public, one of the most fruitful sources of demoralization and crime. The wretched criminal whose language, looks and deportment are chronicled as matters of general importance, become first an object of interest, then an idol, to those of his own class. If, as we know to be the case, men are led by the force of example to the commission of suicide, why not of any other species of crime? If a fashion may spring up, and prevail for a time, of leaping headlong from the top of a monument or the parapet of a bridge, through the publicity given to such acts by means of the press, how shall the exploits of the felon or the assassin escape imitation when made the subjects of a far more extensive and pertinacious publicity, and paraded as they are before the world with all the importance they can be made to assume? There can be no question but that this practice of pandering to a morbid taste for a detestable species of excitement results largely in engendering the very crimes which certain public writers find it so profitable to detail at such length. The performer on the Old Bailey stage becomes a veritable hero in the eyes of the mob of readers for whose especial delectation his history is periodically dished up, and they gloat over the recital of his acts with a relish and a gusto which no other species of literature can awaken. So great, indeed, of late years has grown the appetite for violence and villainy of all kinds, that our romance-writers have generously stepped forward to supplement the exertions of the last-dying speech patterer, as a pendant to whose flimsy damp sheets they supply a still more " full, true, and particular account " in the form of three volumes post octavo. Thus, besides the certainty of being hanged in the presence of ten or twenty thousand admiring spectators, the daring and darling desperado who · dies game " stands the enviable chance of becoming a literary property in the hands of one of these gentlemen, and of running a second course, " in half calf and lettered," to interest and instruct that very community whom it was his life-long occupation to rob, to plunder or to slay.

Pondering such discursive philosophy as this in my mind, I stood still on my threepenny eminence until the crowd had sufficiently cleared away to allow me to retrace my steps so far as Ludgate-hill without inconvenience. Then, having no great relish for the cadaverous jocularity which generally characterizes the scene of an execution during the removal of the body of the malefactor, I descended and turned my back upon the ignominious spectacle, with a feeling of disgust for the multitude of my fellows who could find recreation in the elements of cruelty and horror and with anger and vexation at myself for having added one to their number.

CHAPTER XII.

The Printing Season—A "regular Fly"—Blue-book Labors—Half a pint of Beer—Office suppers and night work—A Sleepy House—Birth of a Blue-book—Destiny of the majority of them—I am promoted and enter the closet—The Printer's Reader—His peculiar position, and the reputation he bears—A model Reader—Candidates for the Closet—His real Character—Slanders concerning him—His habits of neatness and punctuality—His amusements—His 'den"—The Reader at work—The Reading-boy, and his predilections—His duties and habits—The reader his oracle—Specimen of the tribe—A stipendiary Billow—Virtues of the Wave—His one failing—I am called up to be reprimanded—Marvellous erudition of my Employer.

My merry Christmas and first matrimonial plum-pudding, which I had a hand in compounding—the sprig of mistletoe which I bought for home-consumption, the walks in the parks and the skatings on the Serpentine during the two days' holiday, the various visits to the grand gastronomic displays of butcher, confectioner, and poulterer; the oratorio at Covent Garden Theatre, where Lindley, Mori, and Dragonetti played together: these are some of the pleasant reminiscences of our first wedded winter, and though similar scenes have been re-enacted a dozen times since then, the first impressions seem to have reserved no room for succeeding ones, which have left but a transient trace behind them. The new year came in with a very icy face, under which encouraging aspect a crop of beggars sprung up in the streets, and filled the air with the proclamation of their woes. Ellen, shocked at their shivering misery, would have relieved, as far as she could, the whole vagabond tribe had I not, with some considerable difficulty, relieved her of the unnecessary load of sympathy which weighed upon her conscience, by showing her the true state of the case.

As tne time drew near for the opening of the session of Parliament, we began to prepare at the office for the renewal of business under the customary pressure of sudden and impatient demand. As usual in the month of January, the overseer was now daily and hourly besieged by applications for employment from hands out of work. As a matter of policy, old faces were preferred to new, but old and new together soon filled the house, until every available frame was occupied. The Queen opened Parliament, to the great satisfaction of crowds of hungry and thirsty typographers; and that small vial of moonshine, the royal speech—fit symbol of the forthcoming utterance of the two great logocracies of the nation—was for a moment in everybody's mouth, and then vanished. Thanks to Joseph Hume, at whose instigation the types began to dance merrily a few hours after the House had met, we had not much time for criticising her Majesty's speech or anything else Colonial papers, reports of committees, election returns, prison statistics, accounts, and fifty things besides, poured in upon us thick and fast Every one was hurried to its rapid and slovenly consummation by the pressure of another demanding immediate attention; and, as a general rule, everything once taken in hand was prosecuted to its conclusion, unless retarded by some unwelcome interference from "another quarter" Occasionally, however, exigencies of a peculiar nature would occur, when a certain subject of real or fancied importance, eclipsing for a time all others, would peremptorily call for the production of a blue-book instanter. Such panics of impatience on the part of our sage senate give rise in the printing-office to what compositors are in the habit of calling "a spurt," or in extreme cases, "a regular fly." I shall describe the birth of a blue-book under these circumstances for the benefit of the unsophisticated public, and of that portion of them in particular, our friends, the buttermen and trunkmakers, who apply so many of them to purposes of real usefulness.

The first inkling of a "regular fly," is derived from a rumor circulating among the men—often originating in a hint from the overseer, and as often arising from suspicion aroused by certain prophetic signs which they understand well enough—such, for instance, as a withholding of work while there is plenty in store. By this they know that the order to print has been issued, and that the temporary lull will soon be succeeded by a storm. By-and-by comes a regular sequence of porters from Westminster, each bearing a batch of copy. These ingenious gentry understand their profession to a miracle. Instead of competing for employment, by emulating each other in matters of punctuality and despatch, they make common cause together, and most probably share the aggregate profits. At any rate they split their packages into small portions, so small, indeed, that it will take a dozen of them to cary a ream of paper—a division of labor which, as each receives a shilling compliment from the printer, is found to answer in a manner perfectly satisfactory. The manuscript received, collated and folioed, and a few other necessary preliminaries first settled, a general order is issued for all hands to suspend everything in progress, to mount cases of a certain specified type, and prepare for copy. Then there is a general burrowing and rummaging in all the dark holes, dusty corners, and damp cellars of the crazy edifice for the type in request, and no small amount of squabbling and skirmishing for its possession when found. The foraging, at length successful, furnishes material for the rapid and pattering shower of wet metal into the dusty cases. While this leaden sleet is descending, the clicker of each companionship, who has received his allotment of the copy, gives notice to all that it is waiting in readiness, and the men as they successively finish "distribution," apply to him for a "taking;" generally a few leaves is sufficient to employ them for two or three hours. In the meantime the "quoin-drawer-man" drags forth fresh stores of type from the hoarded stack in the cellar, being specially charged to continue the supply to prevent the possibility of delay through lack of material. At one o'clock the men are admonished by the clicker that the "line is on," or in other words, business recommences at a quarter to two. Some few, who live at a distance, thereupon send for dinner to the nearest cook-shop, and dine in the office, resuming work after a hasty meal. At two o'clock the overseer makes the round of the office, visiting every room, either in person or by deputy, to ascertain that every frame is filled and that every occupant is in a condition to do his duty. A significant silence prevails, broken only by the low whispering clatter of type rushing into periods and paragraphs. The overseer retires, and soon after the word is passed for night-work—a word far from welcome to any, but particularly disagreeable to the older hands who have had too much experience of the tax it levies upon the constitution, without any compensating contribution to the pocket. During the afternoon hundreds of thousands of type are lifted into line. About four the kettles are singing on the fires, and at five Mrs. Grundy and her maids bring round hot tea on trays for those who decline the trouble of brewing for themselves. There is a cessation of labor for half an hour, the men congregating round the fire, and thrusting lumps of bread on long toasting-forks between the bars of the grate. Having "tippled their twankay," and consumed the short interval of repose, the men resume work. The first few sheets of the forthcoming volume are by this time made up into pages, and the noise of mallets used in locking up the forms resounds from different quarters. The clicker runs to the stair-head and bawls out 'Proofs!'" at the top of his voice, and forthwith appears a pressman with a quire of wet paper across his naked arm, and, perhaps, an inking roller in his hand. He pulls the proofs at one of the thousand and one identical old wooden presses at which Benjamin Franklin wrought as a teetotaller fourscore years ago. The proofs, when pulled, with the copy of each sheet folded within it, are carried to the overseer's closet.

As evening draws on, Pluto, the pewter Ganymede from the public-house in the lane below, makes his welcome appearance, bearing in each hand a bunch of pewter pint pots, each containing half-a-pint of beer. He carries a memorandum-book and a pencil to keep score, and vociferates, as he walks rapidly round, "Beer, gentlemen—gentlemen, beer!" If he utter anything besides, it is *sotto voce*, and for private edification. His half-pints meet a ready sale; and it might be imagined, seeing that they are vended in pint pots, that he is under the temptation to dispense very apochryphal measure. The believers in beer have, however, discovered an ingenious check to any attempts of the kind. I have heard some of them boast that their capacity of swallow was an exact half-pint, and that they could detect a fraud of a thimbleful by the guage of their own throats. Without questioning their exactness, which, however satisfactory to themselves, could not be demonstrated to the satisfaction of another, I prefer the mathematical mode of measurement adopted by the many, which is simple and susceptible of demonstration. It is the briefest operation imaginable: when a thirsty comp suspects that he has an unfair half-pint, he immediately depresses the pint pot to an angle of forty-five degrees, which of course brings the grateful beverage to the very verge of the vessel; he then knowingly glances towards the bottom of the pot, and if any portion of that is not submerged in the liquid, he knows that he holds short measure in his hand, and he knows, too, to what extent it is short; "because," says he, "a half-pint is a half-pint, length-ways or breadth-ways, and no mistake about it."

But we cannot waste our time upon beer. We labor on with the utmost expedition, and in the course of a few hours from the commencement of composition a bundle of sheets of first-proofs have accumulated on the overseer's desk, and he now despatches them, with the copy, to the several readers to whom the volume has been allotted. After an interval of no great length, the proof-sheets marked with corrections begin to return to the respective companionships. As they arrive the sheets are delivered by the clicker to the compositor whose matter commences the first page; he immediately sets about the disagreeable business of repairing his own blunders, and, that done, passes the proof to the companion whose name is marked at the head of the next "taking;" and so on until the whole is corrected, when the man who comes last "locks up the form" and carries it to the press, where a second proof is pulled for the press-reader This proof being compared with the first, and the forgotten corrections re-marked, is read with careful deliberation, and then corrected again, by one compositor, with equal care, after which it is sent down to be worked off, and while it is making ready a third proof is corrected, if necessary, on the press or the machine. Supposing the work to have commenced at twelve o'clock in the day, before eight in the evening all the operations are going on together, and the whirl, bustle, and Babylonish din of a printing office are at their height The banging of mallets, the sawing of "furniture," the creaking of the old press, the shuffling feet of messengers, the bawling of twenty voices, and the endless gabble of reading boys in the little closets which abut upon the composing-rooms—all together form a concert of sweet sounds which tells unfavorably upon the labor of him who has not sufficient power of abstraction to concentrate his attention upon what he is about.

At half-past nine or ten the men begin to think about supper, and the old stagers, knowing the effects of night-work upon the system, are careful to victual their garrisons for the siege they have to undergo. For supper come smoking sheep's-heads in halves, pork and mutton pies, "slap-bang" or boiled beef, and "spotted dog," a very marly species of plum-pudding, from the cook-shop, together with loaves of bread, pats of butter, and lumps of cheese, and the indispensable pots of foaming beer. The temptation to prolong this repast to an inconvenient length is dissipated by the vision of the overseer flitting past the out-skirts of the party, or by the sound of his voice in an adjoining room—at which the relics of the meal are swept aside and the work resumed. Towards midnight there is another vision of the pewter Ganymede, who, walked completely off his legs by miles of burdensome stair-climbing, declares himself " dead beat;" and having dispensed the last allowance of nectar, vanishes with the determination to " go in for the horizontal in less than no time." Under the impetus of supper the work now progresses rapidly. For three or four hours there is neither pause nor relaxation, but towards two or three in the morning—the hour " when deep sleep falleth upon men"—though there be no delay, there is a marked change in the character of the scene. The conversation, at first spirited and general, has flagged by degrees until every voice is hushed into silence, and the only sounds to be heard are those produced by the various operations of labor. I have often fancied at such seasons that I had derived some sort of refreshment from the comparative lull of a few hours, although they were hours of close application to a process not altogether mechanical—and that the body, which is as much the slave of habit as the mind, had actually undergone some restorative action, although defrauded of its natural rest. This may be a mere notion, though I don't think so—but I leave it to wiser heads to determine the question, if it be worth determining.

Morning, dank, misty, and foggy, looks in upon the hot, smoky, and reeking den. By this time, the atmosphere of the series of black caverns in which business is carried on is become disgustingly nauseous, as well as stiflingly hot. Notwithstanding the cold and raw weather without, the perspiration streams from every face within. The entire building is one huge vapor-bath of dismal stenches, from the rank steam of which the soot-black walls and ceilings glimmer with moisture. The most severe and inveterate catarrh is sweated out of the system, to be renewed with increased intensity at the first contact with the out-door air. As the dull wintry light steals on by slow degrees, the candles one by one disappear, and now a few of the hands who, from feeble health or advanced age, had been allowed to escape the night-work, reoccupy their frames. Coming in from the fresh air, they are struck aghast with the horrible odor which prevails, and make some attempts at ventilation, which being clamorously resisted by the majority, they are compelled to relinquish. Breakfast now comes to recruit our flagging energies, and the true value and virtues of hot coffee are brought home to many a thirsty conscience. After breakfast most of us are lively and animated as ever, and the work goes on with unabated energy, except in the case of men past the meridian of life, who, by way of economizing their strength, stick pretty fast to their stools. By eleven o'clock comes the Ganymede again, with his bunches of clean pots, but the same unwashed face as yesterday. "Beer, gentlemen!—gentlemen, beer!" meets the same ready response as usual. By-and-by the overseer passes round with a satisfied expression on his countenance, and we learn, from hints dropped to the clicker, that we are breaking the neck of the business, and shall accomplish the undertaking in time if we "look alive." At one, all hands run off to dinner, but not without an admonition that time is precious. A return within the hour is hardly to be expected, and a little tardiness at this crisis, if not allowed, is wisely winked at by the managers. By half-past two, however, all are again in their places, refreshed with a wash and a clean shave, and some few, perhaps, with a brief nap. But the rate of progress is sensibly diminished from that of the same hour on the previous day. When darkness comes on and the candles are lighted, they burn red, emit a visible smoke, and do not give above half the light they would yield in a pure air. The five-o'clock tea has lost its refreshing qualities, and when it is over, we drag ourselves unwillingly from the sleepy fire-side. The tripping foot-fall of the boys and lads is transformed to the lounging lethargic tread of the clodhopper. Reading-boys and apprentices are missing from their places, and do not answer to their names when loudly called for, and at length are discovered snoring in some dark and out-of-the-way recess, whither they had stealthily slunk off to sleep. Men, too, here and there stretched under their frames, forget themselves, in the hope of being themselves forgot while they smuggle a surreptitious "forty winks." Though generally discovered, they are allowed to lie for half an hour or so before they are "kicked up" and again set to work.

Notwithstanding these and various other trifling drawbacks, before daylight dawns upon the second sleepless night, the whole of the formidable blue-book is standing in type, and the corrections only remain to be done. As this process will furnish occupation but for a small number of hands, lots are now drawn for the liberty of going home to bed; and those who are lucky enough to win, start off without beat of drum, and leave their less fortunate companions to finish the business. A young fellow fresh from the country, when left in this predicament, presents but a sorry spectacle to the view. A vigil of it may be more than fifty hours, passed in an atmosphere that would poison a vulture, has added twenty years to his aspect, and, indeed, he will never thoroughly regain his former look. He begins to wander in his speech—answers incoherently to questions, and staggers about in a semi-somnolent state—and does the last necessary office to his last sheet more like a prize-fighter collecting his exhausted forces for the last "round" than anything else I can compare him to. When the concluding sheet is at length despatched to press, the readers crawl forth from their dusty cribs, and the composing-rooms are empty for the remainder of the day. In the meanwhile, the operations of the pressman or machinist, the warehouseman and the bookbinders have all gone on simultaneously with, or else followed so closely upon, those of the compositors, that by twelve o'clock in the day the blue-book is born into the world, and a small but sufficient number of damp copies are in existence to lie upon the table of "The House."

It would be interesting were it possible, to follow the history of the majority of these blue-books thus convulsively propelled into being. The first stage is the delivery by the agency of the printer of a single copy to each of the honorable members of the Commons' House, or, more properly speaking, to each honorable member's footman, porter, or cookmaid, through whose economical offices an immense proportion of them find their way to the butter-shop before they are a week old. The butter-man, who buys at twopence or threepence a pound, and who will take any quantity, supplies the stall-bookseller, who thus manages to make a fair profit upon this very doubtful species of goods, in spite of the government, which shuts itself out of the regular market by allowing only half the usual gains of the trade upon its publications. When the very ephemeral interest which such volumes for the most part excite has subsided, they fall into the hands of wholesale collectors, who make their monthly rounds, and buy them up at the price of twenty-eight shillings the hundred-weight, and despatch whole stacks of them, in bundles of about a ton each, to play the part of waste-paper to every town in England. Others are hauled off in wagons to the mills and crushed into *papier maché*, a manufacture for which they are peculiarly adapted, seeing that, from the nature of the nondescript fabric upon which they are printed, but very little crushing is required to reduce them to a pulp. The public records of a century back, when the papermakers made paper, would not at all answer for this purpose, and would be rejected as so much impracticable material by the modellers of so-called paper ornaments. At the close of each session a certain number of copies of every-thing printed are collated in bulky volumes, re-paged in manuscript, and bound up with new titles and indexes for deposit in the Museum, libraries and record-offices of the United Kingdom. From the wholesale and sudden destruction that awaits nineteen-twentieths of the blue-books in the first year of their existence, it not unfrequently happens that a new edition is called for even before that year had expired. There is no doubt that this fact is very largely attributable to the convenient size of the blue book page, which the shopkeeper regards as the very model of an envelope for butter, cheese and sausages; and there would be no great risk in prophesying that an edition in small octavo would enjoy an existence of comparative longevity.

With the advance of spring came the short recess of the Easter week, soon after which I found myself in a new position, being promoted, if promotion it is to be called ; and henceforth did duty in a sort of watch-box, in three compartments, as a printer's reader from morning to night, and very often all night long. As the character, habits, and predilections of the very little known and somewhat mysterious class of functionaries of which I now became a member have hitherto been but cursorily noticed, I shall endeavor to introduce the printer's reader to the public. It is very certain that to them he is in some sort a benefactor, although no man ever dreams of acknowledging his good offices, while the dullest blockhead in the world denounces him as an ass. A grudge, a shrug of the shoulder, an ill word—these are the small coin with which the reading public acknowledge his services. The blunders of other men, however enormous, die and are buried, and in time fade away from the remembrance of their fellows. With the printer's reader, the case is altogether reversed ; his merits are still-born, in fact to be merits they must be so, while his blunders are immortalized and last longer than himself. From this very cause he has, time out of mind, been cordially hated by the authors and writers of books, all and sundry. If, as sometimes happens, they are forced to communicate or correspond with him, they snap at and snub him, and would summarily scotch him like a viper, did they dare. Even the pious and gentle-hearted Cowper grows wrathful at the bare thought of him, and spars and kicks at him, and maligns and slanders him by anticipation, having never yet submitted to his good or ill offices. Thus, in a letter to Mr. Unwin, dated May, 1781, writes the author of the "Task," previous to his first appearance in print: "I shall now have an opportunity to correct the press myself, an advantage especially important. A single erratum may knock out the brains of a whole passage. * * * * There is to be found in a printing-house a *presumptuous intermeddler*, who will fancy himself a poet too, and what is still worse, a better than he that employs him. The consequence is, that with cobbling, and tinkering, and patching on here and there a shred of his own, he makes such a difference between the original and the copy that an author cannot know his own work again. Now as I choose to be responsible for nobody's dulness but my own, I am a little comforted when I reflect that it will be in my power to prevent all such impertinence."

The "presumptuous intermeddler" is of course the printer's reader, who is the established butt and target for all abuse levelled at "that confounded printer." Scrub, in the "Beaux's Stratagem," says, "I knew they were talking of me, for they laughed consumedly;" and by an analogous process of reasoning, the unfortunate "reader" knows when authors storm and furiously rage about the blunders of the press, that it is at him that their deadliest wrath is levelled—and he puts on a "damned look" accordingly and instinctively. But if he is hated by authors, he is detested and abominated by compositors, to whom he is indeed a standing, or rather sitting, nuisance and scourge all the days of his life. His grey-goose stump is the whip that lashes them into good behavior; or, worse still, the cat-o'-nine-tails or the knout that avenges their delinquencies. They, of course, have to correct their own blunders at their own cost, and every one that he marks down upon the sheet is so much additional work to be done for nothing, and therefore a subtraction of something from the Saturday night's wages. They wish him at Jericho, or a worse place; and yet, on the principle of holding a candle to the dark gentleman, uniformly treat him with a kind of deferential civility. They fear lest he should resent an affront by a superfluous exercise of his ingenuity in fault-finding upon their proofs; a fear I am persuaded, for the most part, without foundation, seeing that, unless new to the business, he has no energy to spare for purposes of resentment.

The hatred of the author on the one hand, and the compositor on the other, is but indifferently compensated by the estimation in which he is held by his employer, who looks upon him as a kind of necessary nuisance, which it is equally impossible to regard with complacency or to get rid of from the premises. A model "reader," in the eyes of a master-printer, would be a man with a constitution of about forty-horse endurance; who, to a knowledge critically grammatical of all languages living and dead, should add an intimate familiarity with the exact sciences, and a tolerably copious acquaintance with the past and current literature of all nations, and who should be willing 'to exercise his limited faculties at all hours of the day and night (without a disreputable regard for filthy lucre as a compensation for overtime) for the consideration, say of forty shillings a week. There is yet one qualification still more necessary than any of the above in the eyes of an employer, and that is, a perfect and practical acquaintance with the business of a printing-office in all its departments. It follows, of course, that the model reader is never found in the reading-closet, and his place has to be supplied by men for the most part self-educated; and who, like the writer of these reminiscences, have done their best to appropriate such scraps of information as came in their way in the intervals of a life of labor. It is in vain that needy masters of arts, bankrupt pedagogues, "stickit ministers," and cleaned-out gentlemen, flock to the printing-office as candidates for the office of corrector of the press; wanting a practical knowledge of the business, they are of no avail; and this fact has now been so long settled by experiment that masters have ceased even to give their services a trial. A compositor, ignorant perhaps of the very names of the Greek letters, would probably correct the proofs of a Greek Testament more efficiently than would a university professor of the language unused to the patient and scrutinizing routine of press reading. As a specimen of the value, relatively, of scholarship and unschooled but practical lynx-eyed observation, I may mention a fact which came under my own notice some few years back. A new edition of a well-known lexicon was brought out by a publisher in the Row, the editorship being confided to a scholar of high reputation, at an expense, it was said, of five guineas per sheet. The proofs returned by him to the printer, during upwards of four months, contained an average of *sixteen* corrections on each sheet. Before going to press they were again carefully read by a young fellow from the north of the island, who possessed but a moderate reading acquaintance with the language, who spent a day-and-a-half over each sheet, at a cost to the printer of nine or ten shillings, and made additional corrections, averaging through the whole period *fifty-three* per sheet!

Looking at such things as these, of which the printer's reader has good store in his remembrance, it is not much to be wondered at that he has no very great veneration for authors and editors. The scorn they bear him is, in short, pretty freely returned, and that man must be a genius indeed, a Scott or a Dickens at least, who is a genius in *his* estimation. Still, even though he suffer indignity at their hands, he will do his duty by their "muck," as he is pleased to term it, and even condescend to pitchfork it together to get it into a readable shape. The only revenge he is ever known to take upon an irritable scribbler, in return for an affront, is to let him have his own way when he sees him blundering in matters chronological, typographical, or other, instead of setting him right—a species of revenge which he can indulge in every day if he choose.

The habits of close and patient investigation to which in the course of years he becomes in a manner naturalized, beget in the printer's reader a faculty of continuous and dogged perseverance, of which the laborious works which some of them have accomplished remain as lasting memorials. The "Commentary" of Macknight, and the "Bible Concordance" of the eccentric and unfortunate Cruden, and the elaborate compilations of certain living writers, there is but little doubt owe their existence to a faculty thus nurtured and matured. These unobtrusive functionaries are the index-writers to the book-making profession; and not a few of them, when worn out by the long hours and foul atmosphere of the printing-office, subside in their premature old age into literary hacks, translators, transformers, disguisers, and compilers—the pigeon-livered shuttlecocks of booksellers and publishers. There is no instance upon record of one of them ever being convicted of crime, or, that I know of, ever facing a jury in the character of a criminal, although a malicious report circulates among the trade that a "reader" was once hanged. This unfounded slander must have originated in the fact, by no means uncommon, that one who had the misfortune to be not quite infallible, was denounced by his employer as deserving to be hanged for some unhappy blunder—the omission of a comma, perhaps, in that tender part of a volume, the title-page, or something equally awful and tremendous. This report is, however, avenged by another, which originated among the readers themselves, to the effect that one of their number was, some years ago, pensioned off, after having grown blind from the effects of forty years of small print in a dark closet, and allowed to retire, at the age of sixty-five, upon an annuity of thirty pounds a year. The malice of this report is considered, among those who keep it alive, as far exceeding that of the other. For my own part, I believe neither. It is not at all a likely thing that a man who suffers a month's melancholy from a mis-spelled word, who gets the nightmare through having printed an i without a dot, who starts "like a guilty thing upon a fearful summons" when asked whether he read such or such a sheet—it is not likely, I say, that such a man would have spirit under any circumstances to deserve hanging, even though hanging were always as cheap as Lord Sidmouth made it in his day On the other hand, it would be doing the master-printers a gross injustice to suppose that any one of their number would venture to set so bad an example to the rest as to throw a blind man thirty pounds per annum, after having paid him forty shillings a week for forty years. No—the fact is that the " reader" does not retire; he generally sticks to his stool as long as he can, and unless driven from it by actual incapacity to crawl, lives out his last week of life in his peculiar den. If his eyesight fail him, he prudently says nothing about it, knowing that it will be discovered all too soon for him in spite of his silence on the subject. My assertion as to the blameless character of the " reader's" life will perhaps be contradicted by a reference to that clever rogue Hardy Vaux, who was transported; but in truth he was not a printer's reader, but an ingrained and constitutional knave, to a different manner born, who, for the short time that he assumed the reader's function, probably read his proofs as dishonestly as he did everything else.

In personal appearance the reader is neat, precise, and as gentlemanly as his finances will allow him to be. His attire may be worn and threadbare, but it is cleanly and well-fitted. If he have little nap on his well-brushed hat, he has less stubble on his daily chin His morning boots may eschew the mud, but they reflect the sun. He would " dele ' a stain from his skirts as readily as a blunder from his proof-sheet, and would no more tolerate the absence of a shirt-button than an " out in copy." In all his habits he is punctual as the hands of the clock-dial. A secret attraction which he cannot withstand, rolls him out of bed, while yet asleep, at half-past seven in the morning, and he wakes, with his face in the wash-basin, to the consciousness of his daily duty. At a quarter before eight he sits down to his hasty breakfast, and at a quarter past shuts the street-door after him, as he starts, from his cottage or lodging in the suburbs, on his five-and-forty minutes' walk to the office. The clocks are striking nine as he dons his working coat for a four hours' spell at the damp sheet, in conjunction with his *alter idem*, who has attended an hour before to light his fire and dust his desk. The stroke of 'One" summons him to dinner at the coffee-house or cook-shop—he has no time to walk home and back again. Dinner over, he makes the tour of the streets, and studies the world in its multifarious aspects—or he lounges at a book-stall and cheapens an Elzevir edition of some desiderated classic—or handles, with no intent to purchase, the newest publications of the day. While thus engaged, the sight of a work he has himself corrected for the press will send him off like a shot, lest some undiscovered blunder should meet his eye and banish his tranquillity for a month. His daily rambles about town, during the hour when it is most alive with business and pleasure, supply him with a fund of materials for sly and caustic remark. From the unamiable habit of his profession, he sees the seedy and faulty side of everything, and, unfortunately for himself, is seldom attracted by anything else. For him there is a cloud in the clearest sky, a stain on the most faultless reputation, a freckle in the fairest face—and it is a question whether the discovery of imperfection does not yield him more pleasure than the conviction of its absence could afford him. He cherishes a private hobby of some sort or other, and drives it with more or less vigor, according to his age or temperament. He is sure to be a linguist of more or less pretensions, and in his desk is a collection of grammars and dictionaries, rescued from the bookstalls, and which he consults when he suspects an author to be at fault or when his manuscript is illegible, and which he studies in the few intervals of business which the slack season may offer. As he never knows at what hour of the night he shall quit the office, he tells his wife not to expect him home till she sees him. This regulation, by which the domestic affairs go on the same whether he be absent or present, leaves him at liberty to do as he likes with his evenings, which, unless he be a lover of his own fireside, he spends as often at the half-price pit or gallery, the concert-room or the debating-club, as at home.

If you visit him in the theatre of his labors, it is ten to one but you find him

> Placed in a chamber of neglect,
> Encompassed round with disrespect.

There he sits in what seems a sort of cupboard gutted of its shelves to make room for his old mahogany desk, the flap of which is half whittled away. Over his head hangs a smoke-blacked festoon of spiders' webs. A few rays of light find their way in through the upper squares of broken and paste-patched glass which do duty as a window; in the centre pane is a tin ventilator of the whirligig make, but which finally ceased its whirling twenty years ago, and which he has covered up with brown paper to stop out the draught. The plaster has dissolved partnership with the walls, and the naked bricks are in places polished to a rich brown by the friction of his old writing-coat, as he leans back against them a dozen times a day, to get, as he terms it, the corner of the desk out of his stomach. Here he sits upon a stool the padding of which burst its cerements seven years ago, and has since been represented by a foot of inch-plank, sawn by himself from a letter-board—and here he passes the days of the years of his life, plying his goose-quill to the tune of such music as the following, intoned in a rapid and monotonous gabble, without a single pause or stop, save when his reading-machine, that pale-faced boy on the short stool, relents a moment for want of breath ·

Reading-boy *loquitur:* " This *ruling passion* two ital par the most enduring of all the passions which obtain a mastery over the mind close is described in Pope's eps thus turns odious in woollen 'twould a saint provoke close were the last words that poor narcissa spoke turns no let a charming chintz and Brussels lace wrap my cold limbs and shade my lifeless face one need not sure be frightful though one's dead and Betty." (Here the reader dips his pen in the ink, and the boy takes the opportunity to blow like a young grampus for a few seconds, and then resumes.) "Give my cheek a little red close turns again I give and I devise close old Euclio said and sighed turns my lands and tenements to Ned close turns again your money sir close turns again my money sir what all why if I must close then wept turns again I give it Paul close turns again the manor sir close turns again the manor holds close he cried turns again not that I cannot part with that close and died pop ep one oct ed p two five three."

Everybody knows the above passage, but everybody does not know that in order to insure its correct printing it is thus interlarded with technical terms in the reading-closet. Any one who thinks it worth while may learn what these insertions signify by comparing the passage as it stands above with the original. It is true there is no reason upon earth why the boy should ignore the art of punctuation as he invariably does; but, in fact, he knows nothing about it, and the printer, whose sole object it is to get over the ground as fast as possible, would find it but a waste of time to teach him. In reading a foreign language the cacophonous intonations of the pale-faced urchin are infinitely worse, and would be utterly unintelligible to a stranger. In reading Welsh in English houses the attempt at pronunciation is abandoned, and the boy spells the work through, letter by letter.

The reading-boy, ignorant though he be of punctuation, is a mercurial and wide-awake genius, whose knowledge of the world is astonishingly precocious. If a good hand at manuscript, he has seven or eight shillings a week for his services; though if less skilful, or only available for reprint, he will be valued at four or five. But whatever his wage, it is more than probable that he has to maintain himself with his earnings; and this he manages to do by the aid of the occasional twopence an hour for overtime, and even contrives to save a stray sixpence now and then for a visit to the gallery of the theatre at half-price. It is ten to one but he is the possessor of a brace of iron swords, manufactured at tenpence the pair, for purposes of melodramatic slaughter; these he keeps stowed away in some cranny or recess in the closet, and he watches his opportunity to steal off with them, while his reader is occupied in revising, in order to enjoy a comfortable battle with the upright beam in the cellar. Here he will hack and hew away as long as you please, vociferating the while all the defiant blank verse he can call to mind, and evincing an astonishing fertility of imagination in the invention of horrible terms of scorn and detestation, which he launches volubly against the caitiff beam aforesaid. When his services are in requisition he has to be sought out, and another of the tribe is despatched on the search. The messenger knows well enough where to find him, but being also dramatically inclined, he instinctively joins him in a "terrific combat," or in a combined assault upon the delinquent beam, and neither of them makes his appearance in the closet until both are hounded back to it by a third, or by the angry voice of the reader himself bawling at the stair-head. Besides his iron swords, and perhaps a tin-helmet, the reading-boy is master of a collection of dramatic literature in odd sheets, selected from the stall-keeper's twopenny box—soiled, and dogs-eared copies of the acting drama—lives of actors and actresses, and, perhaps, a volume or two of Shakespeare in very old type. These he has ample time to study, as, for several hours daily his master is engaged in the silent duties of revision or comparison. It sometimes happens that a boy thus situated has the sense to turn his position to advantage, and to pick up a knowledge of grammar, or even the elements of a new language, under the direction and with the assistance of his experienced companion; but such instances of sensible foresight among boys from eleven to fourteen or fifteen years of age are comparatively rare.

The ability to read manuscript, often perpetrated in a manner so villanous as to puzzle the writers themselves, is not very common among boys; and hence it continually comes to pass that lads who have entered the reading-closet with the distinct understanding that they would be received as apprentices after a certain length of service, are hindered from that consummation by the very talent which should in justice hasten it, and are kept dawdling on from year to year, adding, perhaps, an additional shilling to their weekly gains, at each recurring season, until they become reading-men (but not " readers"), old enough to marry and settle in life, with incomes something under the average of that of a bricklayer's laborer.

As the reading-boy is from one year's end to the other almost the sole working companion of the reader, the comfort of the latter depends very much upon the good-temper, aptness, and docility of disposition, or the want of such qualities, in the former; and in houses, though I know not if there be more than one, where the mean, despicable, and despotically dishonest practice prevails of making the reader pecuniarily responsible for a mistake, by saddling him with the expense of a cancelled sheet, his slender purse may lie very much at the mercy of his careless or incompetent coadjutor So there is generally a good understanding between man and boy, and in some sort a community of interest and feeling The boy is the reader's messenger and confidant; he brings him refreshment from the ale-house or the coffee-shop, and is his medium of communication with the overseer or the compositors. If from any unusual cause his master is behind time in the morning, the boy never discovers the fact, but conceals it if possible, he watches the coal-cellar, and if he catches the door open, makes a prize of a lump or two to supplement the short allowance for the winter's fire, to which, as he bakes his own potatoes in the ashes, and grills his six-ounce chop on a three-halfpenny gridiron, he pays a not altogether disinterested attention. On the other hand, the reader is the boy's authority in all matters, political, social, religious, or other, not forgetting things dramatic. What are Tories? what is a Whig? a Conservative? a Radical? a Socialist? What's the meaning of *scandalum magnatum?* What is the balance of power? Who invented the pragmatic sanction, and what is it like? Why are doctors' prescriptions wrote in Latin? Who found out short-hand, and why ain't everything printed in it? What's meershaum made of? Where do the new fashions come from? Why do the old chaps in the Chancery Court wear horse-hair wigs? Who pays all them fellows for sitting there? Who made the thirty-nine Articles? and am I obliged to believe them all? Who was Timon of Athens? Is Hamlet true? Are ghosts a humbug? Did you ever see Mrs. Siddons? Who was Mr. Siddons? Did the Romans smoke tobacco?—such are some few of the interesting queries which, as difficulties occur to him, the boy prefers to his reader, and from the ready replies he obtains contrives to enlighten himself on small matters by slow degrees.

The knowledge of the reader himself, though sometimes sufficiently various, is generally anything but profound Though, in the course of fifteen or twenty years' practice, he may have read detached and fragmentary portions of ten thousand volumes, it is probable that he has never read a dozen through from beginning to end. Poetry, philosophy, ethics, sermons, history, tragedy, belles-lettres, polemics, metaphysics, scientific treatises, politics, Acts of Parliament, and all the ologies besides, may come under his notice in the course of a single month; and he must possess an extraordinary power of classification and retention if from such a course of reading he derive any intellectual pabulum. Instead of cultivating such a faculty in practice he pursues an opposite course, and, by abstracting his attention from the spirit and concentrating it upon the letter of literature, is able more efficiently to perform his functions than he could do where he to indulge in speculations upon the subject under his hand. So thoroughly is this accomplished by some members of the profession, that I have known a reader employed for years together on an evening paper, every line of which he read and corrected professionally in the course of the day, who yet called for the same paper and read it regularly over his pipe and glass of grog in the evening, with the design of making himself acquainted with the news.

When, having paid the customary footing, and drank a sober glass to the health of my new companions, I was admitted a member of this erudite fraternity, I set about the novel function committed to me as industriously, but at the same time as cautiously, as possible. An old stager in the house tendered me a friendly warning on the danger of immoderate speed, and informed me at the same time that what I did would be infallibly subjected to the criticism of the head of the firm, who amused himself every morning by looking over the printed sheets of the previous day, and invariably called the readers to account for any real or imaginary delinquency. A little round-faced mannikin, of the "tiger" genus, was allotted to me as a reading-boy, and I had good hopes, from his ready wit and active motions, of speedily training him to perform the duty satisfactorily. When he had finished reading my maiden sheet, and while I was looking it carefully over to see if aught had escaped the first reading, he bounced from his stool and began a series of solemn genuflexions and salaams in the middle of the floor, which he continued for some minutes with a perfectly grave face, to my utter astonishment and no small alarm, as I suspected he had suddenly lost his senses.

"What are you doing?" said I. "Is anything the matter with you?'

"O lor' no, sir; I'm as right as a trivet."

"Then what are you kicking about in that way for?"

"Kicking, sir! I'm a learnin' my part."

"What do you mean? You will learn nothing that way, I'm sure."

"Beg pardon, sir; but I goes on at Dewry-lane to-night in the afterpiece, and I'm a practisin' my part."

"Indeed! Pray is this your first appearance?"

"T'aint no appearance at all, sir. I goes on under a green blanket in these same togs what I got on."

"Under a blanket! and pray, if I may be so bold, what part do you play?"

"I'm one of the waves of the sea, sir."

"Ho, ho! now I understand; and so you tumble about under a blanket to represent a rolling billow?"

"Not exactly, sir; tumbling about won't do—you must bob up and down gently six times reg'lar, and when you comes up agin the dungeon wall you throws out your arms so, and falls flat on your face, and then you crawls off back to the wing while another cove is a comin' on. Oh, ain't it dusty jest a bit at the bottom of the sea!"

"And pray what do you get a night for that clever performance?"

"I git a bob, and goes on three times a week; that's three shillin's a week."

"And pray did you ever perform any other part?"

"Oh, yes, sir. I've a done the goose in the pantomime many a time; but I'm growed out o' that now. I done the dragon last Christmas."

"Well, suppose you do the Mercury now. Take this proof to Mr. T——, and ask for the following sheet." With that the Christmas dragon pounced upon the offered prey and disappeared in a twinkling.

I found this small scion of Thespis astonishingly docile and intelligent. He read manuscripts of average legibility with perfect readiness and with an utterance as distinct and almost as loud as the town-crier's; and brought a considerable share of ingenuity to bear in deciphering the cramped, blotted, and entangled pothooks, with which it would appear to be indispensable that gentlemen and noblemen in high office should conceal rather than express their opinions. Further, his early familiarity with the boards of a theatre had taught him the necessity of punctuality, and he kept his time upon all occasions with the precision of an actor pledged to an audience ; and he would read over his copy to himself when an opportunity offered, previous to reciting it aloud, in order that he might acquit himself creditably, without boggling at the hard words. Then he boiled the kettle, made the tea, and washed up the cups and saucers with the neatness and dexterity of a practised abigail. Unfortunately, however, these virtues and accomplishments were counterbalanced by one failing in his character, or perhaps a peculiarity in his constitution, which effectually marred his usefulness, and compelled the overseer at the end of a few weeks to get rid of him. Whatever the moral atmosphere of Drury-lane at that period may have been, I am afraid that that which prevailed among the band of associated billows under the blanket, in the flatulent entrails of the goose and dragon, and indeed in the whole of the property department, was not the most favorable for the culture of right notions on the important subject of *meum* and *tuum*. Be this conjecture right or wrong, certain it is that nothing of a conveniently portable shape could be left long within the boy's reach without vanishing mysteriously to appear no more. Pencils, penknives, straps, hones, india-rubber, books, halfpence, handkerchiefs, all disappeared so surely as they were left to his guardianship. Whether he gobbled them up in his capacity of goose, devoured them in that of a dragon, or, looking upon them in his character of a wave of the sea, as so many waifs, swept them all off accordingly, it is not worth the trouble to determine. As a matter of course, he never knew anything about the missing articles, and he was too much an actor to betray by his countenance the slightest indication of the consciousness of wrong-doing. But he was not cunning enough to escape a trap that was laid for him; and being at length caught with stolen articles in his possession, he was dismissed as a vagabond billow without a character, and his place supplied by another.

I got on tolerably well with my new duty, and received the best proof of success by the absence, for several months, of remark from any quarter. Freedom from blame being the only praise which a reader ever gets, I naturally looked upon that state of things as encouraging, and began to feel secure upon my stool. But, one fine summer's morning, about eleven o'clock, the counting-house bell rang, and I was ordered to make a prompt appearance before the head of the firm, whom as yet I had never seen. I obeyed immediately, and was ushered into the presence of a gouty sexagenarian, upon whose rather childish and naturally good-humored countenance a frown, got up for the occasion, sat with a very ill grace—and between whom and myself the following brief dialogue ensued:

"Mr. ——," said the elderly gentleman, "you are the new rweader, I undershtand, and, of courshe, a man of education, as a rweader ish. I am rweally ashtonished, shir, zhat you should make shuch a shtoopid blunder as shish—do you shink I pay you forty shillinsh a week for zhat, shir?"

"Allow me to ask what has gone wrong, sir?"

"Why, shish has gong wrong, shir"—and he handed me the sheet.

"Will you have the goodness to point it out, sir? I see nothing wrong"

"Don't pretend to be blind, shir! You know zhat we alwaysh put '*bonâ fide*' wizh a shircumflexh â, and you have left it out, shir"

"No, I have not, sir—with submission the words '*bonâ fide* do not occur in the page."

"Why, what do you mean by zhat, shir?" (pointing to the words '*bona fides*.') "What's zhat but *bonâ fide* in zhe plural? Of courshe, if we have a shircumflexh in zhe shingular, we have it in zhe plural too."

"Excuse me, sir, you have made a slight mistake · *bona fides* is not the plural of *bonâ fide*. The word *bona* in the one instance is in the nominative, in the other it is in the ablative case: it would be a blunder to use the accent in the nominative."

"Nommany!—nommany! ablaty!—Oh, ish zhat it? I musht talk to my shon about it.—Ha! I daie shay you are right, Mr. ——; *bonâ fide* in zhe plural don't carry zhe acshent, you shay. Oh, very well; if zhat's zhe cashe, itsh all right. Zhat will do, shir—you may go down now, shir—good morning, shir."

I bowed accordingly, and returned to my stool below; and thus ended my first interview with the erudite principal, who never summoned me to a second conference—at least, on the subject of a blunder.

CHAPTER XIII.

Overseers, their Duties, Temptations, Virtues, and Failings—Playfair—Screw—Screwdriver—The Printer's Weigh-goose—Who pays the piper—Non Nobis Domine—Silence for the Cha-a-ar!—The Governor's Speech—Incomprehensible Moonshine—The Overseer's Speech—Moonshine accompanied with muttered Thunder—Social Harmony—The Tables turned—Strange Gospellers—Laborious Fanaticism—Three in one pulpit—Oh for a dose of Physic!—Dearth of Religious Knowledge

THE business of the session went on prosperously. I contrived to maintain a fair character to the end of it, by which time I found my constitution considerably shaken through the demands made upon it by night-work, and by the effects of foul air, and sadly in need of repair through the sole medium which would avail me, fresh country air and early hours. Some time in autumn comes the printer's "weigh-goose," the solemnization of which is in most offices dependent upon the fiat of the overseer, who sometimes makes it a kind of laudatory ovation to himself. I shall give a few paragraphs on the subject of the overseer, and then exhibit him presiding at the weigh-goose, the climax of his glory.

The overseer in a large office is much more than the term designating his function implies. He not merely overlooks the whole concern in all its departments, but he manages, rules, and governs the whole with the authority of a despot. In a large house it is indispensable that he possess *all* power, or else he will virtually have none. He engages, employs, suspends and discharges the whole of the working-hands at the promptings of his own will or caprice. He degrades or promotes, without question or demur, or the chance of appeal;

and he appoints every man his special duty, and employs as many deputies as he chooses to see that his behests are obeyed. Where the principals are men of independent fortune, who decline to interfere, or where they are men who are not practical printers, and cannot interfere, the overseer is lord paramount; he gives estimates, and signs and fulfils contracts for work, and orders and purchases all necessary materials as they are wanted. Of course, having everything under his control, the one thing indispensable in an overseer is a character for high principle and unimpeachable integrity. Unless these qualities are at the helm, somebody is sure to suffer, and where, as is too frequently the case, they are altogether wanting, every man on the premises becomes in his turn a victim, in a greater or less degree, to the cupidity or malice, or both, of the managing rogue. I shall fabulize the three classes of overseers, the better to do them justice, premising that the existence of the three distinct specimens is anything but a fable, their prototypes being readily come-at-able; and I shall call them Playfair, Screw, and Screwdriver.

Playfair came of a respectable family in the middle walk of life; and he was brought up in the perfect knowledge of the fact that he would have to make his own way in the world; that whatever position he occupied in life he would have to achieve for himself; and that truth, honesty, industry and fairplay were necessary to achieve anything worth having, and to retain it permanently and creditably. Impressed with this conviction, the lad set to work to act it out in the performance of his daily duties. He rose rapidly into notice and repute, and actually managed the business of his employer before he was out of his apprenticeship. At the end of his term, a larger house offered a premium for his services; but he refused the offer, preferring to travel in England and France for a few years, during which he added something to his knowledge of the world, and qualified himself for a better situation. At thirty he undertook, at the request of the proprietors, the management of an old-established house The result of his management was soon apparent in the increased efficiency of the staff, the order, and comfort and cleanliness prevailing; and the marvellous diminution in the wear and tear and loss of material, which in all printing-offices has to be periodically renewed Another result is the respect of all whose respect is worth having, and the avoidance of the house over which he presides by the ragged and beery multitude of shags, scamps, tramps and pretenders, who disgrace the whole body of journeymen-printers, and who could not tolerate the precision, order, and neatness, which are rigidly maintained, and by which the transaction of business is rendered less costly to the firm, and the annual profits increased. Playfair is the model overseer; he is the bulwark alike of the master and the workmen; and it is fortunate for the latter, and for the interests of the trade, that we are able to point to many of whom he is the type.

Screw is a personage who was cast in a different mould. His father was a journeyman who wrought at press, a " pig" of the old school, who spent the greater part of his earnings in lubricating his larynx, and yet, in spite of all his libations, swore a husky oath to the day of his death. Young Screw contrived to scramble through his boyhood by exercising a sharp wit in catering for an appetite still sharper, without being more than half starved. When apprenticed, it cost him a prodigious effort to learn to spell and to punctuate, but his determination and his hunger combined carried him through; and then he began to acquire the reputation of a " whip," from the unusual quantity of type he would manage to hustle together. His headlong speed was the occasion of his promotion, upon a sudden vacancy, to the overseership ; and now a larger field opened before him, and brought into play his peculiar talent for self-serving. As he awoke by degrees to the capabilities of his new post, he improved them accordingly. He learned to judge of the qualities of printer's ink, before he gave a large order, by the flavor of Messrs. Lampblack and Bones's old port, a hamper of which was found by accident at his lodgings. A ton of new type he perceived to be of the hardest metal and handsomest mould when viewed through the transparent texture of a Bank of England note. The tradesmen who supplied the materials to the office first foolishly taught him the value of a bribe, which he learned so well that in one short year he had transformed the printing office under his control into a rotten borough, of which he carried all the votes in his own pocket. Every business-transaction that passed through his hands he sweated to the tune of seven and a half per cent. Paper, ink, type, presses and machinery, even repairs, as well as all sorts of stock, paid blackmail to Screw, as the indispensable condition of its purchase; and by this means he is known to have well-nigh doubled his salary. His administrative talent consisted of an unlimited and inexhaustible fund of oaths and abuse, and a species of bawling, bullying oratory, which, terrifying the timid and disgusting the well-meaning workman, bore down before it opposition of every kind. The lordship of Screw was of short duration. At the end of three or four years his system of management blew itself up, and him along with it. He was summarily kicked out of office. With the proceeds of his plunder he set up as a publican, and drank himself into the *Gazette;* or he speculated in railway shares, and fed the maws of greater and greedier sharpers than himself; or he turned printer to some obscene, unlicensed publication, which drained him to the last penny, and then landed him in Whitecross-street; or if not by either of these modes, then by some other, equally speedy and effective, he got rid, under the Devil's belly, of what he had so ravenously clawed together over his back, and reduced himself to his original level of "a hand at case," with a character in rags and tatters, in keeping with his costume. This consummation achieved, he applies for work, and pleads his misfortunes as a recommendation to the very firm whose affairs he had so footballed to his own purposes; where, in all probability, he gets taken on again, and, insensible to shame as to honesty, brags of his past overseership and the amount per annum he made it worth to him. I have seen this instructive drama played over again and again within the last twenty years, and it is to be seen still, with some slight variations, by those who choose to look for it.

Screwdriver is a kindred spirit, who, more rogue and less fool than Screw, has more enlarged views of his function, has a wider field for action and a more unlimited sway within it. His employers leave the whole establishment, with its population of three or four hundred men and boys, to his sole management and control. They pay him a gentlemanly salary weekly, and further augment it by a liberal quarterage, and imagine he is content—little dreaming that he levies a few hundreds a-year additional by ingeniously diverting a portion of the weekly wages from their natural channel into his own pocket. Under the pretence of training young hands to a particular kind of work, or some other pretence equally specious, he selects half-a-dozen lads, and, with the permission of his principal—a permission which no employer who knew his own interests would give, and which journeymen, to whose prosperity it is murderously ruinous, would, if they were wise, prevent—he binds them apprentice to *himself*. In a few months these lads, if well chosen, are almost as efficient as any men on the premises. Screwdriver pays them from a quarter to a half of their earnings, pocketing the overplus, with the deduction of a penny in the shilling, which is carried to the credit of the firm. His own boys are, as a matter of course, located in the best companionship, or at any rate that in which they labor speedily becomes the best. They are kept perpetually going, upon the most lucrative work the house affords, from morning to night; and they write such bills during their apprenticeship as they never perhaps equal in the whole course of their lives afterwards. In slack seasons the rest of the house may be standing still, and one may see scores of the old hands, with families dependent upon their industry, lying about under the frames, playing at cards, dominoes, drafts or chess, waiting for employment, while excellent work, in which they have a just claim to an equal share, is monopolized by the companionship with the boys in it, who are working till ten o'clock every night for the benefit of the plundering overseer. Sometimes the game is played with turnovers instead of apprentices; in this case it is equally lucrative, while it is far less troublesome; as the turnover comes to his business well taught, and is an efficient workman from the moment of his engagement. Nothing short of actual stagnation and stoppage of business is ever allowed to relax the labors of Screwdriver's tender flock; they are the first to begin and the last to leave off; and they have no objection to this, as their pay is a settled proportion of their earnings. When, at the expiration of their indentures, they get turned out of the favored "ship," and have to tug at the oar in the common boat, I have heard some of them declare that the half-earnings of their apprenticeship during the season were worth the entire earnings of their journeymanship for a similar period. With such abundant and facile means of replenishing his purse, Screwdriver can afford to disdain the peculations committed upon the ink-maker, type-founder, brass-cutter, &c., by such fellows as the blackguard Screw. He passes with the tradesmen for a gentleman; and if he receive a compliment occasionally in the way of business, it is not to be interpreted as a bribe. His unfortunate vassals, however, know him for a robber, and do not scruple to give him his right name when he is out of hearing and his spies are not in the way. He knows perfectly well that his proceedings are no mystery to the men under his command; but if he have a host of enemies in the unfavored companionships who suffer from his malversation, he has a band of warm friends among those who, working in the same room with his boys, divide with them the advantages of the continual flow of lucrative employment, which adds some thirty or forty per cent to the value of their labor. He lives in an atmosphere of continual alarm and distrust, and he has lived in it so long that it is become his natural element. His hand is against every man, because he knows that every honest man's hand ought to be against him. Hence he is almost as busy with the gratification of his malice and resentment as in providing for his personal emolument. He will discharge a man who ventures to manifest a disapproval of his practices—if a compositor, by the summary process of a fortnight's notice; if a reader, by oppressing him with work until he make his berth untenable, while he will connive at the most glaring delinquencies of a partisan, and even pay him his wages though he have been absent the whole week from his post. Thus much on the subject of Overseers.

The printer's weigh-goose is an annual feast, of which all the inmates of the office who choose to do so may partake; there are in most houses a few who make a point of absenting themselves, but these are hardly five per cent. of the whole, so that the affair may be looked upon as general. The expenses of the day are defrayed by subscriptions from the tradesmen who supply the office with materials, and who are called upon by the stewards for their donations. The overseer usually gives a guinea or two, and the employer contributes a round sum. It is an error to suppose that the fines levied in the office are reserved for this occasion; they are invariably liquidated and imbibed the moment they are paid, and sometimes before. If any money is wanting to complete the necessary amount, it is made up by a moderate poll-tax; and if the sum collected is more than is required to defray the charge of dinner, as is usually the case, then there is so much surplus to spend for the evening's jollification. The weigh-goose is invariably held in autumn, when there is a general relaxation of business. Occasionally, the proprietor of the office will preside at the dinner, but this practice is not universal; if he do dine with the men, he leaves soon after, as his presence would probably be a restraint on their enjoyments. These enjoyments are of a very uproarious description; they consist of grog-drinking and the intonation of songs with tremendous ear splitting choruses; and they endure just so long as there is any money remaining to be spent.

The annual festival at which we were about to be present comes off on a fine day in the middle of September, in some suburban tavern, in which there is "ample room and verge enough" for two or three hundred men and boys to disport themselves at pleasure within doors or without—say Highbury Barn, which will do as well as anywhere. The dinner is to be on the table at four o'clock; a junior partner is to honor the meeting with his presence, and will of course take the chair. The printing-office is shut up for the day—perhaps it is the only day in the year on which it will be found completely void. By eleven or twelve in the morning the men have found their way to Highbury, and, all in their neatest trim, begin to saunter in by twos and threes to amuse themselves in the gardens, skittle-grounds and paddock. Bowls, rounders, trap and leap-frog are played *con spirito*; and a good appetite is earned by exercise in the open air. As the time draws near, the gardens are crowded with the guests; and a few minutes after the hour has struck the dinner-bell peals out, and the whole troop flock in to victual their individual garrisons. The men who were elected to the office of stewards have already dined by themselves in a private room, and are now prepared to assist in serving their comrades. There is abundance of room—no unsightly scrambling for places; and in a few minutes, the young governor having arrived, and grace being said, the hum of conversation gives place to the clatter of knives and forks, which endures for the best part of an hour, during which time astonishing execution is done upon a substantial and well-dressed dinner. That great fact being satisfactorily accomplished, it is succeeded by a desperate attempt at "Non nobis Domine"—an attempt which is, however, knocked on the head by the hammer of the "Vice," upon his discovering that two-thirds of the voices are instinctively gliding away into "We won't go home till morning." Then the cloth is removed, wine is placed upon the table, glasses are charged, and the health of her Majesty is drunk with "three times three."

The overseer now proposes the health of the junior partner, at the mention of whose name there is a rattling storm of knuckle-bones upon the table, and of heels under it, threatening the demolition of the glasses. Bumpers are filled with zealous haste; "hip, hip, hooray" from two or three hundred throats shakes the very dust from the ceiling; the bumpers are simultaneously inverted, and the spontaneous explosion from every lip of the sing-song stave, "He is a jolly good fellow," attests the jovial affection of the company. When they have informed the good-natured gentleman how good and jolly he is some fifteen or twenty times in succession, and added half-a-dozen times at least that "he is one of us," which is undoubtedly the perfection of a compliment; and when at length they are hesitating and seem doubtful as to the propriety of impressing him any longer with the fact of his goodness and jollity, a voice in a red waistcoat and beadle-cut coat, standing magisterially at the rear of the table-head, roars out like the crack of doom, "Silence, gentleman, for the Cha-a-ar!" At the signal a hundred mouths bellow 'Silence!' with the full force of their lungs, until, as "all noise is stilled by a still greater noise," they are reduced to order by the reiterated banging of the hammer in the vigorous hands of the "Vice;" and something approaching to silence being at last obtained, the junior partner gets upon his legs.

A very short extract from the speech of the great man will suffice for the reader. "Gentlemen," he begins, "this is one of the important and—hm, haw—gentlemen, pleasant occasions —hm-m—an opportunity, I may say—hm—yes, when the heart expands—hm—expands, gentlemen, with delightful emotions and sentiments—hm, haw—as I said, gentlemen, with delightful, and pleasurable, and congenial sentiments. (Hear,

hear, and cheers.) Gentlemen, I thank you for the expression of your sympathy. Hm, haw—yes, sympathy, and sentiment, and fraternity, you know, gentlemen, are the order of the day. (Loud cheers.) The stupendous fact, gentlemen, has dawned —hm, he, haw, yes—I make bold to aver, and to announce, gentlemen—hm—and to fearlessly assert, and to say, yes, to say, that the stupendous fact has dawned—has dawned, my dear friends, upon the moral perceptions of universal man, that everybody is everybody's brother—(tremendous cheers, shouts of "bravo!" "go it!" and waving of glasses and handkerchiefs) —and sister of course; for the ladies, bless their hearts! the ladies, gentlemen, are not to be forgotten on this delightful occasion. (Hear, hear.) It is in the order of Providence, gentleman, yes—hm, he, haw—yes, gentlemen, it is in the order of Providence, as I said, that one man should wear a better coat than another, though that, as I am sure you will agree with me, does not prove him to be a better man. ("Hear, hear, hear," and "Thrue for you," from a notoriously lazy, drunken Irish bully.) No, gentlemen, it is not the garb that makes the man—(hear, hear)—nor the noble mansion—(hear, hear)—nor the gilded coach—(hear, hear)—nor the large landed estate—(hear, hear)—nor the hoarded thousands in the bank— (hear, hear)—nor anything of that sort, gentlemen. (Hear, hear.) No, gentlemen, it is the honest heart that beats as often in the breast of the working-man as a king upon his throne. (Uproarious cheers, mingled with knuckling and stamping, during which a reading-boy slily remarks to his chum that that last paragraph *won't read*, and gets a kick for his criticism from the Irishman aforesaid.) Now, gentlemen, there are certain considerations—hm, haw—yes, what I would propound is simply this. there are certain circumstances to be taken into consideration in connexion with the ramifications of our social organization; yes, gentlemen, our social organization, which, viewed in relation to—hm, haw—yes, in relation to the various idiosyncrasies and temperaments with which Providence—

Providence, gentlemen, has thought fit to endow us individually —for every man, you will bear in mind, is an individual in all the elements of his being—(hear, hear)—gentlemen, you understand me, I hope—hm, haw—I speak in reference to certain inherent specialities existing in all the multitudinous variations and types of the *genus homo*—(hear, hear)—and which have all their manifestations—their manifestations, I say, gentlemen, in what is commonly designated under the term inclination, or perhaps, gentlemen, I should say more properly—yes, more properly, propensity. Had we time to enter upon this question at length, it would, unless I am very much mistaken—it would be seen, gentlemen, that there is—hm, haw—yes, that there is an ever-springing fountain of true philosophy, welling up, so to speak, within and around us—around us, my dear friends— and that all the circumstances of all possible states of existence, and the innumerable modes of being and feeling, and habits, and predilections, and antipathies of the immense cosmical combination of which we fluttering, wind-borne and unsubstantial atoms—who are but the animated dust that fringes the eternal ever-changing road-track leading to the universal essence—have but a very feeble consciousness." Here the learned orator goes off into the misty realms of incomprehensible moonshine, where he disports himself with amazing volubility; and, finding himself quite at home, drops his ' hms" and "haws" and hesitation, and talks at nothing like a cataract for a full half-hour or more, to the perfect bewilderment of his auditors, who, bestowing an occasional cheer and "hear, hear" at some passing allusions to their profession, wonder impatiently where and when it is to come to a close. Having at length accomplished his grand flight, he condescends to alight upon terra-firma; and, winding up his peroration with an assurance that he is the friend and brother of the working-man, or he is nothing, concludes by thanking them for the honor they have done him in drinking his health, and, amidst a general clamor of applause, prepares to depart. He walks slowly and condescendingly through the living lane which is formed for his egress, and shaking hands as he goes with all who are near enough to lay hold of his fingers, leaves his friends and brethren to the enjoyment of their own peculiar pleasures, and, stepping into his carriage at the door, drives off.

The young governor being gone, the overseer seats himself in the vacant chair. The vice, according to immemorial prescription, proposes his health, the proposition is noisily welcomed by his personal adherents and partisans at the crosstable. The overseer's health is drunk upstanding by all, with "three times three" by the partisans gathered around him, and with three times nothing, save an audible groan by way of termination, by those who consider themselves aggrieved by his administration. Then comes the usual stereotyped speech, the component parts of which are again moonshine, and nothing but moonshine, kept bottled up for the occasion, and regularly uncorked once a-year. Its delivery, with its grumbling running accompaniment, comes off much in the following fashion:—

Overseer.—" Gentlemen · In thanking you for the honor you have done me in drinking my health, you will allow me on the present occasion to make a few remarks, and to express the obligation you have laid upon me during the past year. I need not tell you that the amount of work we have got through this season has been unprecedentedly great. We have had to make extraordinary efforts to meet the demands of the season. We have worked night and day, Sundays and week-days. I should be ungrateful if I did not express my sense of your manful co-operation in the arduous task. I trust the endeavors which I have always made to render equal justice to every man in the establishment have been fairly appreciated by you all. It has always been my object to stand between the employer and the working-man in the character of a fair arbitrator, to protect and to assert the interests of both :"—

And so on and on, to the length of a newspaper-column, the

flashes of moonshine occasionally interlarded with the muttered thunder of discontent growled at a safe distance, and swallowed up in the applause of the favored coterie clustered round the chair. The speech concludes, as all such speeches are destined to conclude, with vociferous cheering and a round of applause; and the applause terminates in the ejaculation from a multitude of mouths of that significant class of interjections to which invalids are in the habit of giving spiteful utterance after swallowing a nauseous dose of physic.

The business of the meeting thus despatched, the harmony supervenes. Glees are seriously chanted by men with solemn faces, and the private doings and histories of monks and friars who are very fond of fat bucks, and fairies frisking about, with little pigs which make the very best sort of bacon, and horn-blowing foresters green, and salt-sea pirates—of monarchs who deal out destiny to trembling mortals, and of "murphy-merchants" who deal out baked "taturs" to hungry ones—of heroes going on horseback to glory, and of other heroes going in carts to the gallows, and of a host of remarkable worthies too numerous to mention—all married to immortal verse, are deliberately sung in tolerable strains by the few who have voices and ears— each verse being put to a sudden, violent and murderous death by a crashing chorus of intolerable discord from the bawling multitude who have only lungs. Duets, solos, and most astounding recitations succeed to the glees. After each vocal or rhetorical display, a health or a toast is proposed and duly honored; and if the wine be plentiful, and last long enough, every small functionary gets an ovation, and makes a speech, and is celebrated in chorus as " a jolly good fellow."

As the evening grows late, and the fumes of the wine and grog begin to operate upon cerebrums and cerebellums only proof against beer, the more sober part of the assembly slink away silently. The mirth now becomes more noisy and less orderly and regulated. The chairman in vain calls to order; the voice in the beadle-coat and red waistcoat is by this time become so hoarse with shouting that he gives up his vocation in despair, and retires. The chairman follows his example, sidling off without beat of drum When his absence is discovered, the "vice" is installed in his place. In vain he bangs with his hammer upon the table till the glasses dance around him; he rises to speak, but it is impossible to hear a word that he utters. Confusion grows every minute worse confounded. Five different vocalists, men of one song, are each roaring his peculiar ditty; and as many different orators, who loudly claim a right to be heard, are thundering away upon what each conceives to be a subject of the most vital importance to the assembly. One who has a genius for figures and grog is bitterly impeaching the conduct of the stewards, who, he declares, have mismanaged the funds. He is indignant that no more wine or spirits is coming to his share, and demands brandy-and-water round, and is ready to prove, from the account which he has kept, that there is money in the stewards' hands to pay for it. Another orator is eager for the restoration of quietness and the resumption of harmony: he is laboring for an opportunity to sing his crack song. A third has some remarks to make on the young governor's address, the true drift and signification of which, under the inspiration of his third bottle, he has just been enabled to perceive, and is charitably anxious to enlighten his comrades. In the midst of the tumultuous din, gabble, and bawling, a half-tipsy subject leaps upon the table, and commences the rapid and dramatic enunciation of "My Lord Tom Noddy," which, as he is celebrated for doing it remarkably well, and it being considered an exceedingly graphic and interesting narrative, collects a crowd of admiring auditors. In the comparative lull which he creates the voice of the chairman is at length heard calling gentlemen to order. His imperative call is resented by several voices retorting, "Order yourself!—don't disturb the harmony." Before "My Lord Tom Noddy goes home to bed" the chairman has formally resigned his office, and retired.

What takes place afterwards I do not pretend to know, never having had the patience to sit out to the end of the saturnalia. How some got carried home to bed by their companions—how others got locked out, and wandered the streets all night—and how others again were laid up, disabled by over-indulgence in eating and drinking: these are things which I can speak of only from report. Such trifles are considered as matters of no importance; and to the generality of working-men they form rather a pleasant appendage to the annual jollification than anything to blush for, as they add a few piquant features to the history of the enjoyment when it is over, and nothing but its history remains to talk about.

Somehow it generally happens that this brief moment of relaxation is immediately followed by a tightening of the reins of government, and a rather rough assertion of authority. As if he were fearful that the delightful sentiments of universal brotherhood with which the hearts of employers expand convulsively and regularly once a-year should be mistaken for anything more than they were meant for—to wit, mere figures of speech and flowers of rhetoric—it is ten to one but the very next day will find the benignant orator harping upon a very different string, enforcing some obsolete law with a rigor hitherto unheard of, or in the character of a Draco, enacting new ones of cruel severity. The " brother of universal man" is perhaps turning the house upside-down by a stormy and abusive inquisition into a fancied overcharge of sixpence, which, after an enquiry of three or four hours, turns out to be perfectly correct; or he has taken it into his head to revise the charges for overtime, and after a dogged and ill-tempered investigation for three or four days, and the petulant examination of half the time-hands in the house, he succeeds at length in reducing by the sum of twopence the money-value of the Sunday, which the workman is compelled to sacrifice whether he like the bargain or no. At the heels of the weigh-goose, too, there not unfrequently comes the "bullet," as it is termed, or the sudden discharge, which sends a third or a half of the hands adrift after a fortnight's notice. The printing business is invariably slack at the fall of the year, and seldom becomes brisk again until after Christmas, or when Parliament is on the eve of sitting. To meet this crisis a singular custom prevails, the philosophy or humanity either of which is not very apparent. One half of the men in a large establishment get their discharge, in order that the remaining half may be retained in full employment, from which we must necessarily infer that, in the estimation of master-printers, it is better that fifty men out of a hundred should have no bread to eat than that the whole number should be reduced to half a loaf!

One evening when, during the recess of Parliament, I was returning early from my work, I stumbled accidentally upon a congregation of laboring men assembled for religious worship. I had been tempted by the prospect of a brilliant sunset to prolong my walk by making a leisurely circuit round the outskirts of the northern part of the city. At twilight, I found myself threading a winding lane with black brick cottages on one side and stunted aspen-trees on the other. Lying back about a dozen paces from the row of mean habitations, I saw a pair of small arched chapel windows, though which lights were glimmering; and I knew from the strange mixture of sounds that greeted me that something unusual was going on within. Creeping softly along the narrow flag-stone pavement, I opened the door and entered as stealthily as possible, and was startled by what certainly must be considered an odd phase of divine worship—if it were not something else. The building was a chapel of some thirty feet square, with two small galleries, one on either side of the entrance. In the pulpit was an unshaven orator addressing an audience in the highest state of excitement, and consisting apparently of laboring-men and their wives, with a good sprinkling of young children. Every sentence uttered by the speaker was received with audible demonstrations of rapturous enthusiasm. The individuals who occupied the pews which filled the centre of the area rose every now and then upon their feet, and looked anxiously and scrutinizingly around—casting compassionate glances upon about a dozen dimly-seen proselytes who appeared to be struggling upon their knees in comparative darkness among some benches under the gallery. Suddenly, a laboring-man rose from a form in the aisle, and making staggeringly for the agonizing group, plumped himself down among them, which was the signal for a simultaneous shout from every lip of "Another! another! Glory to the Father, another!" followed by the instinctive explosion in chorus of a verse of a hymn celebrating the victories of Immanuel to the tune of Rule Britannia," most vociferously and discordantly yelled out. That was no sooner finished than the black beard in the pulpit roared forth, "Let us help them, my friends! let us help them!" and then in a solemn voice, "Let us pray!" Then he began a passionate prayer to the Great Being, whom he violently conjured to come down that instant and assist his creatures in the throes of the new birth. The voice of the preacher was lost in the exultant responses of the congregation, many of whom prayed much louder than their leader; and when they paused for breath for a moment, the wailing and sobbing from the wretched creatures floundering about among the benches, and lifting their clasped hands and screaming, distracted and grimy faces now and then into the light, filled up the intervals in a manner truly characteristic and deplorable.

While this strange scene was going on, I could not help closely remarking the behavior of a pale-faced, starveling operative of about five-and-twenty, who stood near me, with the remains of a dirty and dog's eared hymn book, the leaves of which he kept on greasily thumbing over, in his hand. He looked like, and probably was, a poor working-shoemaker of the lowest class; but whatever the actual misery of his lot, and he was wan, meagre, and ill-clad in the extreme, his present rapturous condition was such as would have mocked at compassion. He was in a perfect ecstasy of saintly delight, though from the vocabulary in which he expressed it in fitful and incoherent mutterings, I suspected he was but a new convert himself, to whom some savor of the old Adam yet remained, which he no doubt would have got rid of if he could "Oh, glory!" he muttered to himself, while his whole frame trembled with excitement, and swam in perspiration, "ain't this a precious Pentecost?—thirteen sinful souls at one haul!" Then he would bawl an Amen to the petition of the moment; and again, in an under-tone, "Oh, crikey! here's a blessed manifestation" Anon, he would read a verse or two during a pause in the proceedings, and press the leaves of the book to his livid lips, and then, unable to control or repress the expression of his satisfaction, would burst out with such involuntary ejaculations as, "Gemini, here's an adorable go! Here's a stunnin' outpouring!" with sundry others of a similar and even less orthodox description, which I have no inclination to record.

The united prayers being ended, the preacher came down from the pulpit, and beckoning a couple of followers from the precentor's desk, the three together pulled, hauled, and carried their now prostrated and exhausted converts into the vestry in the rear, where it is to be hoped they gave them something more restorative than a second course of jobation, though what they there did with them I had no means of knowing. Another speaker mounted the pulpit stairs, and, after a short address, and a hymn which was sung exultingly to the tune of "Jolly Dick the Lamplighter," dismissed the congregation with a benediction and an appointment for another service for the morrow night.

This reads very like a piece of gratuitous exaggeration and caricature, and yet it is nothing of the sort; indeed, I might have shown the affair in a much more ridiculous aspect, and yet have adhered to the truth. Some years have elapsed since I stumbled upon the scene above described, but the same thing is observable at the present hour by those who choose to look for it. No later than the month preceding the opening of the Great Exhibition, I was accidentally witness of a scene equally preposterous and far more miserable and melancholy. In the very heart of the metropolis, and within hearing of the roar of the traffic of Fleet-street, a small band of the self-styled elect, almost exclusively of the lower and laboring ranks, had met together for the purpose of deprecating the wrath of God about to be let loose upon a guilty land to avenge the national sins consummated in the erection of the Crystal Palace, which was relentlessly doomed, as the great temple of Mammon, to a sudden and horrible destruction, together with the rebellious city which had raised it in mockery of the Most High! The grieving and groaning community of some sixty or seventy jaundiced-looking individuals, occupied the floor of the chapel, the galleries being shut as useless, and left to the dust of years. Three long-visaged messengers of woe entered the pulpit at once. The first who spoke launched out into such a violent strain of prophetic denunciation as soon elicited a chorus of dreadful groans from all present. He shot forth every tenth syllable from his lungs with such tremendous force as would have drowned the crack of a rifle, and actually raised the dust in the forsaken galleries to such a degree that he and his compeers stood aloft in a mist, through which their magnified forms loomed like evil genii threatening horror and ruin. In the exercise of his Christian charity he compared the modern metropolis to the Sodom of old Judea, and declared that it came off "second best" in the comparison. He assured his audience that all the real Christians in London (perhaps he mentally excepted the present company) might be trundled out of town in one of the omnibuses then rolling along the Strand.

When he had tired himself out, which he did in about

twenty minutes, another followed in the same strain, though he at least condescended to give a reason for the doom he threatened, and that reason was, he said, the sins of the aristocracy, whom he accused of having gone after strange gods in worshipping Jenny Linds.

The third speaker, a sallow north-countryman, half-choked with the Northumbrian burr, graciously directed attention to the sole means of averting the impending calamity, which he solemnly declared was only to be accomplished by the urgent prayers of the faithful then and there present; "that small and chosen band were the remnant who had not bowed down to idols, and they held in their hands the destinies of the modern Babylon; and deliverance, if it came at all, must come from the sacred violence of their united and unwearying prayers, which alone had power to stay the avenging arm of an insulted God!" All this was received by the poverty-stricken, sickly and woe-begone assembly as the veritable utterances of prophecy, and was responded to by a chorus of gasping sobs and groans from a dozen or two of male and female "sweaters," cobblers, shoebinders, and slop-makers, whom foul air, confinement, want of exercise, and semi-starvation had first etiolated, then endued with a saffron-colored skin, and at last landed in the monomania of religious fanaticism. I could not help thinking, as I looked upon them, that three grains of calomel round, with a double dose for the orators, followed at a proper interval by a general participation in a social bowl of salts and senna, would have sent their peculiar and truly pitiable piety to the right about, and restored them to the perception of common-sense; and I would gladly have paid the expense of the entertainment had it been practicable.

When the last speaker had blown his wailing blast, and the three together had disappeared in the dusty mist they had raised, a man plumped himself suddenly on his knees on the table beneath the pulpit, and began a very noisy and desperate kind of oration which partook as much of the nature of a

330   A NOTE TO BE NOTED.

public announcement as it did of a prayer, at the end of which the assembly broke up.

The above are some of the forms in which the religious sentiment finds embodiment among the lowest and least educated section of the working classes.* I forbear to make

* The working ranks in large towns enfold men of every variety of religious opinion and profession. The greater part of them, as might be expected, professedly belong to the Established Church, and nine-tenths of these are the individuals who make up nearly the whole of that immense body who never enter a church or chapel nor hear a sermon once in ten years. Among the denizens of the workshop, to dissent is at least to have the character of being religious to a certain extent, while to belong to the Established Church is too often to have a character for no religion at all. The marked distaste for the inside of a church which these professed adherents to the religion of the State display, may well arise from the fact that Christianity, as it is there offered to their acceptance, assumes a garb and an attitude which are offensive to them. When the workingman contrasts the cushioned pew in which the fat cit snores at his ease, and pursy respectability reclines so comfortably swaddled, with the cold, damp stones and narrow, hard bench proffered for the accommodation of his weary limbs, he looks upon the whole affair as a kind of scurvy joke, in which the laugh being all against himself, he declines to take a part. On the subject-matter of Christianity he is often as ignorant as a Blackfoot Indian, and, indeed, in this respect is precisely on a level with his clod-hopping brother who stumbles at the plough tail. He knows nothing either of its doctrines or its history, and has no more idea of what the Reformation effected, or was intended to effect, than an Esquimaux has of the Eleusinian mysteries. When, at a period which there is no great risk in presuming to be not far off, England shall be again spiritually subjected to the Roman Pontiff, there will be no necessity for any jesuitical perversion of the million masses that compose the industrial army. The vast majority of them are at the present moment every whit as good Catholics as they are Protestants, without knowing it. The wisdom that should have enlightened them has been hauled on ship-board by a pious press-gang, and transported beyond seas to illuminate the savages and cannibals of Polynesia and New Zealand. It is so much more gratifying to our favorite phase of Christian philanthropy to behold a converted cannibal jabbering and grimacing on a missionary platform, than it is to see a fellow-countryman rescued from the slough of ignorance and vice, that we send thousands of talented men and hundreds of thousands of money on a journey to the Antipodes, to prevent Quackoo from griddling his grandmother, while Peggy Styles at home poisons Big Bob, her husband, for the sake of four pound ten—which we are content to denominate a very shocking procedure, and say no more about it. It will be no proof of the soundness of this economy, even should the bulwarks of the Protestant faith be found in Australia or New Zealand when its outworks are assailed at home.

any comment upon them, because a sincere zeal for what a man considers to be the truth, however mistaken he may be, has some claims to respect. If these things be repulsive to well-ordered minds, they will ascribe their existence to the right cause, which is the low state of knowledge among the populace on the subject of Christianity. Had the Church of England done her duty during the two centuries last past—had her priests and bishops really earned but a tenth part of the money they have been paid for instructing the people, such doings as these would never have been witnessed. They are the wild weeds of a religious soil—the natural out-croppings of a religious necessity, in a region which has been the subject of unprincipled neglect from the preferment-hunting crew whose bounden duty it was to have cultivated it with care.

CHAPTER XIV.

I cut off my own tale, and wind up that of others—My last visit to the paternal roof—A Domestic Scene—A Sabbath Evening Walk—Worship *al Fresco*—Wagon-loads of Eloquence—a travelling Prophetess—a startling Surprise—My old Friend of the Revolution—An Infidel turned Evangelist—Death a stern Teacher—N——'s History—Consummation of Dick D——, the tippling Cockney—Profitable Policy of the 'own Correspondent,' and his mysterious disappearance—Last news of my Sheep's-head Friend—The Fish once more; his successful courtship and prosperous marriage—Parents and Friends in the Silent Land——Conclusion

I AM warned by the length to which the above desultory sketches of my experience have proceeded, that I have not much further space to occupy, and that I must therefore bring them to a close. Were I to relate the incidents of my life from the events detailed in the last chapter up to the present moment, they would present but the repetition of an often-told tale, and would afford matter of very little interest to the general reader. The personal adventures of a journeyman printer, who travels about from place to place, are often sufficiently varied and amusing, so long as he is free to follow the caprices of the moment, to play the bird of passage, and to come and go where and when he chooses. But marry him to a wife and surround him with a family, and, by the very means which enhance his moral and social value, you cut off the romance of his condition, and reduce him from the mirth-exciting exaltation of an amusing vagabond to the dull and dead level of a useful member of society, for whom and for whose destiny and doings nobody upon earth cares a straw. That this has been pretty much my own case during the last dozen years of my life is a fact which, just in the ratio that it has been important to me and mine, is uninteresting to the rest of the world. In beginning this narrative, I admonished the reader that I had no story, in the proper sense of the word, to tell. I have neither done, nor seen, nor suffered anything very extraordinary during the course of my humble career; and I had no intention of claiming any man's applause, or his compassion either, by anything I thought fit to record. But I thought, and I think still, that to every mind there is a history belonging, which however imperfectly written, will repay the trouble of perusal; and in presenting the public with so much of mine as I judged it worth while to disclose, I have endeavored in some sort to show the operation of circumstances in determining the mental bias. If I have not succeeded also in delineating some characteristic peculiarities of the class to which I have belonged nearly all my life, it must be because I have no talent in sketching from nature, to whom alone I am indebted for my models.

It remains for me now, ere I take my final farewell of the reader, to give a parting glance at some of the characters with whom he formed an acquaintance in the earlier pages of my narrative. For reasons already mentioned, I shall not further recount my own personal history; but I must advert to one or two events which, being connected with the *dramatis personæ* of my tale, derive from that cause an interest they would not otherwise possess.

Of all the personal friendships I ever formed among the members of my own class, there has been none so close or so warmly reciprocated as that which sprung up spontaneously with N——, my literary, republican, and infidel companion, in the printing-offices of Paris. From the first month of our acquaintance down to the present moment, I have never, when reflecting, as I sometimes do, on the constitution of my own mind, been able to divest myself of the consciousness that very much of its character is due to my association with N—— at a period when I was unconsciously collecting that experience from which character results I never corresponded with him after I had quitted Paris, because, owing to the unsettled state of affairs at the time of my departure, it seemed very unlikely that he would remain long there. Thus I lost sight of him; and when many years had passed away without his calling on me in London, where he would have found me readily upon inquiring among the trade, I concluded that I should see him no more. I was, however, mistaken.

One morning in the middle of September, 1840, while the atmosphere was yet glowing with all the heat of summer, having obtained a fortnight's holiday—a bonus which it is never difficult to procure from a master-printer in slack seasons, seeing that he does not pay wages to an absent servant—I started with my wife to pay a visit to the old friends of her youth in the little quiet village in the valley of the Avon. The Doctor's pony-chaise was in waiting for us at the railway-station at Bath; and in six hours from the time of leaving Paddington, we came in sight of the villa where I had spent the two most tranquil years of my existence. The good doctor, upon whom age was now stealing fast, had got rid of his types and press, having refused sundry offers made by a printer in the district, and made, as he conceived, a better bargain, by bestowing them upon a young beginner in business. He was still as fond of the angle as I had found him at my first acquaintance, and having first dined in the old library, we spent the evening together at the roach-hole at the river side, and covered a small grass-plot with the shiny scales of the victims we drew to land. I spent two hours afterwards in tuning up the old piano, not having much experience in the business, and having got it into trim, we closed the evening by singing some of the old gentleman's favorite Church music. Next day we visited all the old places, the old faces and the new mill, and filled a few sheets of paper with some hasty sketches of scenes which we wanted at home to complete our remembrance of the valley. Everybody laid claim to a property in my wife, and I never caught sight of her save at the end of the day, when we both had news to tell, and I the fruits of my artistic labors to produce. Thus time passed on, in rambling, riding, and driving about, now with a companion and now without, while I drank fresh draughts of health with every passing hour, and before I had been a week away from the smoky haunts of London, had completely recovered strength and spirits.

I set off on the first Saturday morning to visit my parents, and to carry them an invitation from the Doctor and his lady to return with me, and spend the following week at F——d. The walk of sixteen miles was a delightful occupation for the forenoon. I found the old couple awaiting my arrival ere they sat down to dinner, and they agreed to return with me next day, if the conveyance upon which they relied were procurable. Ned came home to dinner. He had commenced business for himself in a modest way; and having sold a couple of easy chairs, and taken an order for a dining-table that morning, was in capital spirits with the prospect of "making a do of it." He promised to drive us over, and set off to Tom's in the afternoon to see about the horse and chaise.

There was a family gathering in the evening, among whom there were several new members who had come into the world since my last visit, and with whom I had to make acquaintance. The old people were astonishingly merry at the multiplication that had taken place—and merry were we all till it was time to put the babies to bed—and then the mothers moved off, and the fathers lighted their pipes, and mixed their temperate grog, and drank affectionately to my health and prosperity, and blew a cloud of smoke that sent the sparrows twittering from their roosting-places in the trellice-work overhead. Then we went in-doors to supper, with the home-made loaf and the country cheese; and then came the old family Bible and the worn-out dogs-eared prayer-book, and the tremulous voice of my good old dad, as he read deliberately the psalm and the prayer, as in the days when I lay in my mother's lap, while she soothed little Ned to silence in her arms. Then came the bed-room candles, and we kissed each other all round; and I went to my own little room, and crept between the sheets, and lay watching the harvest-moon flashing broad and red between the vine-leaves as they fluttered in the cool night wind;.then the voices of other days sounded in my ears, and the scenes of the years of infancy among the fields and crystal streams of my native place swam again before my eyes; and the joys and the sorrows of childhood were re-acted once more, as I slept—it was for the *last* time—in my father's house.

After the morning service, flavored with the damp smell of the old family pew; and after a hot dinner, which had cooked itself at the kitchen fire, while the whole household were at church, my brother Tom made his appearance with a horse and gig, which, the four-wheel having broken down the day before, was the only conveyance at his command. As it would only contain two persons, my father and mother got into it, and Ned and I resolved to walk off together an hour or two later, so as to reach F———d by supper-time, after which Ned would return with the horse, who would have had a few hours' rest. We took an early cup of tea in the garden, and about five in the afternoon set forth on our way. Ned, who was well acquainted with all the short-cuts and field-paths in the neighborhood, chose a route which avoided the high-road altogether, and leading me through corn-fields, where the sheaves of a late crop were yet standing, and through shady forest coverts and copses of underwood, where the hazel-nuts "in milk-white clusters hung," beguiled the way with talk upon the events of the past, and the confidences of the present hour, and the hopes and probabilities of the future. From a high ground, which we reached after an hour's walking, we could hear the clattering call of the church-bells of half a-dozen different villages, and could discern here and there between the trees the white smock-frock and the bright scarlet mantle of the husbandman and his wife, as, in answer to the appeal, they led their prattling children towards the square little grey towers from whence the summons rang forth. On either hand, too, we could see the two famous cities of the west—Bristol, with her countless bottles of black smoke perpetually uncorked, begrimed with the scoriæ of a thousand commercial volcanoes, and reeking in a perennial mist; and beautiful Bath, reclining like an Oriental queen upon a couch of emerald, and bathing her feet in the tepid flood. Below, the languid river wound along like a thread of silver, and over-head a cloud of rooks mingled their hoarse voices with the clang of the Sabbath-bells, the drowsy tinklings of the flocks and the lowing of the distant herds. Descending the hill, we entered a wood, through which our path continued for more than a mile, and which was alive with parties of nutters, some bent on pleasure and some on profit—shop-boys and apprentices from the neighboring cities, full of frolic and fun as they pursued their "merciless ravage" among the hazel trees—and poor, ragged, half-clad wretches, who, begirt with capacious bags, and crook in hand, pursued their unlicensed trade in stealthy silence, but with an earnestness and activity that showed the importance to them of the harvest they were surreptitiously reaping at the rate of a bushel or two a-day.

We soon left the wood behind us, and mounted to a high and open down of level table-land, which we traversed for a mile or two, and, at an abrupt turning in the bye-road we were then pursuing, came upon a sort of natural basin hollowed out of the side of the hill which we had to descend, where a singular spectacle awaited us. A large wagon, three-fourths of the length of which was covered in with clean white drapery, and the remaining portion occupied by a raised platform, was drawn up across the road, which was little more than a mere horse-track. Several other smaller vehicles were grouped on either side, in a semi-circular form, whose concavity fronted, and in a manner completed, the natural grassy amphitheatre of the hill-side From one of the tented vehicles arose a thin stream of smoke, and the aroma of coffee was perceptible in the air. As many as five or six hundred persons, nearly all seated on the grassy declivity, were grouped in front of the wagon in profound and motionless silence, and on the little platform a hoary-headed man knelt and prayed.

We were irresistibly drawn to the spot, and in less than a minute had joined the congregation. The scene was wondrously strange and picturesque. Behind the wagons a straggling group of tall and graceful birches threw their slender branches up into the sky; and between their speckled trunks the eye roamed at will over a vast level and cultivated plain, mapped out in white roads, and spotted with homesteads and villages, and terminating, at the distance of eleven or twelve miles, by the abrupt wall-like ridge, that marks the south-west boundary of Salisbury Plain, upon which the Westbury white horse was seen prancing gallantly.

As the tremulous voice of the old prophet wavered in the wind that fluttered his white locks, some passing cloud-shadows flickered over us, and a few drops of rain fell upon his face. He took advantage of the circumstance in his prayer in a manner so eloquent and touching as drew audible sobs from the rough group around him. When he rose from his knees, a younger man, with lungs well used to the work, gave forth a hymn, which all joined in singing with hearty good-will, and an energy expressive of the prevalent state of feeling, repeating the last verse three or four times with added nerve and voice.

The psalm ended, a woman of about thirty years of age, of a pale and intellectual cast of countenance, clad in white garments and wearing a fillet of white around her brows, gave an infant she had been soothing to slumber to the old man, and stepped forth upon the platform. Tall, graceful, and wan as marble, she stood like a Sybil statue upon a pedestal, with the distant landscape, now sinking into shadow, for a background. As the warm drops of rain still continued to patter down at intervals, a few of the auditors who stood beneath and close to the wagon had hoisted their umbrellas. She looked at them —a half-compassionate, half-reproachful look—turned her large orbs to the sky, and said, "My friends, put down your umbrellas, I cannot speak to whalebone and cloth; I want to see your faces; the God I serve will cork up the bottles of heaven, and bid the sun to shine." In an instant the cause of offence was removed, and, strange to say, in another instant the clouds had passed away, and the warm red rays of the sinking sun shone upon every face. She spoke for a quarter of an hour upon the subject of man's duty to his fellow-man, and spoke, too, in a vein of perfect propriety, considering the place and the audience she addressed, and with a fluency and a simple elegance of diction that could not have been surpassed. When she had finished her short harangue, she disappeared in the tent. The young Stentor then stepped forth, and shouted, " Praise God!" At which signal the whole audience, who had been there ever since morning, and had not moved from the spot the whole day, burst into a simultaneous roar, which took the air of the Old Hundredth Psalm.

As we had yet five miles to walk, I motioned Ned, at the termination of the strain, to follow me out of the crowd, as it was full time to proceed on our journey. We had cork-screwed our way to the front of the wagon, and were in the act of passing within a few feet of it, when two syllables from a well-known voice caught my ear, and caused me to look up. Had it been possible to have fallen to the ground in the crowd in which I was jammed, I verily think I should have been prostrated in mortal astonishment at the spectacle that met my gaze. I clutched my brother by the arm, and stood staring in mute bewilderment at the figure on the platform. The last rays of the sun shone upon his head, which he had turbaned with a handkerchief. He had uttered the words

"My friends!" and was about to commence his address, but paused a moment or two with a commanding gesture, imposing silence on the multitude. As he stood for an instant collecting his thoughts, an echo from a distant rising ground repeated the last line of the old tune with a distinctness so startling that one might have thought it the response of living voices. Hardly crediting the evidence of my senses, I stood with eyes riveted to his face, awaiting the repetition of the words which had spell-bound me. I had not long to wait. The old voice, the old action, and forcible volubility of expression were not to be mistaken. There stood my old friend, N——, the oracle of the printing-office, the unanswerable infidel advocate and declaimer of 1826, the revolutionary combatant and disappointed republican of 1830—now a wayside and unbeneficed preacher of the doctrines which it seemed once to have been his very instinct to deride and to condemn. I resolved, if it were practicable, to speak with him; and with this view sent Ned on to the villa, with the information that I was on the way, and should follow him in an hour or two at the latest.

My old friend had lost none of his ancient energy and enthusiasm He had always possessed the faculty of making the subject upon which he spoke appear a subject of importance, and now that he had taken upon himself the office of an evangelist, he spoke with such zeal, and ardor, and fluency, and authority to boot, that I was not at all surprised at the responsive chorus of groans, and sobs, and sighs with which his untutored audience acknowledged the power of his eloquence. He caught my eye as I stood gazing up at him in amazement; and, when he had ended his discourse, and dismissed the assembly with a short prayer and benediction, he sent a young fellow to conduct me to the rear of the encampment, where I found him busy with others in preparing coffee for the refreshment of the party. Their day's work, he said, was concluded, and they were on the point of breaking up, and only awaited the arrival of the horses and the owners of the vehicles, who had lent them for that day's service, before they left the ground.

The horses came before the temperate repast was finished, and then N——, bidding a brief adieu to his companions, seized me by the arm, and demanded "Now, my friend, whither bound?" I told him my destination, and hoped he would favor me with his company a part of the way. "All the way," said he, " were it ten times as long. I have much to say, and I hope good news to hear; God grant it." The sun had gone down, but the broad moon, who had looked him in the face as he sunk behind the hill, gave us the benefit of her light, as we went on our way. N—— was silent for some minutes, when I, anxious for information, naturally asked where he had left his charming wife.

"In Pere la Chaise," said he, with a dismal attempt at firmness.

"Dead?" said I, stopping short in my walk.

"Dead!" he replied. "Come," said he, after a pause, "you used to be fond of the children; why don't you ask after them?"

"You cannot mean it," said I, "God forbid that it should be so. Do not tell me so!"

"Man! I must tell you the truth. Wife and children are all dead—and buried—in one grave—in one day."

I dared not again break the silence, and we walked on for some time without a word.

He recovered his self-possession at length, and told me calmly and manfully the history of his life since we had parted last. He had stayed in Paris after the Revolution which had given a throne to Louis Philippe. He had found friends and patrons there who were willing to serve him. But the cholera came in '32, and his wife had fallen a victim to her compassion for a suffering servant who was struck down in the street; the children sickened on the same day, and within a week he was left widowed and childless. He said the streets of Paris became a horror to him after this, and he flew to the coast, whence he soon after sailed for America. He had bought land in the Far West, and cleared it and sold it again. He had sought forgetfulness in the haunts of cities and the solitudes of the forest, but it was not to be found; but he blessed God that he had at length been led by a voice, to which he listened for the first time in an Indian settlement, to seek and to find a better cure than oblivion for the sorrows of the human lot.

"I have been anxious to see you," he said, "God has granted my wish. Let me hear from your own lips that the blasphemies I have often uttered in your presence did not alienate you from the truth; give me that satisfaction, if you can." I set him at rest on that point, by declaring my adherence to the principles in which I had been brought up; and I told him candidly, that if I had not answered his arguments against Christianity, it was not because I thought them unanswerable, but because I knew him to be so much the cleverer disputant that I stood no chance with him. He was greatly relieved by this declaration, which he said had removed a load from his breast. He then questioned me as to the events of my own life, of which he was ignorant; congratulated me on my prudent marriage, and gave me a great deal of very serious and excellent counsel, which I am afraid I have not followed so rigidly as I ought to have done. "I am but a stranger in my own country," said he, in conclusion, as he drew near the house. "I have joined these good people, because they offered me an opportunity which I dared not refuse. The few relatives that I have in England believe that I am yet in America, and I shall not undeceive them until the eve of my return thither. I shall go back in the spring to the work which Providence has allotted me to do; it will last my life. Alas! it would last a thousand lives. God bless you, my dear fellow; perhaps I may see you again in London before I sail." By this time we were at the garden-gate. I tried in vain to prevail upon him to enter; he shook me heartily by the hand, called the blessing of Heaven upon me and mine, turned away with a bound, and a moment after I heard him leap the stile which divided the paddock from the road, and walk with rapid steps towards the village. I never saw him again.

Those among my readers who entertain any sympathy or curiosity on the subject of Dick D——, the tippling cockney, will not be sorry to learn that after lying in the hospital for three months, during which he was visited by the lovers of liberty of both sexes, he at length recovered of his broken head. Upon his restoration to society, he found himself at once a patriot and a teetotaler, before teetotalers had sprung into existence, in spite of himself; a patriot, because he bore the scar of an honorable wound on his pericranium, supposed to have been battered in by the butt-end of a grenadier's musket —and a teetotaler, because he was compelled to total abstinence from alcoholic beverages of all sorts, through the painful sensibility of his injured scalp to the slightest fumes of spirituous liquors ever afterwards. He was nursed and coddled through his convalescence by a lively French cook-maid, a trifle faded, who became enamoured of *le brave Anglois*, who had perilled his life in the cause of honor and *la belle France*. Her devotion to his comfort and convenience was most touching and exemplary; she plastered his plate, and slopped, and gruelled, and souped, and ragoued, and fricaseed, and biftecked, and pôt-au-feud him till he got well and hearty, and then she married him by way of completing her good intentions. His reputation for valor procured him a lucrative employment in one of the Government offices so soon as he was in a condition to go to work. He retained it for some years, but must have relinquished it, though I know not for what reason, before the year 1839, as I then began to meet him occasionally taking the air, in company with his wife, on Waterloo-bridge. He honored me with a nod of recognition on several occasions, but testified no inclination for a renewal of our former intimacy, which also, on my own part, there was no wish to revive. I understood from a fellow-workman that he subsequently relapsed into his ancient partiality for the manufactures of Barclay and Perkins, and that he died in 1842, from his persistence, in spite of surgical warning in the use of draughts of "cool porter," to assuage the fever of his brain. After his death, his widow returned to Paris, where she yet, I believe, keeps a humble sort of lodging-house, chiefly inhabited by English workmen.

E——, the "own correspondent," who showed his prowess during the three days of the Revolution by locking himself in his room and shaking beneath the bed-clothes, having thoroughly mastered the German language, effected an engagement with a London paper, in virtue of which, being furnished with the necessary introductions, he transferred himself to Vienna, whence for many years he regularly transmitted communications intended for the enlightenment of the British public on the subject of Austrian affairs. Here he not only lived in a style of respectability, but amassed besides a considerable sum of money. With a prudence out of all proportion with his valor, he contrived to double his gains by selling himself to both parties. The salary paid to him by his employers in London, and which was sufficient to maintain him genteelly, was of course the price of the information which he collected and detailed for their use; and this salary was paid over again by the tools of Metternich and the Austrian Cabinet in compensation for the pains he was willing to take in cooking all his despatches to their taste ere they went sent off. Thus the British public were crammed for some twelve or fifteen years with Austrian delineations of Austrian diplomacy; and thus and by similar successful tamperings with other venal scoundrels, it was that we were all so gloriously ignorant of Austrian atrocities in relation to Hungary almost up to the very hour when Kossuth, having got the whole blood-sodden dynasty in his mailed grasp, was blockhead enough *not* to clutch them with a mortal grip, and sacrificed the independence of his country and the liberties of Europe to a qualm of ill-timed leniency. When the popular outbreak first made head in Vienna, E—— was seen working at a barricade, and sporting a tricolored cockade in his cap; but he vanished, no one can say how or where, at the first sound of a shot. It is not known whether he is at present living or dead He had saved a good sum of money, and his relations in London would be glad to know what has become of it. He left behind him in Vienna the reputation of having been hanged by Bem as a spy; but, from what I know of his character, I feel assured that is not the truth, as he never could have mustered courage to undertake the office.

My first London friend and considerate adviser B—— continues to thrive, to live as jovially and to dress at times as luxuriantly as ever. He is now the proprietor of a comfortable little jobbing business in a provincial town, and has almost realized a competence; he talks, however, of "going in for a coach or a coffin" by investing all he is worth in starting a newspaper. That he will make the attempt I have not a doubt, though I have great doubts of its resulting in anything else than the absorption of his superfluous energies and his superfluous cash. Time has grizzled his curly hair, and puckered his dauntless visage; but he has made up his mind never to grow old, and therefore he never will. His eldest son, Jem, emigrated with a wife and a young family two or three years ago, and in all human probability he is at this moment up to the eyes in the auriferous soil of the Australian Ophir.

Of my old friend and press-mate, the "Fish," I heard and saw nothing, notwithstanding the diligent inquiries which I regularly made whenever I travelled westward, for more than eleven years after I parted from him upon his rupture with the widow in Paris. He had, in fact, almost vanished from my mind and memory when, one day, happening to be cited as a witness to one of our metropolitan minor courts of justice, I heard myself while waiting my turn to be called upon, addressed by a once familiar and grateful voice as "Master Charles." I turned round involuntarily, and there, arrayed in an ample gown of office, and bearing a black and gilded wand in his hand, stood the ancient and veritable "Fish" of former times, but amplified from the lither, ling line outline of my juvenile days to the broad-breasted, turbot-shaped volume of judicial portliness. Matrimony had done it all. He had returned to London and procured employment at case in a small office. The window by which he stood at work day by day commanded a view of an alderman's dining-room, in which a buxom housekeeper made her appearance every afternoon at three o'clock to lay the cloth for her master's dinner. Whether from the lady's resemblance in some respects to the merry widow of the Rue de la Harpe I do not pretend to say, but the Fish was again caught in the net of Cupid. He began making advances in dumb show, and in spite of the coyness of the fair one, soon succeeded in establishing a set of telegraphic signals indicative of a growing good understanding between them. After he had coquetted for a few weeks in this way between a couple of closed windows, he hoisted a signal, which he had printed in large type, proposing a meeting at a particular spot at a certain hour. The lady blushed, but nodded acquiescence. She kept her appointment, and the upshot of it was that the Fish married the housekeeper of the alderman, who, taking a fancy to him, had patronized him and inducted him by degrees into his present comfortable and corpulent position, which left him, he said, nothing to wish for. All this I learned from the Fish's own mouth while waiting until my turn came to kiss the book. When the court broke up he doffed his robes of office, and inviting me to his residence, which was not far off, introduced me to his better, and, large as he had grown himself, bigger half. He resided on the basement floor of a noble house in one of the inns of court, and over his head dwelt the magistrate who presided in the court of justice where he officially attended, and of which he was a mere stalking ornament, and nothing more. He paid no rent, and enjoyed certain perquisites besides the privilege of occupation, in return for which he took charge of the key of the street-door, which he opened and shut once a-day. Neither he nor his wife have much else to do but to take care of themselves—an occupation in which they suffer very little interruption, and in which, judging from appearance, they succeed to perfection.

The cottage and the garden in the Gloucester-road have long ceased to be. The advance of modern improvements has blotted them out. The lease of the little place expired seven years ago; but it endured long enough for the shelter of my parents, both of whom had taken up their abode in a narrower house before the little cottage where they had lived so happily was condemned to fall. Within the last ten years I have stood by the graves of many dear to me, and I have seen all trace of their peaceful and blissful existence obliterated from the earth. The stately mansion and trim gravelled walks of one of Bristol's merchant princes occupy the spot which was once the centre of our hopes and affections. Other hopes and other aspirations are busy on the same spot; and these in their turn shall pass away to make room for more in infinite succession. The good old Doctor and his rather rigid lady have travelled the same road which the rich and the poor, the proud and the humble, are all compelled to take; and the villa has passed into other hands. I believe that all these changes, though they be bitter to endure, are yet just as they should be. There is a compensation for every calamity under the sun, save those which deservedly entail shame or dishonor upon the sufferer, and it is often to be drawn from the very circumstances of the evil we deplore. Hearts that have loved and lived together continue to live more wisely and to love more truly when the bonds of a common suffering have been added to those of a common affection. There are gifts among the numberless bounties of Heaven which must be rent away from us before we can ever possess them as we ought, and the loss of which, moreover, can alone arouse us to the full value of those we are allowed to retain. But a truce to such reflections as these; I have no intention of tagging a moral to the end of my story, which finishes here. One parting word with the reader, and I have done.

When I commenced these desultory reminiscences of my personal history at the suggestion of the gentleman who was then the proprietor of TAIT'S MAGAZINE, and to whose kind and encouraging advice I shall ever feel largely indebted, I did so without much consideration of the subject, trusting to the suggestions of a rather voluminous experience as a journeyman printer to supply matter for what I intended to be but a very brief chronicle. I was astonished to find that the first few numbers aroused the spleen of certain editors of newspapers, who denounced them as the work of a hackneyed fictionist, and not the production of a working-man at all. I forgave them the gratuitous falsehood. Some of them have since discovered their mistake, and tacitly acknowledged it. Many more have awarded me a far greater meed of encouragement than I am conscious of deserving, for which I beg to return them my hearty thanks. Numbers of my old companions have recognized some of the events of my story; and if I have not answered the numerous letters I have received from them, it is because my time was too much occupied to attend to all, and I was unwilling to make any invidious distinction. I have thought it my duty to take the opportunity which has arisen in the course of my narrative of exposing certain abuses which exist in the details of the trade to which I was brought up; but in so doing, I have sought to avoid anything like personality, and have been prompted by no other motive than a sincere desire for the correction of existing evils. With unfeigned thanks to the reader for his long-continued indulgence, I now respectfully bid him adieu.

APPENDIX.

A WORKING MAN'S NOTIONS ON SOCIALISM

To start fair in a survey of the workings of Socialism, we must suppose all distinctions of rank and class to be abolished, all previous right to every species of property at once and for ever abrogated, and the whole of the pecuniary debts and obligations of all the individuals of the state to each other to be for ever cancelled. This done, and a general equitable and impartial divison of the whole of the property of the community effected, under the direction of functionaries elected by the whole— what follows? To-day all are equal, equal as were the sons of Noah when they stepped out of the ark. But what would be the state of affairs to-morrow? or this day month? "Oh, but," says the Communist, "we should pass a law that the gains of every man should go to the common stock! Be it so; then the whole property of the state is a common stock, and you at once abolish individual right and individual accumulation Let us see how that will work. Every man is supposed to exert himself, and to do his best for the benefit of the common stock. You have put all upon an equality, as far as the right to, and enjoyment of, the stock in hand are concerned; but you have not equalized the power of production. "That is of no consequence," says the Socialist; "if each one does what he can, it is all that the community has a right to expect. Further, we shall not estimate the services of the statesman or the artist higher than those of the field-laborer; all labor is equally honorable, and merits the same reward, and would receive it from a reasonably-constituted society." Very well; be it even so if you will. But there are yet other things you have not equalized, and some of these are the honesty, the integrity, the industry, and the will to exercise it, which characterize different individuals so variously. Under your system idleness thrives as well as activity. What will you do with your drones? You can deprive them of nothing, for individually they have no property, nothing to be deprived of. Thus, your Utopia will inevitably become the paradise of laziness and criminal inaction It would be easy to show, also, that, desirable as it may appear to some now groaning under the curse of unrequited toil, it would soon become the purgatory of the industrious, skilful and well-intentioned; because there would be no reward for superior talent or superior exertion, in the estimation of the generality of mankind Some few noble minds are to be found in all ages among all societies, with whom considerations of personal advantage are not the moving principle, but unless all the members of the communist kingdom, or at least the great majority of them, were men of this rare mould, there would be but small progress among them, and less harmony. The ambition even of the highest order of minds, by which the world has profited and is profiting so much, is not of that refined and ethereal composition which disdains and rejects the solid advantages attendant upon distinguished success in any pursuit whatever, rather is that distinction from the common herd, which great success carries with it, coveted by most on account of those very advantages, which are all, be it observed, connected with the enjoyment of the rights of property, and of individual and exclusive possession. The advocate of the new social doctrines pretends that their general adoption would put a period to the existence of individual ambition of this old-world character as a motive to personal exertion. It would be a miserable event for human progress and happiness if his views in this particular should ever be realized; for we may gather from the history of the human race, whose lessons have been going on for thousands of years, that wherever these incentives to exertion have been wanting, there the improvements desiderated have not sprung up, and the race has not advanced in its social condition.

Although perfect equality has never been known to exist, even among savage tribes, as all have their chiefs, and many their degraded classes, yet that approach to it which is masked by the lax notions of property which obtain with them may be fairly considered as one of the causes of their weak and degraded condition. This, indeed, is partly shown by what takes place when savage societies are brought into friendly contact of juxta-position with the civilized It is then seen that energies and aspirations which had before lain dormant, and elements of improvement and progress of which no symptoms had before appeared, start at once into active operation. Thus, some of the Indian tribes of North America, from constant association with their white brethern, learned to cast off the habits and customs of savage life, and have assumed those of the civilized community with whom they are in contact. An Indian newspaper in the Indian language and conducted by an Indian editor, is one among many tokens of the partial emergence of a barbarous race from the degraded level of uncivilized equality. The history of the New Zealanders, and of the inhabitants of the Polynesian Isles, affords further testimony, as well of the debasing tendency of the nearest approaches to actual equality with which we are acquainted, as of the social amelioration which ensues among a people so nurtured whenever the motives and incitements which characterize the civilized condition are made to operate upon them. From the lowest level of embruting apathy, ignorance and self-indulgence, some of these islanders have risen to be the rivals and emulators of their teachers and benefactors; and that plainly from the instigation of motives which a state of settled equality could never supply. If we consider these facts in connexion with what took place in France after the senseless and socialist Revolution of 1848, when an experiment was actually made, upon no small or unimportant scale, of the practical working of one portion of the equality system, we may probably arrive at conclusions pointing to the truth in reference to this great question. I allude, of course, to the operations in the national workshops in Paris, which were intended to show the world the superiority of guaranteed employment and certain and equalized wages over the system which left employment and wages dependent upon character and industry. It must be within the recollection of all who paid any attention to the subject, that the experiment resulted in the clearest possible manifestation of the mischievousness and absurdity of the plan which it was intended and expected by its advocates to recommend. It is no exaggeration to say that that experiment operated, as far as it was possible for any experiment to do, in bringing into play all the meanest, least honest, and most disgraceful characteristics of the laboring ranks. Instead of practising their different callings with the zeal and emulation which their would-be benefactors had vaunted for them, not only did the positive reverse of such conduct appear, but they seemed carefully to vie with each other in maintaining a system of fraudulent and dishonest inactivity, by which, at one and the same time, the Government were atrociously plundered, and themselves more deeply disgraced and demoralized

Such experiments as these show plainly the tendency of the doctrines of equality when reduced to practice. There is very little doubt, it appears to me, that if the world were doomed by an irrevocable and unavoidable decree to have recourse to a system of universal equality—organize it how we might—a few short cycles would behold the most advanced and civilized of the nations relapsed again into barbarism, and reduced to a condition of primitive wretchedness and inefficiency. It is perhaps possible that those indispensable labors of man without which he could not exist would be continued to be carried on with something like regularity, under the pressure of necessity and threatening famine. Perhaps, too, under a system of equality, the very highest departments of science might flourish for a time, even more than they have ever yet flourished; because these are generally the pursuits of men to whom worldly gains and honors are of less than secondary importance, and because the operation of such a system might by possibility admit to the peaceful prosecution of such high studies certain orders of minds, now shut out from it by adverse and necessitous circumstances. But admitting all this (and it is admitting a great deal), society would not be much if at all advantaged by their endeavors and their success, and that for a reason for which we have not far to seek. There is a medium class of intellect, which, making a spoil or a quarry of the fruits of that of the highest order, obtains both profit and popularity by reducing them to purposes of practical utility, or where, which is but seldom, utility is out of the question, to the grasp of general comprehension. It is plain that to the operations of this class of persons the whole advantage from the pursuit of science which accrues to the entire community must, mediately, be owing; and that, were it not for them and their exertions, the funds of knowledge which have been accumulating for ages would never have been made available to the masses of the people; and those numberless social ameliorations and cheap luxuries which distinguish the present age of the world from the period of our Saxon ancestors, and which have mostly resulted from the application of scientific discoveries to the practical ends of comfort and convenience, would never have had an existence at all. Now mark—this class of persons, comprising the most active, useful, provident, and sagacious members of the commonwealth, live and move and have their being in the atmosphere of profit—that is, of personal and individual gain. This is the very air they breathe; it is their natural and necessary element, and without it they die, or rather would never live. For though the originators of so much that is essential to the advancement and well-being of the world, they are themselves the result of that very constitution of society which permits and sanctions inequality, and from the dead level of ignorance and barbarism calls into being all the aids and accessories of talent and civilization, by the promise of individual distinction and reward. That this is so no man can doubt who knows anything of human nature. There is indeed a pride of intellectual majesty that, intent on the search after knowledge for its own sake, may care little or nothing for the applause or rewards of the world; but this belongs not to the men who meddle with details, and reduce to purposes of every-day utility the facts and principles they may realize; and were it not for the men of practical mind, the greatest benefactors of the human race might have spent their lives in a round of comparatively unproductive toils.

It would appear from what has been already briefly hinted, that the founders and advocates of communism and equality have left out of their estimate of the human character one of its chief and most prevailing elements—that is, individuality. Man is essentially an individual, and practically, however much socially amalgamated, he abhors the thought of losing his individuality, and being lost and swallowed up in an undefined general mass. From the very earliest dawn of his consciousness, we find him, while yet an unjudging infant, aiming at distinction—endeavoring, as it were, to separate himself from the general aggregate of his fellows. It is this feeling that makes every child constantly anxious to have something it can call its own, because property is the first means of individualization suggested to a child's mind Hence children constantly appropriate articles to themselves and call them "mine," and ' yours," even though the articles in question be the property of others, or not property at all, as clouds, stars, floating straws, or flying birds From the youngest child to the oldest man, and through all ages and races, this desire for appropriation exists and prevails, and must exist and prevail, for the single reason that private property is, and is intended to be, the strongest of all social bonds, as well as the means and medium of the highest civilization and refinement. In order that it may operate to this great end, the Creator of the human mind and faculties has so constituted his creatures that every acquisition they make, whether of property or capability, which is itself a kind of property, is accompanied with pleasure. If we learn a language, or acquire an accomplishment, we feel, and properly feel, a pleasure in our success, but this pleasure is connected with the idea of profit to be reaped in some form or other from what we have attained. In the same manner, if we acquire a house, a horse, or a portion of land, or any other species of property whatever, we feel a pleasure, which if not in nature precisely similar to the pleasure resulting from mental acquirements, is yet in some measure analagous to it, because the same idea of profit is connected both with the material and the mental acquisition. It is from this idea of profit or personal appropriation, which presents to the minds of masses almost the sole means of individualization, that the exalted passion for independence has its source; which passion is nothing more than an earnest desire to emerge from the general crowd of one's fellow-men, and to be recognized as a separate individual. It is no argument against accumulation as a fit and natural occupation of the human energies, to say that love of property leads to covetousness and avarice. As well may we repudiate or denounce any other natural propensity common to every one, because when exercised to excess it degenerates into vice. This, indeed, is the case with them all. Carried to excess, eating becomes gluttony, drinking grows to intoxication, sleeping to sluggishness, and the virtues themselves may, by the same process, be turned into vices—as prudence in excess becomes parsimony, zeal is changed into bigotry, moderation into ascetism; and even the ornaments and graces of character may by excess be metamorphosed into the accessories of caricature, and become repugnant to decency and common sense

It is greatly to the assaults made upon this natural desire for individualization common to the whole human family, that the failure of all the socialist experiments hitherto made must be attributed. We have seen in the case of the working-men of Paris, how its partial suppression operated in the destruction of all energy, and the production of a thousand petty vices of character, all combining to defeat the objects of those who sought, by doing violence to a natural principle, to obtain an improvement upon the results of natural laws. The experiments of Mr. Owen, at New Harmony, and the St. Simonists of France have shown how much, or how little, success must invariably result from such combinations. It appears to me that the degree of success attainable from any similar experiment may be pretty safely and surely predicated—given, first, the condition in life of the parties composing the colony. Supposing the party to consist chiefly of persons of the middle or comfortable class (anything above this grade is out of the question), and supposing them to have cast their separate quotas into the common stock, it appears plainly that the elements of dissolution must begin to operate upon the very day and hour that the colony commence their common labors. In an active, industrious, middle-class community, it would be impossible to quell the feeling of individualization; and the hope of diverting its energies to any other object than the accumulation of private property would, in a colony consisting of anything more than a very limited number, be utterly vain and futile. Some, from the possession of qualities acceptable to the whole body, would gain character and consideration; and discontent, with equal certainty, would be the portion of others. Disagreement would supervene upon dislike; and after mutual quarrels and recrimination, the colony would break up and separate, each resuming his own again, if he could get it. But, supposing instead of a middle class, one of a much lower grade, a class of operatives and laborers who had little or nothing beyond their labor to contribute to the general stock. In such a case the instinct of individualization would not be so strong; men sunk in poverty and destitution have long ceased to attend to its promptings; its voice, indeed, cannot be heard above the clamor of necessity, while it is ever loudest in the atmosphere of civilization and luxury. So long, then, as the joint labors of the whole colony merely sufficed to supply their necessities, they might go on with comparative equanimity. Poverty, indeed,—the general poverty—as it was the originator of their compact, would also be their bond of union; the general necessity would guarantee the general harmony. But with the very first advent of prosperity would arrive also the seeds of disruption. With the prospect of substantial amelioration the principle of individualization would assert its natural dominion, and under its growing energies the spirit of philanthropy, once the boast of the community, would become less and less prevalent among its members, until at length the more active, talented, and ambitious among them would demand and obtain a general and final division of the proceeds of their mutual labors—unless, indeed, which is perhaps equally probable, a general scramble took place, and each, helping himself as he best could, betook himself off to pursue his fortune in some preferable locality, where the bugbears of philanthropy, benevolence, and universal sympathy did not blunderingly interfere between his industry and that independence which God and nature hold out as its appropriate reward.

In concluding the subject of socialism, I may add that there is but one possible condition of life in which perfect equality would be either desirable or practicable—and that would be a condition which it has not pleased the Almighty to bring about since the fall of our first parents. . . . In the paradise of Eden, where for a time was neither disobedience nor sorrow, equality might be reasonably supposed to dwell. When man first disqualified himself for an associate with his Maker, he laid the sure and fatal foundation for that inequality of condition among the future races of the world which will always be, as it has ever been, the principal characteristic of their varying lot. With the very first step in violation of the command of God, our frail progenitor planted in his unborn offspring the first seeds of antagonistic emulation with each other. The very first infraction of His law severed the sacred bond of brotherly love which was dependent upon its fulfilment. Until man shall again walk the earth the image of God, morally pure and undefiled, he shall sojourn upon it the member of a class, the disciple of a sect, the struggler for pre-eminence. Despised of some and envied of others, he shall show what an overruling Providence, in directing for thousands of years the present organization of the social world, has intended him to show, namely, that the progress of our race towards that social perfection which they are ultimately destined to achieve is owing more to individual effort prompted by mutual emulation, and rewarded by individual aggrandisement, than by any other agency whose operation it is possible to trace through the facts of mundane history.

We frequently hear the partisans of communism adverting to the existence and practice of their system among the early Christians, who are described in the Acts of the Apostles as "possessing all things in common." Much stress is laid upon this fact by some of the more sober and serious of their party, who contend that such was the natural and unavoidable result of the action of *pure* Christianity upon the mind and heart. Such persons are slow to perceive that this community of goods *is merely related as a fact*—that it is nowhere held up as an example, nor its continuance recommended. The terrible doom of Ananias and his wife shows that it was liable to be the instigator of the greatest deception, and may perhaps have contributed to its discontinuance. However that may be, it is certain that communism prevailed but for a short time among the early Christians; for we find Paul, at a period not much later, carefully organizing a regular system of collections and contributions for charitable purposes—a system which there could have been no grounds for establishing during the practice of communism. Is it unreasonable to suppose that to the clear-headed sagacity of that courageous man the overthrow of communism was due? and that he was the first to perceive that a practice which originated in the child-like sincerity and simple faith of the first members of the first Church was at least as much liable to abuse as to disinterested imitation among the indiscriminate crowds that day by day were added to the number of converts? May he not also have perceived that a constitution of society which placed all its members upon an equality was not a constitution best adapted for the cultivation and increase of that charity which is the vital principle of Christianity, but the exercise of which in its most palpable form it is the nature of equality to preclude?

In submitting the above as my own views on the subject of communism, I feel confident that I do but represent the opinions of a very large portion of the class to which I belong. Whether that section of the working ranks who have arrived at the above conclusions form the wiser portion of the whole body it is not for me to say; certain I am, however, that as a general rule, they do embrace among their number those who are best off. If any one thing more than another shows the estimation in which the system of socialism is held among working-men, it is the fact that its popularity is ever on the wax or on the wane in a degree corresponding with the scarcity or abundance of employment. A long-continued period of slackness in trade recruits the ranks of the socialist army, and the return of prosperity and well-paid employment as effectually disbands them; and this shows us that independence is much dearer to the workman than any advantages which he has yet learned to recognize as derivable from the communist plan, which he has recourse to as a *pis aller*, and only accepts when the hope of independence is withheld from him.

If I am right in the views above expressed, then the evils under which working-men at times so grievously suffer are not to be redressed by a recourse to the socialist practice. Neither does combination, under any phase which it has yet assumed, appear to me to offer a remedy; because while a deficient amount of employment has to be shared among a redundancy of hands, the fact of laborers combining together cannot remove the discrepancy existing between the work really to be done and the quantity it would be desirable to have to do. If all combine, then all will inevitably compete; and in lieu of starving individuals, when trade is unprosperous and employment fails, we shall have starving companies and bankrupt combinations. It may be likely that a new law of partnership would enable the *élite* of the class to do something for their own advantage: but it is probable that their success would be prejudicial to the main body. The partial prosperity of the partnership *en commandite* in France is no proof that a similar system of doing business would succeed with English workmen. The chararacters and habits of both are dissimilar in many respects: the amount of labor and wages which would satisfy a Frenchman, and enable him to enjoy himself to his heart's content, would keep an Englishman in a state of perpetual anxiety and grumbling ill-humor. A Frenchman will sacrifice a day's work at any time for the sake of effecting a trifling improvement in the article he is producing, while the Englishman would rather string beads all his life at thirty-shillings a-week than he would co-operate in the noblest achievement of human skill at a wage of sixpence less. For my part, I have more faith in an old adage than in any new system. "Every man for himself" sounds like a very churlish motto: but when every man has learned to rely upon himself, the plethora in the labor-market will be very much reduced; thousands will emerge from the ranks of working-men, and take post as something better, and a more even balance will be struck between the labor to be done and those who have to do it.

THE END.

BIBLIOLIFE

Old Books Deserve a New Life
www.bibliolife.com

Did you know that you can get most of our titles in our trademark **EasyScript**™ print format? **EasyScript**™ provides readers with a larger than average typeface, for a reading experience that's easier on the eyes.

Did you know that we have an ever-growing collection of books in many languages?

Order online:
www.bibliolife.com/store

Or to exclusively browse our **EasyScript**™ collection:
www.bibliogrande.com

At BiblioLife, we aim to make knowledge more accessible by making thousands of titles available to you – quickly and affordably.

Contact us:
BiblioLife
PO Box 21206
Charleston, SC 29413